George Orwell, the Secret State and the Making of *Nineteen Eighty-Four*

By Richard Lance Keeble

Published 2020 by Abramis academic publishing

www.abramis.co.uk

ISBN 978 1 84549 761 3

© Richard Lance Keeble 2020

All rights reserved

This book is copyright. Subject to statutory exception and to provisions of relevant collective licensing agreements, no part of this publication may be reproduced, stored in a retrieval system, or transmitted in any form or by any means, without the prior written permission of the author.

This book is sold subject to the conditions that it shall not, by way of trade or otherwise, be lent, re-sold, hired out, or otherwise circulated without the publisher's prior consent in any form of binding or cover other than that which it is published and without a similar condition including this condition being imposed on the subsequent purchaser.

Abramis is an imprint of arima publishing.

arima publishing
ASK House, Northgate Avenue
Bury St Edmunds, Suffolk IP32 6BB
t: (+44) 01284 700321

www.arimapublishing.com

Richard Lance Keeble is Professor of Journalism at the University of Lincoln and Honorary Professor at Liverpool Hope University. He has written and edited 42 books on a wide range of media-related subjects. The chair of the Orwell Society (2013-2020), he edited *Orwell Today* (2012) and *George Orwell Now!* (2015). He is also the joint editor of *Ethical Space: The International Journal of Communication Ethics* and *George Orwell Studies*. In 2011, he gained a National Teaching Fellowship, the highest award for teachers in Higher Education in the UK, and in 2014 he was given a Lifetime Achievement Award by the Association for Journalism Education. In 2020, Routledge are publishing a collection of his essays under the title, *Journalism Beyond Orwell*.

Contents

Introduction
Exploring the Ever-Expanding World of George Orwell　　　Page 1

Section 1. New Perspectives on *Nineteen Eighty-Four*
Chapter 1. The Secret State and the Julia Conundrum　　　Page 12

Chapter 2. *Nineteen Eighty-Four* and the Spooks　　　Page 26

Chapter 3. Orwell – by his Great Friend David Astor　　　Page 39

Chapter 4. Beyond Big Brother: The Story of Surveillance in Britain and America　　　Page 44

Chapter 5. Two Wonderful Ways to Celebrate *Nineteen Eighty-Four*'s Anniversary　　　Page 47

Chapter 6. *Barnhill*: Missing the Crucial Astor Factor　　　Page 52

Section 2. Orwell and the Journalistic Imagination
Chapter 7. 'The Art of Donald McGill': Orwell and the Pleasures of Sex　　　Page 58

Chapter 8. 'There is Always Room for One More Custard Pie': Orwell's Humour　　　Page 72

Chapter 9. 'Such, Such Were the Joys' (and Pains)　　　Page 88

Chapter 10. Orwell's Film Reviewing: Another Look　　　Page 110

Chapter 11. Struggle with the Prose (Just About) Worth the Effort　　　Page 116

Chapter 12. Far Beyond Mere Hackery: Orwell's Journalism　　　Page 120

Section 3. Orwell's Afterlife: Beyond 1950
Chapter 13. Appreciations: Just Months After he Died　　　Page 126

Chapter 14. Gordon Bowker: So Wonderfully Insightful into Orwell, the Man and his Writings　　　Page 131

Chapter 15. Orwell and Leveson　　　Page 137

Chapter 16. A Deliberately Provocative, Fascinating Feast of Racy Writing and Orwellian Musings　　　Page 140

Chapter 17. Mrs Orwell – A Review and a View　　　Page 143

Chapter 18. The BBC – And the Political Economy of Broadcasting	Page 146
Chapter 19. Orwell – The Proto-blogger	Page 150
Chapter 20. The Orwell/Self spat: What it Reveals about Contemporary Culture	Page 153
Chapter 21. 'Two Titans of the Fight for Individual Freedom'	Page 155
Chapter 22. Jura Days	Page 157
Chapter 23. Retracing the Steps of George Orwell	Page 162
Chapter 24. Orwell, the University and the University of Life	Page 166

Introduction

Exploring the Ever-Expanding World of George Orwell

I was lucky to have a whole-year sabbatical from City, University of London, starting in September 1999 and was determined to write something on Orwell. Since becoming a sub-editor on my local newspaper in Nottingham in 1970 (immediately after leaving Oxford University where I studied Modern History), I had always found his journalism for radical, progressive journals an inspiration. From Nottingham, I moved to *Cambridge Evening News* in 1974, to the *Teacher*, the newspaper of the National Union of Teachers in 1977 – and then to City in the appropriately Orwellian year of 1984 to run the International Journalism MA with Bob Jones.

In 1999, the field of Orwell Studies seemed already far too crowded. But as I read Orwell's writings and about his life it occurred to me that in the academy interest in his journalism remained very much on the margins. Orwell was primarily seen as a novelist – *Animal Farm* (1945) and *Nineteen Eighty-Four* (1949) being universally considered masterpieces – and the author of such essays as 'The Lion and the Unicorn' (1941), 'The Art of Donald McGill' (1941) and 'Politics and the English language' (1946). His part memoir/part fictional *Down and Out in Paris and London* (1933), his investigation into poverty in the north of England in *The Road to Wigan Pier* (1937) and his frontline account of his time fighting with Republican militiamen during the Spanish civil war, in *Homage to Catalonia* (1938), were also the focus for academic analysis. But his frontline reporting on the Continent for the *Observer* and *Manchester Evening News* during the final days of the Second World War and his regular columns for the leftist journal, *Tribune*, between 1943 and 1947 had been completely ignored. So here were just the openings I needed to venture into the world of Orwell.

Once completed early in 2000, I sent my essay on Orwell's 1945 war reporting to Bob Franklin, editor at the academic journal *Journalism Studies*. It was immediately accepted and so my venture into Orwellian research was well and truly launched. I never looked back. By the time I had my analysis of Orwell's 'As I Please' columns in *Tribune* published in *The Journalistic Imagination: Literary Journalists from Defoe to Capote and Carter* (which I jointly edited with Sharon Wheeler, Routledge, 2007), I had come to understand the broader historical, cultural, political and ideological factors accounting for the marginalisation of the study of Orwell's journalism – and journalism as a literary genre in general – by the academy.

Since their emergence in the early seventeenth century in Europe's cities, particularly London, the 'news media' (variously known as corantos, diurnals, gazettes, mercuries and proceedings) have been associated with scandal, gossip and 'low' culture. During the 1720s, Grub Street came to be associated with an impoverished area of London where poor writers lived just as the word 'hack' came to be associated with writers and prostitutes – basically anything overused, hired out or common. On a basic level, journalism has provided writers with an income. Yet this very fact has reinforced journalism's position as a sub-literary genre. For literature is considered the fruit of 'scholarship' – hence pure, disinterested and above market considerations, including those of being readable and accessible – while journalistic writing is viewed as distorted by the constraints of the market, tight deadlines and word limits (Keeble 2007: 3-5).

All this has meant that journalism has long struggled to be considered a worthy academic discipline and a genre worth special attention for its literary elements. Thus, until quite recently the journalism of writers such as Eliane Brun, Angela Carter, Charles Dickens, Marguerite Duras, George Sand, Willa Cather, Mahatma Gandhi, James Joyce, D. H. Lawrence, Mary McCarthy, R. K. Narayan, Oscar Wilde and Virginia Woolf, (to name but a few) had not drawn the attention of the academy. Moreover, writers themselves have often looked down on their journalism: Virginia Woolf, in her poem 'Fantasy', represented the journalist as a bug, repellent and blood-sucking. George Orwell even looked down on his journalism as 'mere pamphleteering'.

New Perspectives on *Nineteen Eighty-Four*

Since those early forays into the world of Orwell, I have had four main ambitions:

- to continue examining sensitive and previously unexplored areas in my own research (such as those, for instance, relating to sexuality, his humour, his possible ties with intelligence);
- to encourage the spread of Orwell Studies globally through editing both collections of essays by international scholars and a new, peer-reviewed, academic journal;
- to promote an understanding of Orwell's life and writings through my involvement in the Orwell Society (of which, in recent years, I have been chair);

- and to maintain a critical awareness of the publications constantly appearing about the man and his writings (so various book reviews are dotted about this text).

One of the most controversial aspects of Orwell's life surrounds his deathbed decision to hand over his 'little list' of 38 crypto-communists to Celia Kirwan (née Paget) who was working as Robert Conquest's assistant for the secret state's propaganda unit, the Information Research Department (IRD), recently established by the Labour government. Most commentary sees this decision by Orwell – the vehement critic of totalitarianism and the Big Brother surveillance state, the human rights campaigner, the archetypal 'decent' chap – essentially as an aberration (possibly linked to his ill-health and liking of the very attractive Celia Kirwan). My research, however, suggests that the act (which I feel was a gross error on Orwell's part) is perhaps best seen as consistent with those of a man already caught up for a number years with intelligence.

Orwell was introduced to the world of the secret state by his great friend David Astor. And my research into his war reporting assignment in 1945 for Astor's *Observer* and the *Manchester Evening News* suggests that he may well have attended the first conference of the Committee for European Federation, bringing together resistance groups from around Europe, in Paris, as part of some kind of intelligence mission (Keeble 2001). Adding to the mystery is the fact that Orwell was closely followed by intelligence since he began his journalistic career in Paris in the late 1920s – as his 39-page MI5/Scotland Yard file, released in 2008, reveals (see Chapter 2).

During my 1999-2000 sabbatical I was living in Great Abington, close to Cambridge, and so would go regularly to the university library and read the original hard copies of the *Observer* and *Manchester Evening News* where Orwell's war despatches were carried. What a privilege this was. I was also during my sabbatical keen to interview Astor (one of the wealthiest men in England). I thought that through hearing his clipped, old-Etonian accent I could perhaps get a sense of Orwell's voice. After all, though Orwell worked from 1941 to 1943 for the BBC, the corporation had kept no record of him speaking. In the end, I was amazed at how easily I managed to secure the interview with Astor. I simply looked in *Who's Who?*; saw there his home telephone number; spoke to him briefly to arrange our meeting. And for around two hours I chatted to him in his substantial terrace house just round the back of the MCC Cricket Ground in Marylebone, London. Amazing (a transcript of the interview is carried in Chapter 3). His deep affection for Orwell was clear; he saw that I was also sincere in my appreciation of the man

– and so we chatted on. Of course he denied that Orwell had any dealings with intelligence…

Strangely, Orwell's own complex relationship with intelligence is rarely linked to the analysis and understanding of his masterpiece, *Nineteen Eighty-Four* – that stark warning about a Big Brother surveillance society engaged in constant warfare against manufactured enemies – and in which spies and telescreens follow citizens' every move. Equally strange has been the reluctance of commentators to consider Julia a possible Party spy luring Winston Smith, with whom she has a passionate, clandestine affair, into a honeytrap. Look closely and you'll see how Orwell drops many hints that Julia may well, indeed, be a Party spook. But Orwell is far too clever to present a definitive picture since, in a totalitarian world dominated by the myths and lies of intelligence, nothing is certain – as I highlight in the book's opening chapter.

Orwell the Literary Journalist

My study of the literary elements of Orwell's 80 'As I Please' columns for the leftist journal *Tribune* between 1943 and 1947 was the first such analysis and appreciation. Examining the texts was a complete joy for me. They were so witty and original and diverse in subject matter – I had a permanent smile on my face as I read and studied them. The publication of my essay on the columns in my book *The Journalistic Imagination* (2007: 100-115) also led to me being invited to give the keynote address at the annual conference of the International Association of Literary Journalism Studies (IALJS) in Chicago in 2009. Since then I have made many friendships with IALJS colleagues, jointly edited a number of books with academics I have met there examining the spread of literary journalism (LJ) worldwide – and deepened my understanding of the many fascinating debates surrounding LJ as both journalistic practice and academic discipline. Moreover, in my analyses of Orwell's literary journalism I have sought to raise other previously marginalised elements.

For instance, the central place of sexuality in Orwell's writings has been largely missed by critics and biographers. In contrast, I place my study of his remarkable 1941 essay about the sexy seaside postcards of Donald McGill in the context of his representation of sex in a range of his works (Chapter 7; see also Keeble 2019). Thus it explores his daring treatment of homosexuality (at a time when it was illegal in the UK) in *Down and Out in Paris and London*, the homo-eroticism in *Homage to Catalonia* and his almost New Mannish frankness about his own sexual development in his remarkable prep school memoir, 'Such, Such Were the Joys'. Yet Orwell's celebration of sexuality is best seen in his McGill essay in which he combines *faux* shame with a joyful affirmation of the hedonistic, Sancho Panza attitude to life – and a celebration, nothing less, of the pleasures of sex.

Orwell is, also, too often associated with the dull, dystopian world of *Nineteen Eighty-Four* and misrepresented as lacking in humour. For instance, the *Oxford Book of Humorous Prose* (Muir 1990) fails to include any piece by Orwell. I would actually argue that Orwell is one of Britain's greatest humourists. In my role as chair of the Orwell Society I often give public talks on the man – his life and writings. All I have to do is read excerpts from his writings (always so vital and accessible) and people laugh. In my study of Orwell's humour (Chapter 8), I examine the lighter side of his personality, the humour amidst the horror of the Spanish trenches in *Homage to Catalonia*, the constant high spirits and droll wit in his 'As I Please' columns for the leftist journal *Tribune* between 1943 and 1947, the many satiric elements in *Nineteen Eighty-Four* – and his polymathic knowledge of (and highly opinionated views on) English humorous writing in his 1,884-word essay 'Funny not vulgar' (first published in the *Leader*, on 28 July 1945).

Much of the debate over Orwell's essay 'Such, Such Were the Joys', about his years at St Cyprian's prep school, concentrates on the extent to which his recollections are truthful or imagined. Little attention has been directed at the literary elements of the essay. Thus here, in Chapter 9, I examine in detail the literary devices Orwell uses: such as dramatic narratives, verbatim dialogue, the balancing of tones and attitudes, the sexually explicit, the polemical, confessional and intimate voices, historical generalisations, the journalistic style and social/cultural analysis.

Moreover, Orwell's stint as a film reviewer for *Time and Tide* (the vaguely right-of-centre journal edited by Margaret, Lady Rhondda) between October 1940 and August 1941 has been largely ignored by commentators – or his reviews have been dismissed as dull. In Chapter 10, I challenge that view arguing – along with my late friend and colleague John Tulloch (2012) – that Orwell often came up with original insights in his film reviews and displayed an awareness of its possibilities as both an art form and propaganda tool – and its potential for remaking the way we understand the world.

Orwell's Afterlife: Beyond 1950

As Dorian Lynskey points out in his excellent 'biography' of *Nineteen Eighty-Four*, of 2019 (reviewed in Chapter 5), Orwell never merited an entry in *Who's Who* until the year of his death and won only one award (a $1,000 literary prize from *Partisan Review*). And he was never to experience and take pleasure in the enormous success of his dystopian masterpiece since he died tragically young at the age of 46 just days after its publication. Indeed, as

Orwell's fame quickly spread and sales of *Animal Farm* and *Nineteen Eighty-Four* mounted globally, his legacy became a sort of ideological battleground between the right, left and centre during the Cold War and beyond with each faction claiming him as one of their own.

One of the first appreciations appeared just months after his death (considered in Chapter 13) in a special edition of *World Review*, a journal published by Edward Hulton, describing itself as 'a monthly devoted to literature and the arts and all other aspects of our cultural interests'. It had previously carried Orwell's Appendix on Newspeak from *Nineteen Eighty-Four* (then shortly to be published) though without any background explanation. Around selections from Orwell's Notebooks (from 18 May 1940 to 28 August 1941), which lie at the core of the journal, are contributions from a glittering array of (all male) journalists and intellectuals: Bertrand Russell, Tom Hopkinson, Aldous Huxley, John Beavan (little did he know that he had been included in Orwell's 'little list' of crypto-communists), Herbert Read, Malcolm Muggeridge and Stephen Spender. The collection mixes both celebration and critique. Orwell's personality as much as his writings clearly fascinated many – and this is reflected in the articles.

Intriguingly, Orwell asked in his will for no biography to be written. Was this simply a reflection of the self-effacing aspects of his personality? Did he have secrets which he wanted to remain hidden? We will never know the precise reasons. The request in the will certainly failed to dim the constant curiosity about his life and a series of substantial biographies have appeared over the years helping to reinforce Orwell's iconic position in global culture – by Peter Stansky and William Abrahams (1972 and 1979), Bernard Crick (1980), Michael Shelden (1991), Jeffrey Meyers (2000), D. J. Taylor (2003) and Robert Colls (2013). One of my favourites is by Gordon Bowker (2003) who sadly died in January 2019. I thus took the opportunity in my obituary (Chapter 14) to highlight the originality and richness of his biography. As I comment, through the course of the 495-page text he delves deep into Orwell the man 'providing original and often profound insights into his writings and complex personality. Bowker's prose is always clear yet densely packed with meticulously researched information – and throughout he displays a deep knowledge of the politics and broader culture of Orwell's times'.

Orwell's second wife, Sonia Brownell (whom he married on his death bed) has drawn somewhat mixed reactions from her contemporaries and later Orwell biographers. Her own biographer, Hilary Spurling (2002), paints a glowing picture and argues that the sexually confident Julia character in *Nineteen Eighty-Four* is based on her. Sonia is certainly open to criticism for secretly selling the global distribution rights of *Animal Farm* to the CIA. And yet the *Collected Essays, Journalism and Letters* which she co-edited with Ian Angus in 1968 (published two years later in paperback) helped confirm Orwell's position as one of the most important polemicists, political analysts, journalists and authors of the twentieth century. A new play by Tony Cox about Sonia (reviewed in Chapter 17) reflects the continuing 'afterlife' of Orwell yet fails to provide any new insights into Sonia. As I comment: 'The play is called *Mrs Orwell* yet, in fact, the playwright misses the opportunity to focus more on her – for instance, her relationship with Cyril Connolly, her feelings about her former lover Maurice Merleau-Ponty, her views on Orwell's work and contemporary writings in general. Too often in the histories the women in the lives of "Great Men" (Mrs Bach, Mrs Dickens, Mrs Joyce, Mrs Mahler etc) are marginalised – here was a chance to put the spotlight on Sonia. But still the real emphasis of the play is on Orwell, the man. What a shame.'

Orwell's views on many topics were ambivalent – or shifted over the years. Yet throughout his career he maintained a consistent political/economy critique of the press – which remains highly relevant still today. For instance, Eli Noam's study of 30 countries suggests that the concentration of media ownership continues to escalate with the internet amplifying this process across national borders (Noam 2016; see also Christians 2019).

Significantly, in his first published piece in the UK, 'A farthing newspaper' (for Chesterton's review *G. K.'s Weekly*, in 1928), he highlights the economic factors impacting on its operations and political bias (Orwell 1970 [1928]: 34-37). *Ami du Peuple*, costing just ten centimes, has recently been launched in Paris with a manifesto claiming it is 'uncontaminated by any base thoughts of gain' (ibid: 34). Eric Blair (as he was then known) adds, ironically:

> The proprietors, who hide their blushes in anonymity, are emptying their pockets for the mere pleasure of doing good by stealth. Their objects, we learn, are to make war on the great trusts, to fight for a lower cost of living and above all combat the powerful newspapers which are strangling free speech in France (ibid: 34-35).

He proceeds to deconstruct, with polemical vigour, the paper's pretensions – noting that its proprietor is M. Coty 'a great industrial capitalist and also proprietor of the *Figaro* and the *Gaulois*'. In other words, it is merely putting across 'the sort of propaganda wanted by M. Coty and his associates'. Thus, he is concerned over the ways proprietorial ownership and the pressures from advertisers seriously constrain the press. Later, in 'The Lion and the Unicorn' (1970 [1941]), written during some of the bleakest days of the Second World War when Britain seriously feared invasion by the Nazis, he writes bluntly: 'Is the English press honest or dishonest? At normal times it is deeply dishonest.

All the papers that matter live off their advertisements and the advertisers exercise an indirect censorship over news' (ibid: 88).

Again, in his Introduction to *Animal Farm* (1945) which was only discovered in 1972, Orwell begins repeating the arguments developed over a number of 'As I Please' columns – hitting out at the monopoly control of the press (Orwell 1972: 1037):

> The British press is extremely centralized and most of it is owned by wealthy men who have every motive to be dishonest on certain important topics. But at the same time a kind of veiled censorship also operates in books and periodicals as well as in plays, films and radio.

He continues: 'Anyone who challenges the prevailing orthodoxy finds himself silenced with surprising effectiveness. A genuinely unfashionable opinion is almost never given a fair hearing, either in the popular press or in the highbrow periodicals' (ibid). He directs his critique, in particular, at 'the greater part of the English intelligentsia which have swallowed and repeated Russian propaganda from 1941 onwards'. As an example he highlights the BBC celebrating the twenty-fifth anniversary of the Red Army without mentioning Trotsky: 'This was about as accurate as commemorating the battle of Trafalgar without mentioning Nelson but it evoked no protest from the English intelligentsia' (ibid: 1038).

In Chapter 18, I show how Orwell also applied this political economy critique equally consistently to his comments on the BBC in many of his 'As I Please' columns. As I conclude, he places his analysis in the context of a broader discussion about journalism and broadcasting in general, language, propaganda and censorship. And while he is particularly aware of the political economy of broadcasting as he draws on his own experience of working for the BBC in the early 1940s, many of his insights, critiques and preoccupations remain acutely relevant to any discussion of broadcasting today.

It's always dangerous to predict how Orwell may have reacted to any of the political, cultural, economic, journalistic changes since 1950: in any case, he was essentially unpredictable, would often change his views or hold ambivalent attitudes (such as over pacifism) – attacking a stance vehemently but them befriending its advocates and submitting articles to their journals. But on his attitudes to the blogosphere, it's tempting to say he would have been at home there (though concerned to highlight the political economy of the internet and its global dominance by a few US-based-companies). In Chapter 19, I argue that he may even be considered a proto-blogger. Take a look at those 80 wonderful 'As I Please' columns he contributed to *Tribune* between 1943 and 1947 and see the amazingly close relationship he instinctively establishes with his readers. So often he responds to letters sent to him directly or addressed to *Tribune*. At other times he is running a short story competition or giving his readers a quirky brain teaser to answer. Elsewhere he invites letters, asks readers to answer queries or even point him towards a book, pamphlet or quotation he is looking for.

Indeed, Orwell's close relationship to his readers was crucial to the flowering of what many consider the greatest journalism of the last century. While he realised mainstream journalism was basically propaganda for wealthy newspaper proprietors, at *Tribune* he was engaging in the vital political debate with people he often criticised – but who mattered to him.

Finally, in Chapter 24, I examine the enormous and forever growing impact Orwell exerts today on higher education in the UK: in English Studies, Cultural Studies, Journalism and Literary Journalism. Orwell's virtual invention of the discipline of Cultural Studies is well known – with his commentaries on so many of the manifestations of popular culture which fascinated him such as crime novels, boys' weeklies, women's magazines, cups of tea, Woolworth's roses, common lodging houses, the common toad and handwriting. He is less well known for anticipating the emergence of Media/Journalism Studies with his innovative critiques of the press throughout his writing life. As we have seen, he constantly questions the notion of press freedom, stressing the impact of advertisers and proprietorial control on content. Orwell also adopts many other original ways of examining the press: for instance, deconstructing an issue of the *Daily Mirror* and cheap women's newspapers – to highlight the manufacture of the 'sunshine mentality' – and even damning journalism training at the time (see Chapter 1, Keeble 2020 forthcoming).

Significantly, his reflections on the press culminate in the creation of Winston Smith, the anti-hero of his dystopian masterpiece *Nineteen Eighty-Four*. For Winston is a media worker at the satirically named Ministry of Truth altering the records of *The Times* to conform to the current dogma. So Orwell's damning critique of the press (still so relevant today) persists to the very end.

References

Bowker, Gordon (2003) *George Orwell*, London: Little, Brown

Christians, Clifford (2019) *Media Ethics and Global Justice in the Digital Age*, Cambridge: Cambridge University Press

Colls, Robert (2013) *George Orwell: English Rebel*, Oxford: Oxford University Press

Crick, Bernard (1980) *George Orwell: A Life*, Harmondsworth, Middlesex: Penguin Books

Keeble, Richard (2001) George Orwell as war correspondent: A re-assessment, *Journalism Studies*, Routledge, Vol. 2, No. 3 pp 393-406

Keeble, Richard (2007) Introduction, Keeble, Richard and Wheeler, Sharon (eds) *The Journalistic Imagination: Literary Journalists from Defoe to Capote and Carter*, Abingdon, Oxon: Routledge pp 1-14

Keeble, Richard Lance (2019) Beyond the dystopian gloom: Orwell and sexuality, Joseph, Sue and Keeble, Richard Lance (eds) *Sex and Journalism: Critical, Global Perspectives*, London: Bite-Sized Books pp 88-96

Keeble, Richard Lance (2020, forthcoming) *Journalism Beyond Orwell*, London: Routledge

Meyers, Jeffrey (2000) *Orwell: Wintry Conscience of a Generation*, New York: W. W. Norton and Company

Muir, Frank (1990) *The Oxford Book of Humorous Prose: From William Caxton to P. G. Wodehouse*, Oxford and New York: Oxford University Press

Noam, Eli M. (2016) *Who Owns the World's Media? Media Concentration and Ownership Around the World*, New York: Oxford University Press

Orwell, George (1970 [1928]) A farthing newspaper, Orwell, Sonia and Angus, Ian (eds) *The Collected Essays, Journalism and Letters of George Orwell, Vol. 1: An Age Like This, 1920-1940*, Harmondsworth, Middlesex: Penguin pp 34-37; *G. K.'s Weekly*, 29 December

Orwell, George (1970 [1941]) The Lion and the Unicorn, *The Collected Essays, Journalism and Letters of George Orwell, Vol. 2: My Country Right or Left 1940-1942*, Harmondsworth, Middlesex: Penguin pp 74-134; February 1941

Orwell, George (1972) The freedom of the press, *Times Literary Supplement*, 15 September pp 1037-1040

Shelden, Michael (1991) *Orwell: The Authorised Biography*, London: Heinemann

Spurling, Hilary (2002) *The Girl from the Fiction Department: A Portrait of Sonia Orwell*, London: Penguin Books

Stansky, Peter and Abrahams, William (1972) *The Unknown Orwell*, London: Constable

Stansky, Peter and Abrahams, William (1979) *Orwell: The Transformation*, London: Constable

Taylor, D. J. (2003) *Orwell: The Life*, London: Chatto and Windus

Tulloch, John (2012) Sceptic in the palace of dreams: Orwell as film reviewer, Keeble, Richard Lance (ed.) *Orwell Today*, Bury St Edmunds: Abramis pp 79-101

- I would like to thank the Orwell Society and Pete and Richard Franklin, of Abramis, for allowing me to republish the essays in this book. I dedicate it to four wonderful friends and collaborators over many years: Sue Joseph and Donald Matheson (*Ethical Space*) and Tim Crook and John Newsinger (*George Orwell Studies*). Many warm thanks to you all.

Section 1

New Perspectives on *Nineteen Eighty-Four*

Chapter 1

Nineteen Eighty-Four, the Secret State and the Julia Conundrum

> Secret service history may be a health hazard. It attacks the mind. In long periods immersed in it everything looks different. ... There is no firm ground anywhere: no certainties, no reference points. People turn out to be not what they seemed; institutions do not function as they were supposed to; accepted truths may be deliberate disinformation; spies and moles are everywhere; and the cleverest and most dangerous of them are those who appear most unlikely and innocent.
>
> Bernard Porter: *Plots and Paranoia* (1989: 228)

Introduction

Julia, the 'girl from the English Department' with whom Winston Smith conducts a passionate affair in *Nineteen Eighty-Four*, remains one of the novel's most intriguing characters. This chapter argues that her place in the novel is understandable only in the context of Orwell's complex relationship with Britain's intelligence services. It will explore the various ways in which Julia has been interpreted – by both feminists and (mainly male) Orwellian biographers – and how her representation is part of a more general discussion in the novel about sexuality.

The chapter will go on to present an original and critical perspective on Julia – and its epistemological implications. This interpretation helps give Orwell's celebrated dystopian novel a particularly modern character – making it essentially about the slippery, unstable nature of meaning.

Orwell, Astor, the Spooks and the Making of *Nineteen Eighty-Four*

It is impossible to consider the role of Julia in *Nineteen Eighty-Four* and the ways in which the novel highlights the horrors of a Big Brother surveillance society without considering the crucial role played by his friend, David Astor, in Orwell's final years.

It was Cyril Connolly who introduced Orwell to fellow old-Etonian and millionaire David Astor in 1942 – and after Orwell's wife Eileen died suddenly in 1945, he arguably became the most important influence on his life. Indeed, following their meeting at the Langham Hotel, near Broadcasting House, where Orwell was working as a producer in the Indian Section of the BBC's Eastern Department, the two immediately became friends (Lewis 2016: 22). Astor's family owned the *Observer*; he became its highly distinguished editor between 1948 and 1975 – and, from March 1942, Orwell made regular contributions such as profiles and book reviews to the newspaper until his death.

Significantly, Astor also introduced Orwell to the world of intelligence. Astor's intelligence ties went back as far as 1939 when he did 'secret service stuff', according to his cousin, Joyce Grenfell (Macintyre 2014: 201). Phillip Knightley records that when, in July 1939, Col. Count Gerhard von Schwerin, of the German General Staff, arrived in the UK as a spokesman for the German opposition to Hitler, he was met by David Astor (1986: 131). He served in the early part of the Second World War in naval intelligence alongside Ian Fleming (author of the James Bond spy novels) and Dennis Wheatley (later to become the occult/adventure novelist) (see Cabell 2008: 12, 29, 49) and later with the covert Special Operations Executive (SOE).[1] Thereafter, he maintained close links with intelligence.

Astor also introduced Orwell to other intelligence friends through the Shanghai dining group (named after the Soho restaurant where they met) which he had created with his friend and old-Harrovian Edward Hulton (Purvis and Hulbert 2016: 158). Old-Etonians in the group included Guy Burgess (later exposed as a Soviet spy), Frank Pakenham (later Lord Longford) and John Strachey.

After leaving the BBC in November 1943, Orwell planned to report for the *Observer* from Algiers and Sicily following the Allied landings but the authorities turned him down on health grounds. Orwell then quickly acquired the post of literary editor at the leftist weekly *Tribune*, which he held until February 1945 when he resigned to take on a war reporting assignment for Astor's *Observer* and the *Manchester Evening News*.[2] Was this a cover for an intelligence mission? Intriguingly, most of the men he met in Paris on his assignment – A. J. 'Freddie' Ayer, Harold Acton, Ernest Hemingway, Malcolm Muggeridge – were either old-Etonians, working for intelligence services of one kind or another – or both (Keeble 2012; Chapter 2).

Stephen Dorril, in his history of MI6, reports that in 1944 Astor was transferred to a unit liaising between SOE and the Resistance in France, helping the French underground in London spread the word to groups throughout Europe (Dorril 2000: 457). While in Paris, perhaps inspired by Astor, Orwell attended the first conference of the Committee for European Federation, bringing together Resistance groups from around Europe. The French novelist and editor of *Combat*, Albert Camus, was amongst those present – though they failed to meet. Astor was later adamant that Orwell had no intelligence links[3] and Peter Davison, editor of Orwell's twenty-volume collected works, commented: 'I doubt if Orwell would be involved with intelligence – but that by no means says he wasn't.'[4]

All this suggests that Orwell's controversial decision to submit a 'little list' of 38 'crypto-communists' (briefly and somewhat crudely) to his friend, the sister-in-law of the author Arthur Koestler, Celia Kirwan (née Paget) when she was working as Robert Conquest's assistant for the secret state's newly-formed propaganda unit, the Information Research Department, was not an aberration (as generally thought).[5] Rather, it was an action consistent with his attitudes and behaviour as they developed during the 1940s – particularly through his friendship with David Astor.[6]

Moreover, during Orwell's final years, Astor played an enormously important role. It was he who persuaded Aneurin Bevan, Orwell's old *Tribune* editor, by now Secretary of State for Health in the Attlee government, to allow the special importation of the very expensive drug, streptomycin, from the United States to treat his friend's TB (Taylor 2003: 392).[7] It was he who owned the land on the remote Scottish island of Jura where Orwell spent his final days bashing out the *Nineteen Eighty-Four* manuscript. Astor also paid for the private room (No. 65) at University College Hospital where Orwell was to marry Sonia Brownell (with Astor as Best Man) and spend his last days. It was he who hosted the lunch at the Ritz following the wedding (Orwell was too ill to attend). And after Orwell, the atheist and unpredictable to the very end, asked in his will to be buried in a churchyard, Astor found a plot at All Saints, Sutton Courtenay, Oxfordshire, close to his family estate.[8]

There were clearly many influences on Orwell in the making of *Nineteen Eighty-Four*. Yet, given Orwell's introduction to the world of spooks by his friend Astor, is it not surprising then that his last great novel should describe a world of Big Brother, of child spies and telescreens – and where the state's surveillance intrudes into the individual's innermost private life? Orwell's ambivalent attitude to just about everything was reflected in his responses to the secret state. On the one hand, he supported it and became friends with some of its operators. But he also saw the secret state's growing powers and was horrified. So he dedicated all his energy (in what proved to be his final years) in his remote house on Jura to composing the crucial warning. And his representation of Julia in *Nineteen Eighty-Four* was also profoundly influenced by his concerns over the political and epistemological implications of the growth of the secret state.

Julia: Is she Based on Sonia?

An intriguing number of elements in *Nineteen Eighty-Four* have close personal ties to Orwell. For instance, Winston begins writing his diary on 4 April – the day after the funeral of his first wife, Eileen O'Shaughnessy (in 1945);[9] Eileen had also, significantly, written a poem 'End of the Century, 1984' marking the 50th anniversary of her school in 1934 and looking ahead to the next half century (Bowker 2003: 382); Winston is said to be 39 – precisely the age Orwell's son, Richard, would be in 1984; the place where Winston is tortured by O'Brien at the end of the novel is given the number 101, satirically, after the room at the BBC where Orwell attended many boring meetings during his time working there between 1941 and 1943 – and so on. Inevitably, then, a number of writers have suggested that Julia is closely based on Sonia Brownell. For instance, Hilary Spurling, in her sympathetic, short biography of Sonia, writes (2002: 93):

> Memories of Sonia – her youth and prettiness, her toughness, above all her radiant vitality – fed directly into the book's heroine (who puts in a sixty-hour week or more tending to the literary machines in the offices of the Fiction Department at the Ministry of Truth). Sonia's imagined presence kept company with Orwell on the island of Jura as Julia's comforted his hero, Winston.

But according to Dorian Lynskey (2019: 174), there is little to link Sonia and Julia: 'Orwell was also close to Inez Holden and Celia Paget and he saw more of them while writing *Nineteen Eighty-Four* than he did of Sonia. Sonia and the dark-haired Julia didn't look alike, and they certainly didn't think alike.'

D. J. Taylor suggests the evidence for the Julia/Sonia identification is mixed. On the one hand: 'Orwell, at the time he first asked Sonia to marry him, was in his early forties. In both cases, a distinctly unhealthy middle-aged man is obsessed with an energetic woman in her twenties' (2019: 40). Like Sonia, Julia has a forceful presence but while Winston notes of Julia that 'Except for her mouth, you could not have called her beautiful' Sonia was well known for her striking good looks (ibid). Moreover, Orwell had begun the novel well before he became involved with Sonia.

Taylor suggests that traces of a number of other women are to be found in Julia. The sexual encounters with Julia *en plein air* recall his relationship with Eleanor Jaques in Suffolk in the early 1930s while Julia's 'swift, athletic movements' recall Brenda Salkend, a gym mistress and another of Orwell's loves in Suffolk during the early 1930s (ibid: 41). Julia's significance in the book, Taylor argues, is 'figurative rather than decisive': symbolising youth, impulse, free-spiritedness. Certainly, towards the end of the novel, when

Winston is being tortured with the rats cage in Room 101, Julia becomes the focus of his symbolically ultimate betrayal: 'Do it to Julia! Do it to Julia! Not me! Julia! I don't care what you do to her. Tear her face off, strip her to the bones. Not me! Julia! Not me!' he cries (Orwell 2000 [1949]: 329).

The Feminist Critique

Orwell's representation of Julia has drawn particular wrath from feminist critics. For Daphne Patai, Orwell evokes yet another female stereotype: she is motivated only by a love of sexual pleasure and is totally uninterested in the political dynamics of the society that oppresses her (Patai 1984: 243). When Winston reads to her from the book, supposedly written by the leader of the rebellion, Goldstein, she falls asleep (ibid: 244). Patai also suggests Orwell's naming of the central characters reflects his sexist bias (ibid):

> Julia has only a first name; she is an insignificant female, and Orwell in this respect follows his society's convention of considering a woman's last name a disposable, because changeable, element in an uncertain social identity. O'Brien, at the opposite pole, has only a last name, in typical masculine style. And Winston Smith, halfway between powerless personal feminine and the powerful impersonal masculine, has a complete name, albeit an ironic one in that it combines the legendary with the commonplace.

According to Beatrix Campbell (1984: 129), women simply 'do not appear as protagonists in Orwell's working class'. On *Nineteen Eighty-Four*, she comments: 'Julia is Winston's sleeping partner in sedition. Her rebellion is essentially sexual. She's promiscuous, she's had hundreds of men and her subversion is sealed in an equation between corruption and sexuality.' This reduction of Julia to her corrupt biology renders her rebellion 'as something seething below the threshold of political consciousness' (ibid). Similarly, Deidre Beddoe, in her essay 'Women in the writings of George Orwell', acknowledges that Julia shows courage, flouts the minor and then the major rules of the totalitarian society – and initiates contact with Winston. But she adds (1984: 147):

> The protests of Winston and Julia are inspired by totally different motives. Whereas Winston is inspired by intellectual concepts like the integrity of history and the notion of freedom, Julia is only 'a rebel from the waist downwards'. The sexually attractive and sexually active Julia objects to the regime because it stops her having a good time.

For Christopher Hitchens, hardly noted as a feminist (2002: 105): 'Every one of the female characters [in his novels] is practically devoid of the least trace of intellectual or reflective capacity.'

Male Idealisations of Julia

Contrasting with the damning feminist critique of the Julia representation, the (mostly male) biographers have tended to idealise her. Michael Shelden, for instance, comments (1991: 472): 'For Julia and Winston, sex becomes a form of liberation, a way not only of rebelling against the dictates of the Party, but also a means by which they can enjoy a sense of freedom in the release of passion. ... It is an affirmation of life in the face of Big Brother's attempt to eliminate all signs of vital existence among his subjects.' Robert Colls is almost ecstatic in his adulation (2013: 215-216):

> She is a 26-year-old mechanic – a technical woman, once of the new middle class that Orwell had reached out to in the late 1930s – smart, young, self-aware, unsnobbish and competent in all the ways Winston is not. She does as she pleases. She is practical. She is instinctual. She is effective. She gives him hope. She shows him how. She tells him where. ... The most important words in the book have nothing to do with the proles or Big Brother or Room 101: 'We are dead,' he said. 'We're not dead yet,' said Julia prosaically.

According to Jeffrey Meyers (2000: 284):

> Like Winston she is a symbolic figure. When she brings chocolate to their first meeting the smell of it stirs a troubling memory in Winston. Later, in bed with Julia, he wakes and remembers the day he stole the family's chocolate ration was the same day that his mother and sister disappeared. The chocolate connects Julia with his lost mother's love and helps relieve his guilt for his mother's death. Julia represents the power of instinctive feeling and the continuity of love.

James Preece (2019) even argues that Julia is 'the clearest indication of feminism (in substance, if not in word) in Orwell's late writing', adding: 'Julia's sense of politics comes from freedom – freedom to love, to have sex and to be herself in the countryside.' While for Dorian Lynskey, Julia represents a third way to live under Ingsoc (2019: 174):

> O'Brien claims there is no such thing as objective truth; Winston insists there is; Julia maintains that *it doesn't matter* (italics in the original). Because she can't remember the past and doesn't care about the future, she lives entirely in the present, which is what the Party wants. ... In some ways, she is cleverer than Winston, intuiting that Goldstein and the revolutionary Brotherhood are probably fictions concocted by the Party, but it is a cynical, even nihilistic intelligence.

Nineteen Eighty-Four's Sexual Politics

Sexual politics lie at the heart of *Nineteen Eighty-Four*. According to Cass R. Sunstein (2005: 241):

> Orwell suggests that totalitarian governments favour 'sexual puritanism', which induces 'hysteria', something that such governments mobilize in their own favour. This is the image of patriotic frenzy as 'sex gone sour'. On this view, sexual freedom embodies freedom and individualism, and it is the deepest enemy of a totalitarian state. A state that allows sexual freedom will be unable to repress its citizens.

Orwell represents Oceana as hyper-puritanical: the aim of Party is to remove all pleasure from the sexual act; all marriages have to be approved by committee; permission is refused if the couple give the impression of being physically attracted to one another; the only recognised purpose of marriage is to beget children to serve the Party; sexual intercourse is seen as a slightly disgusting minor operation, like having an enema – and the Junior Anti-Sex League advocates complete celibacy for both sexes (Orwell 2000 [1949]: 75). In addition, all children are to be begotten by artificial insemination (artsem in Newspeak) and raised in public institutions. At the same time, promiscuity is permitted amongst the proles – and pornography is produced specially for them in Pornosec, a sub-section of the Fiction Department (ibid: 50). Towards the end of the novel, as O'Brien tortures Winston, he pronounces (ibid: 306):

> We have cut the links between child and parent, and between man and man, and between man and woman. No one dares trust a wife or a child or a friend any longer. But in the future there will be no wives and no friends. ... The sex instinct will be eradicated. Procreation will be an annual formality like the renewal of a ration card. We shall abolish the orgasm.

In this context, the passionate affair Winston has with Julia acquires added symbolic significance. As Robin West stresses (2005: 248): 'Erotic sex, Winston Smith insists in *Nineteen Eighty-Four*, is a truly *political* and even revolutionary act.' In contrast to the sexually promiscuous Julia, Winston's wife, Katharine, is represented (quite mercilessly) as a frigid bore:

> As soon as he touched her she seemed to wince and stiffen. To embrace her was like embracing a jointed wooden image. ... They must, she said, produce a child if they could. So the performance continued to happen, once a week quite regularly, whenever it was not impossible. ... But luckily no child appeared and in the end she agreed to give up trying, and soon afterwards they parted (Orwell 2000 [1949]: 76).

Daphne Patai is particularly critical of Orwell's depiction of sexuality in the novel. Though Julia is said to have had many affairs, nowhere are the problems associated with contraception and abortion considered (1984: 247). The only reference to the biological facts of reproduction appear when Julia cancels a meeting with Winston because 'it's started early this time' (Orwell 2000 [1949]: 160). 'This delicate reference to menstruation, and the assumption that it prevents intercourse (apparently the sole object of Julia and Winston's meetings) is reiterated when Winston reflects that this "particular disappointment must be a normal, recurring event" in marriage' (ibid: 161).

Is Julia a Spy?

But what if Julia is actually a member of the Party, luring Winston Smith into a honeytrap? Orwell certainly offers various hints that he wants us to at least ponder this question. When Winston first sees Julia at the Two Minute Hate session, she arrives with O'Brien – who first befriends and then turns into his torturer in Room 101 (ibid: 12). Why? Are they friends? Is it just a coincidence? Even Winston wonders: 'The idea had even crossed his mind that she might be an agent of the Thought Police. That, it was true, was very unlikely. Still, he continued to feel a peculiar uneasiness, which had fear mixed up in it as well as hostility, whenever she was anywhere near him' (ibid: 13). He next sees her in the canteen: 'His earlier thought returned to him: probably she was not actually a member of the Thought Police, but then it was precisely the amateur spy who was the greatest danger of all' (ibid: 71).

Perhaps the strongest hint Orwell offers that Julia is actually a spy occurs when Winston, on the spur of the moment, decides to take a walk through London's backstreets. But then, whom does he see walking towards him: none other than the 'girl from the Fiction Department' (ibid: 115). 'She looked him straight in the face, then walked quickly on as though she had not seen him.' And Winston ponders:

> There was no doubting any longer that the girl was spying on him. She must have followed him here, because it was not credible that by pure chance she should have happened to be walking on the same evening up the same obscure backstreet, kilometres distant from any quarter where Party members lived. Whether she was an agent of the Thought Police, or simply an amateur spy actuated by officiousness, hardly mattered. It was enough that she was watching him (ibid).

When Julia and Winston meet for sex for the first time, there is this extraordinary conversation (ibid: 139):

> 'What is your name?' said Winston. 'Julia. I know yours. It's Winston – Winston Smith.' 'How did you find that out?' 'I expect I'm better at finding things out than you are, dear.'

In other words, is not Julia revealing all the attributes of a conscientious spy – knowing the name of her target, for instance? And as if to confirm the reader's suspicions, Orwell adds: 'He began telling her the story of his married life but curiously enough she appeared to know the essential parts of it already' (as, indeed, would not a well-briefed spy?).

Winston is later arrested along with Julia by the Thought Police in their love nest above Charrington's junk shop. But is Julia actually tortured – like Winston – in the Ministry of Love? We never really know. At the end, they meet by chance in a park. Each admits betraying the other under torture. But we can never be sure on anything about Julia.

So What?

Seeing Julia as a spy can lead to two contrasting interpretations. On the one hand it can be seen as subverting the conventional image of her: instead of being a submissive sex object she becomes a highly politicised agent of the state, influencing events in major ways. And her falling asleep just as Winston begins to read from Emmanuel Goldstein's dissident political tract, *The Theory and Practice of Oligarchic Collectivism*, can now appear in a completely different light: it's not because she's unpolitical and unintelligent as Orwell's feminist critics have argued (see Patai 1984: 244) but, as a spy, she is completely uninterested in it.

On the other hand, as Tim Crook (2018) argues: 'There is still a valid feminist criticism of this dimension of the characterisation in deploying and demeaning the woman as a stereotypical Mata Hari-type honeytrap where women feature almost exclusively as the corrupting and seducing agents of sexpionage.'

The Julia Conundrum and Epistemology

The Julia Conundrum is best understood within the broader context of Orwell's reflections on truth and objectivity in both his writings in general – and in *Nineteen Eighty-Four*, in particular. Perhaps with a touch of irony and dark humour, Orwell has Winston engaging in an esoteric, philosophical discussion with O'Brien in the torture room at the Ministry of Love about a wide range of topics: the nature of meaning, truth, metaphysics, solipsism, power, freedom, death and the transience of life, reality, human identity, sexuality, family life, history, the individual's autonomy (or lack of it) and the nature of existence. Added to this brew are some rather strange/spooky readings of Winston's mind by O'Brien. For instance, on the question of objective truth, O'Brien comments (Orwell 2000 [1949]: 285):

> You believe that reality is something objective, external, existing in its own right. You also believe that the nature of reality is self-evident. ... But I tell you, Winston, that reality is not external. Reality exists in the human mind and nowhere else. Not in the individual mind, which can make mistakes, and in any case soon perishes: only in the mind of the Party which is collective and immortal. Whatever the Party holds to be truth, *is* truth. It is impossible to see reality except by looking through the eyes of the Party.

Winston ponders: the belief that nothing exists outside your own mind – surely there must be some way of demonstrating it is false? (ibid: 305). But immediately, O'Brien, displaying remarkable 'mind-reading' abilities, chips in: 'I told you, Winston ... that metaphysics is not your strong point. The word you are trying to think of is solipsism. But you are mistaken. This is not solipsism. Collective solipsism, if you like.' And to illustrate Oceana's contempt for objective truth, O'Brien holds up four fingers and demands that Winston, under torture, admit there are five (ibid: 286).

As David Dwan comments (2019: 153): 'Winston is a convinced empiricist – a firm believer in the "evidence of your senses", or the "evidence of your eyes and ears" as the foundation for knowledge.' And much of the rhetoric in Orwell's writings asserts the importance of democracy's belief in objective truth. Totalitarian regimes not only circulated lies, they attacked the very 'concept of objective truth' (ibid: 144).

In contrast, O'Brien's rejection of mind-independent reality leads him to cast aside (somewhat ludicrously) all external restrictions on the will. 'He makes no concessions to the friction of the world: "I could float off this floor like a soap bubble if I wished to." So O'Brien cannot even tolerate gravitational laws and claims a kind of freedom that many Christians had denied even to God' (ibid: 158).

Yet, as Dwan stresses, while Winston supports the idea of truth, it is significantly never made clear in the novel what truth really is (ibid: 152). Indeed, as on so many issues, Orwell's reflections throughout his writings on epistemological issues were ambivalent, contradictory – or both. He certainly had little difficulty in telling lies for political ends. While working for the Eastern Overseas Services of the BBC in 1942, he confided to his diary for 3 March:

> Our radio strategy is even more hopeless than our military strategy. Nevertheless one rapidly becomes propaganda-minded and develops a cunning one did not previously have. Eg. I am regularly alleging in my newsletters that the Japanese are plotting to attack Russia. I don't believe this to be so (Orwell 2009: 224).

In *Homage to Catalonia* (1962 [1938]), his account of his time fighting alongside Republican militia men during the Spanish civil war, he outlines his ambivalence in a different way: 'I have tried to write objectively about the Barcelona fighting, though, obviously, no one can be completely objective on a question of this kind. One is practically obliged to take sides and it must be clear enough which side I am on' (ibid: 153).

Within this broad epistemological context, then, the Julia Conundrum serves to highlight the essential unknowingness of reality. Is Julia a spy? Orwell typically teases the reader with a number of clues. Indeed, Orwell loved to give the readers of his 'As I Please' column in the leftist journal *Tribune* (from 1943-1947) brain teases – which he dubbed 'brain ticklers' (see Keeble 2007). For instance, on 7 July 1944, he concluded his column with this 'intelligence test' (see Anderson 2006: 160): 'A man walked four miles due south from his house and shot a bear. He then walked two miles due west, then walked another four miles due north and was back at his home again. What was the colour of the bear?' (The answer, given in his 28 July column, is white: the man lived at the North Pole and the bear must, therefore, be a polar bear.) In the world of *Nineteen Eighty-Four*, O'Brien gives Winston a brain teaser: does the dissident Brotherhood exist? And he tells his victim: 'As long as you live it will be an unsolved riddle in your mind.' Similarly, for readers of the novel whether Julia is actually a spy or not will remain forever an 'unsolved riddle'.

Conclusions

This chapter has sought to locate the representation of Julia in *Nineteen Eighty-Four* within the context of Orwell's personal involvement in the secret state – as well as his reflections (and warnings) on the political, social and cultural elements of his imagined hyper-dictatorial Big Brother state and its radical epistemological implications. For in a society dominated by secret intelligence (with all its brutality, Thought Police, torture, constant surveillance, child spies and propaganda) any notion of 'objective truth' is eliminated. Intelligence, after all, can never be double-checked: by definition its source remains secret and exclusive. It could all be fiction – and often is. As a former foreign secretary, Lord Howe, told the Scott arms-to-Iraq inquiry in 1992: 'In my early days I was naïve enough to get excited about intelligence reports. Many look, at first sight, to be important and interesting and significant and then when we check them they are not even straws in the wind. They are cornflakes in the wind' (Norton-Taylor 2003).

Moreover, seeing Julia as a possible spy makes the novel even darker since her secret affair with Winston is one of its very few bright features – allowing Winston at least a few moments of escape from Oceana's grim reality.

Gordon Bowker, in his biography of Orwell (2003: 388), argues that, more than any other novel, *Nineteen Eighty-Four* is concerned with role-playing and deception: the Party is deceiving everyone, Julia is deceiving the Anti-Sex League, Charrington, the junk shop owner, and O'Brien are deceiving Winston, Winston is deceiving himself. He continues, significantly raising questions about Julia's identity:

> 'Truth' is also a deception because the Party controls the present, past and future. Once this 'shifting reality' is established, no one can be taken at face value. Julia seems to be a secret hater of the Party and Big Brother, seems to be a candidate for the dissident Brotherhood, seems to go off to be tortured after her arrest and finally seems to have been purged of her thought-crime. But in the world of the book she could, like O'Brien and Charrington, also be a dissembler leading Winston straight into the arms of the Thought Police. On Airstrip One truth rests on ever-shifting sands, only pain and Room 101 are real.

The Julia Conundrum can also be linked with Orwell's broader literary project. One of the most perceptive analyses of Orwell's *oeuvre* is provided by Lynette Hunter (1984). She argues that his ambivalences, contradictions and inconsistencies emerge from his essential approach to writing and learning:

> The assumption that one can absolutely define Orwell in biographical terms is parallel to the assumption that his writing and message or interpretation are equally clear and fixed. But the very attempt to define and fix into stasis is part of a world view that Orwell rejected. If this is not recognized then the outcome is often the suggestion that Orwell is being inconsistent, hence untrustworthy and deceitful.

For Hunter, Orwell's approach is always questioning and educational as he invites his readers to join him in his quest for learning.

> All too often there is an unwillingness to accept that Orwell might learn, come to appreciate different things and change his mind, and to recognize that this apparent inconsistency overlays a fundamentally consistent belief in the need to evaluate actively, never to assume the quality of axioms and fixed standards (ibid).

Orwell's literary voice, above all, Hunter argues 'does not impose opinion on others but invites discussion' (ibid: 11).

Similarly, David Dwan says Orwell's overall *oeuvre* 'raises troubling questions about his own inconsistencies and doubletalk' (2019: 206). He adds: 'Contrary to what many have assumed, Orwell provides few solutions to our political difficulties, although this was never his job. As Hilary Putnam once suggested, the writer's task is not to deliver solutions but to engage in the "imaginative re-creation of moral perplexities".'

Indeed, highlighting the Julia Conundrum (and the question readers are invited to consider: is Julia a spy?) ties in not only with Orwell's epistemological uncertainties and concerns about the growing powers of the secret state – but it also gives the book a strangely modern character, making it, as Bowker argues (op cit), a novel about the slippery, unstable nature of meaning.

Notes

[1] Knightley, Phillip (1986: 131). In 1956, Astor was persuaded to offer cover for the SIS agent (later to be revealed as a Soviet spy), Kim Philby, as a journalist in Beirut

[2] *Tribune* was later to be distributed to British missions abroad by the Information Research Department

[3] In an interview with the author, London, November 1999

[4] In a letter to the author, 7 December 1999

[5] 'Known' suspects include Labour MPs, the future Poet Laureate Cecil Day-Lewis, authors J. B. Priestley and John Steinbeck, journalist Richard Crossman, actors Michael Redgrave, Charlie Chaplin and Paul Robeson, actor and director Orson Welles, and the historians A. J. P. Taylor and Isaac Deutscher

[6] It is ironic, then, that Orwell was followed closely by British intelligence from the time of his first publication in *Monde*, edited by the communist Henri Barbusse, in Paris, in 1928 until his death (see Keeble 2012). Orwell's great friend, an old-Etonian, the novelist Anthony Powell, had also worked for intelligence during the war

[7] Taylor op cit: 392. The treatment unfortunately did not work

[8] Crick op cit: 580

[9] See https://www.irishtimes.com/opinion/stop-all-the-clocks-frank-mcnally-on-the-influence-of-george-orwell-s-first-wife-eileen-o-shaughnessy-on-1984-1.3923580, accessed on 22 June 2019

References

Anderson, Paul (ed.) (2006) *Orwell in* Tribune, London: Politico's

Beddoe, Deirdre (1984) Hindrances and help-meets: Women in the writings of George Orwell, Norris, Christopher (ed.) *Inside the Myth: Orwell: Views from the Left*, London: Lawrence and Wishart pp 139-154

Bowker, Gordon (2003) *George Orwell*, London: Little, Brown

Cabell, Craig (2008) *Ian Fleming's Secret War*, Barnsley, South Yorkshire: Pen and Sword

Campbell, Beatrix (1984) Orwell: Paterfamilias or Big Brother?, Norris, Christopher (ed.) *Inside the Myth: Orwell: Views from the Left*, London: Lawrence and Wishart pp 128-136

Colls, Robert (2013) *George Orwell: English Rebel*, Oxford: Oxford University Press

Crick, Bernard (1980) *George Orwell: A Life*, Harmondsworth, Middlesex: Penguin

Crook, Tim (2018) On Julia and sexpionage, in an email to the author, 20 September 2018

Dorril, Stephen (2000) *MI6: Fifty Years of Special Operations*, London: Fourth Estate

Dwan, David (2019) *Liberty, Equality and Humbug: Orwell's Political Ideals*, Oxford: Oxford University Press

Hitchens, Christopher (2001) *Orwell's Victory*, London: Penguin

Hunter, Lynette (1984) *George Orwell: The Search for a Voice*, Milton Keynes: Open University Press

Keeble, Richard (2007) The lasting in the ephemeral: Assessing George Orwell's 'As I Please' columns, Keeble, Richard and Wheeler, Sharon (eds) *The Journalistic Imagination: Literary Journalists From Defoe to Capote and Carter*, Routledge: London pp 100-115

Keeble, Richard Lance (2012) Orwell, *Nineteen Eighty-Four* and the spooks, Keeble, Richard Lance (ed.) *Orwell Today*, Bury St Edmunds: Abramis pp 151-163

Knightley, Phillip (1986) *The Second Oldest Profession: The Spy as Bureaucrat, Patriot, Fantasist and Whore*, London: André Deutsch

Lewis, Jeremy (2016) *David Astor*, London: Jonathan Cape

Lynskey, Dorian (2019) *The Ministry of Truth: A Biography of George Orwell's* 1984, London: Picador

Macintyre, Ben (2014) *A Spy Among Friends: Philby and the Great Betrayal*, London: Bloomsbury

Meyers, Jeffrey (2000) *Orwell: Wintry Conscience of a Generation*, New York and London: W. W. Norton and Company

Norton-Taylor, Richard (2003) The BBC now has been got up to obscure the ugly truth, *Guardian*, 28 June

Orwell, George (1962 [1938]) *Homage to Catalonia*, Harmondsworth, Middlesex: Penguin

Orwell, George (2000 [1949]) *Nineteen Eighty-Four*, London: Penguin Classics

Orwell George (2009) *Diaries*, Davison, Peter (ed.) London: Penguin

Patai, Daphne (1984) *The Orwell Mystique: A Study in Male Ideology*, Amherst: University of Massachusetts Press

Porter, Bernard (1989) *Plots and Paranoia: A History of Political Espionage in Britain 1790-1988*, London: Unwin Hyman

Preece, James (2019) The secrets of *Nineteen Eighty-Four*, *International Socialism*, Issue 163. Available online at http://isj.org.uk/the-secrets-of-nineteen-eighty-four/, accessed on 9 August 2019

Purvis, Stewart and Hulton, Jeff (2016) *Guy Burgess: The Spy Who Knew Everyone*, London: Biteback

Shelden, Michael (1991) *Orwell: The Authorised Biography*, London: William Heinemann

Spurling, Hilary (2003) *The Girl from the Fiction Department: A Portrait of Sonia Brownell*, London: Penguin

Sunstein, Cass R. (2005) Sexual freedom and political freedom, Gleason, Abbott, Goldsmith, Jack and Nussbaum, Martha C. (eds) *On Nineteen Eighty-Four: Orwell and Our Future*, Princeton and Oxford: Princeton University Press pp 233-241

Taylor, D. J. (2003) *Orwell: The Life*, London: Chatto and Windus

Taylor, D. J. (2019) Who was Julia? *Nineteen Eighty-Four*'s many heroines, *George Orwell Studies*, Vol. 3, No. 2 pp 39-43

West, Robin (2005) Sex, law, power and community, Gleason, Abbott, Goldsmith, Jack and Nussbaum, Martha C. (eds) *On Nineteen Eighty-Four: Orwell and Our Future*, Princeton and Oxford: Princeton University Press pp 242-260

- This chapter was first published, with the title, '*Nineteen Eighty-Four*, the Secret State and the Julia Conundrum', in *George Orwell Studies*, Vol. 4, No. 1 pp 71-84, 2019.

Chapter 2

Nineteen Eighty-Four and the spooks

In 2005 and 2007 respectively, Orwell's Special Branch and MI5 files were released to the National Archives. From the start of his journalistic career, writing for left wing newspapers in Paris in the late 1920s, his every move appears to have been watched. Later in Spain in 1936-1937, fighting in a Trotskyist militia against Franco's fascist forces, Orwell was closely followed – not only by a communist secret agent but by an agent working for the British secret service, MI5. Back in England and working for the BBC's Empire Service in 1940, he was being followed by Special Branch.

But then in the 1940s, Orwell befriended a fellow old-Etonian, David Astor, proprietor of the *Observer* who was heavily involved in the Special Operations Executive (the military arm of foreign intelligence). And the evidence suggests that, towards the end of his life, he became a part of the intelligence community. He possibly even worked for intelligence on a mission to Paris in 1945 – and on his death bed fed them information about fellow intellectuals. All this throws up a new perspective on Orwell's *Nineteen Eighty-Four*. Here is one of the most famous warnings about the emergence of a totalitarian state dominated by its secret service – written by a man who probably had close links with the spooks. The case study also provides a useful insight into the way in which the secret state can impact so intensely on an artist's life and imagination.

Big Brother Watches Eric Blair

Orwell's first ever signed article, *La Censure en Angleterre*, appeared in late 1928 in *Monde*, a journal which was being edited by the communist Henri Barbusse (Taylor 2003: 95). Soon afterwards three pieces based on his tramping in London appeared in the leftist *Le Progrès Civique*, run by René Nicole and Henri Dumay (see Bowker 2003: 107) followed by an article examining the way in which British tariffs were underdeveloping Burma where he had served in the Imperial Police from 1922-1927.

In a report for British intelligence (code number CX/12650/1988 dated 8 February 1929) Captain Miller, of Scotland Yard, reported on Orwell:

> He is a single man and lodges at 6, Rue du Pot de Fer, Paris, having arrived in France on 7.6. 28. BLAIR apparently states that he is the Paris correspondent for the "Daily Herald", "Daily Express", "G.K's Weekly",

but he makes no mention of the "Workers' Weekly". BLAIR [here, the name of the source is blanked out] states, wrote three articles in the "Progress Civique" of 29.12.28., 5th and 12th January, 1929, entitled "La Grande Misère de l'Ouvrier Britannique". The first article dealt with unemployment in England, which, according to Blair, is due to the war; the second with how the unemployed tramp spends his day; the third with London's beggars. He spends his time reading various news papers, among which is "L'Humanité", but he has not so far been seen to mix with Communists in Paris and until he does consider that the French will not interfere with him.[1]

A later report, dated 11 March 1936 (coded 301/NWC/683), commented:

> Shortly after resigning from the Indian Police, Blair went to France, and for some time eked out a precarious living as a free lance [sic] journalist. Whilst in Paris, he too had an interest in the activities of the French Communist Party, and spent a good deal of time studying "L'Humanité". Information is not available to show whether he was an active supporter of the revolutionary movement in France, but it is known that whilst there, he offered his service to the "Workers' Life", the forerunner of the "Daily Worker", as Paris correspondent.

Special Branch's same report shows the high degree of surveillance directed at Orwell, his every career and life move being recorded. For instance, it records the publication of *Burmese Days* by 'Victor Gollancz, Ltd, 14 Henrietta Street, W.C., a firm which specialises in Left Wing literature'. His time as 'down and out', his becoming a 'master at a preparatory school known as "The Hawthorns", Church Road, Hayes, Middlesex' and then at Fray's College, Harefield Road, Uxbridge, Middlesex until the end of 1933, and his time as a patient at Uxbridge and District Cottage Hospital are all noted.

Later in the report, Special Branch notes that Blair worked at 'Booklovers' Corner' owned by Francis Gregory Westrope who 'is known to hold socialist views, considers himself an "intellectual"' and is suspected of 'handling correspondence of a revolutionary character'. A Metropolitan Police report of 25 August 1936 (301/NWC/683) suggests that they considered charging Westrope for contravening the registration of Business Names Act 1916 – but in the end decided against.

On 24 February 1936, the Chief Constable of Wigan, Thomas Pey, reported Orwell's involvement with the communists while he was researching *The Road to Wigan Pier* passing on a letter from John Duffy, DC 79, to a certain 'Det Insp. Cockram' (catalogue reference MEPO/38/39). Orwell is described as 'about 36 yrs, 6ft, slim build, long pale face'. Duffy continues:

> I beg to report that this man has been staying in Wigan from Monday, the 10th instant at an apartment house in a working class district in this borough. I understand that a member of the local Communist Party was instrumental in finding Blair accommodation. Blair attended a Communist meeting in this town addressed by Wal. Hannington on the 10th instant. It would appear from his mode of living that he is an author, or has some connection with literary work as he devotes most of his time in writing. He has also collected an amount of local data e.g. number of churches, public houses, population etc and is in receipt of an unusual amount of correspondence. … In addition to correspondence from England, he is also in receipt of letters from France and I saw a newspaper which appeared to be the French counterpart of the "Daily Worker". In view of the association which this man has formed with the local Communist Party during his visit to Wigan, I respectfully suggest further enquiries be made with a view to establishing his identity.

Late in 1936, Orwell handed over the manuscript of *The Road to Wigan Pier* to his publisher Victor Gollancz. Intriguingly, a photocopy of a review of the book by Ethel Mannin, in the *New Leader* of 12 March 1937, is included in Orwell's Metropolitan Police file, dated 30 March 1937 (301/NWC/683).[2] She wrote:

> There is a great deal in this book which the informed Socialist will find irritating and even infuriating; sheerly silly, and a tilting at windmills. But it is worth-while for its first part and because, if only they can be persuaded to read it, it will do a great many people who see no case for Socialism so much good.

Orwell, the Spanish Civil War – and the Spooks

The Metropolitan Police report comments:

> It is of interest to note that according to Ethel Mannin's [sic] review, Blair is now fighting in Spain with the P.O.U.M in Bob Edwards' contingent. Edwards left this country on 10-1-37 in charge of a party of I.L.P. recruits who were proceeding to Spain to fight for the Government forces. Special branch file [destroyed] refers.

Indeed, in December 1936 Orwell had headed off to Spain to join a militia of the Trotskyist Workers' Party of Marxist Unification (POUM) in their fight against the fascists led by General Francisco Franco who had staged a military uprising against the Republican government. Orwell later reported on his experiences during the Spanish civil war in *Homage to Catalonia* (1938).

Adding to the extraordinary Orwell spooks mystery is the evidence that he was spied on in Spain by the both the communists and MI6. Orwell's biographer Gordon Bowker reveals that David Crook, a young communist from London, spied on Orwell, his newly married wife Eileen, who visited him on the frontline, and other members of the contingent from the Independent Labour Party (ILP) (Bowker 2003: 219). Crook had been taught the techniques of surveillance by Ramon Mercader, a communist who later, in August 1940, murdered Trotsky in Mexico with an ice-pick. And he took his orders from the Soviet espionage agency, then known as the NKVD and later renamed the KGB. Bowker says of Crook (ibid) that he soon had the run of the ILP offices in Barcelona.

> He slipped into the empty office, stole files, took them to the Russian Embassy, had them photographed and returned before anyone got back. It was a point of pride for him that, in the course of not many days, copies of everything on the ILP Barcelona files were in the hands of his Russian handlers (ibid).

Details of Crook's activities are held in the KGB archives, although Orwell's KGB file is still under wraps. Among his reports was an observation that he was '95 per cent certain' that Eileen was having an affair with Georges Kopp, another ILP member (ibid). Crook had been instructed by the Soviets to seek out the existence of affairs, as such information could enable the communists to blackmail vulnerable targets. He passed his reports to Hugh O'Donnell, another communist from London, whose codename was O'Brien. According to Bowker, Orwell was oblivious to this, 'the fact that the character in *Nineteen Eighty-Four* who first wins the confidence of Winston Smith and then betrays him is given the name O'Brien must be one of the strangest coincidences in literature' (ibid).

Adding further to the mysteries came the revelation in 2006 that Orwell's closest comrade in Spain, Georges Kopp, went on allegedly to spy for MI5, in a case being run by Anthony Blunt (later to be revealed a Soviet spy). Kopp was captured in Spain and tortured but somehow managed to survive (Fenton 2006).

Spooks follow Orwell to the Beeb

In August 1941, Orwell joined the Empire Department of the BBC as head of cultural programmes for India and south-east Asia. During his two-year, largely unhappy stint there, Orwell was closely watched by Special Branch (the source clearly being an employee of the BBC). For instance, a letter dated 20 January 1942 (file number 301/NWC/683), reports in detail on the office politics:

> Eric Blair, who is in the Indian Section of the Middle East Department of the B.B.C. and under the direction of Z.A. BOKHARI (a Punjabi from

Lahore) is in charge of broadcasts in English to India, has been telling some of his Indian friends that his department was endeavouring to get Mulk Raj Anand on the staff, but that the Indian office was strongly opposed to the appointment. He assured his friends, however, that he is going to challenge the right of the India office to dictate as to which people should be employed in his department. BLAIR considers that M. R.ANAND is a well-qualified candidate for the post. Blair was at one time in the Burma Police ... He was practically penniless when he found work with the BBC. This man has advanced communist views and several of his Indian friends say they have often seen him at communist meetings. He dresses in a bohemian fashion both at his office and in his leisure hours. He is particularly friendly with A. SUBRAMANIAN, and has been instrumental in securing occasional broadcasts (presumably in Tamil) for the latter.

The lengthy letter concludes: 'Blair is also mentioned on Special Branch report 402/41/179, dated 10th March, 1941, (copy sent to M.I.5) as having reviewed a book written by Richard Terrell, a well-known communist, on whom M.I.5 asked for a report.' Particularly striking here is the precise detail of the reporting – incorporating references to his friendships, dress and reading habits.

The Crucial Astor/Orwell Friendship

Perhaps the closest clues to Orwell's possible intelligence links lie in his extremely close friendship with David Astor, the millionaire *Observer* journalist whose father owned the newspaper and who was to be its celebrated editor from 1948 to 1975. Astor served in the early part of the Second World War in naval intelligence alongside Ian Fleming (later author of the James Bond spy novels) (Cabell 2008: 12) and later with the covert Special Operations Executive (SOE).[3] Thereafter, he maintained close links with intelligence.

Both Cockett (1991: 94) and Crick (1980: 425-26) report that Astor had been determined to meet Orwell after reading his 'Lion and the Unicorn' (1941) and finally secured an introduction to him through Cyril Connolly, an old-Etonian friend of Orwell, then editing the influential journal *Horizon* and filling in for the *Observer*'s literary editor. They met in a café near the BBC off Portland Place where Orwell was working on broadcasts to India. As Bowker (op cit: 291) records: 'The two became firm and lasting friends. Orwell contributed to Astor's page and became in due course a celebrated *Observer* contributor.'

After leaving the BBC in November 1943, Orwell planned to report for the *Observer* from Algiers and Sicily following the Allied landings but the authorities turned him down on health grounds. Orwell then quickly acquired the post of literary editor at the leftist weekly *Tribune*, which he held until February 1945 when he resigned to take on the war reporting assignment.

Was the Assignment to the Continent a Cover for an Intelligence Mission?
Was it a cover for an intelligence mission? Dorril (2000: 457) certainly reports that in 1944 Astor was transferred to a unit liaising between SOE and the resistance in France, helping the French underground in London spread the word to groups throughout Europe. While in Paris, perhaps inspired by Astor, Orwell attended the first conference of the Committee for European Federation, bringing together resistance groups from around Europe. The French novelist and editor of *Combat*, Albert Camus, was amongst those present. Astor was later adamant that Orwell had no intelligence links[4] and Peter Davison, editor of Orwell's twenty volume collected works, commented: 'I doubt if Orwell would be involved with intelligence – but that by no means says he wasn't.'[5]

Yet significantly most of the men he met in Paris on his assignment were working for intelligences services of one kind or another. One of them was Malcolm Muggeridge who introduced him to P. G. Wodehouse (Wolfe 1995: 215; Muggeridge 1975: 256-257). Muggeridge had been assigned to keep watch on the comic novelist who was suspected of having Nazi sympathies following his broadcasts in the summer of 1941 from Berlin for the American CBS network (Donaldson 2005 [1982]: 259-260).[6] Orwell had written an article in defence of Wodehouse in February just before leaving on his assignment (though it was not published until July in the *Windmill* magazine) and may simply have wanted to express his admiration to the creator of Jeeves and Bertie Wooster (Keeble 2001).

Malcolm Muggeridge (1903-1990) began his journalistic career as Moscow correspondent for the *Manchester Guardian* and during the Second World War served in the British Secret Intelligence Service (MI6) in Brussels, Lourenco Marques in Portuguese East Africa and Paris. Later he worked closely with the CIA-funded Congress for Cultural Freedom and *Encounter* magazine (see Saunders 1999). During the late 1940s he was the *Daily Telegraph*'s Washington correspondent and became its deputy editor before a four-year stint (1953-1957) as editor of the satirical journal *Punch*.

Orwell also met the philosopher (and fellow old-Etonian) A. J. 'Freddie' Ayer,[7] who was in Paris for the Secret Intelligence Service, at that time particularly concerned about the danger of a communist coup (Ayer 1977: 286-287; Rogers 1999: 192). Another writer Orwell saw was Ernest Hemingway whom he had previously met in Barcelona during the Spanish civil war. The American novelist, who was serving as a war correspondent and staying at the Paris

Ritz, had close links with members of the Office of Strategic Services (OSS, the forerunner of the CIA) and his son, Jack, was member of the OSS (Whiting 1999: 104).

Carlos Baker's account of the meeting in his biography of Hemingway (1972 [1969]: 672-673), based on a letter he wrote to the critic Hervey Breit on 16 April 1952, only adds to the mystery: 'Orwell looked nervous and worried. He said he feared that the Communists were out to kill him and asked Hemingway for the loan of a pistol. Ernest lent him the .32 Colt that Paul Willerts had given him in June. Orwell departed like a pale ghost.' Andrew Belsey raises some intriguing questions about this incident: Why did Paul Willerts give a pistol to Hemingway? Where did the pistol come from? Was Willerts authorised to give away weapons that presumably belonged to the military? What happened to the pistol after it was lent to Orwell? Was it returned, or did Orwell retain it?[8] Belsey comments: 'Group-Captain Paul Willerts was Air Attaché in Paris at the time. He was the son of Sir Arthur Willerts, previously head of the press office at the FO, and before that *Times* correspondent in Washington. No doubt both were familiar with the magic circle of intelligence.'[9]

Most evenings in Paris, Orwell dined with Harold Acton, whom he had known vaguely at Eton and who was working as a press censor for SHAEF (the Supreme Headquarters Allied Expeditionary Force) (Bowker op cit: 324).

Orwell's possible links with the security service (MI5) have been explored in detail by West (1992: 162-165). West reports a 'retired CIA officer in Washington' asserting that Orwell worked for MI5 and suggests that he could have developed contacts with Maxwell Knight, head of MI5's Department B5(b) counter-subversion unit and a former pupil of Orwell's prep school, St Cyprian's, in Eastbourne. Yet Anthony Masters (1984) makes no reference to Orwell in his biography of Knight.

Intriguingly, an FBI file (NUMBER 62-69317) on Orwell also exists.[10] Released in October 1999 through a Freedom of Information request, it contains as many as 90 pages, 79 of which have been released, the rest – for some reason – withheld.[11] In one section of the file, Eugene Reynal, vice-president of Harcourt, Brace and Co, publishers of the American edition of *Nineteen Eighty-Four*, is reported to have written to FBI director J. Edgar Hoover, asking him to endorse the book. 'We hope you might be interested in helping to call this book to the attention of the American public, and thus perhaps helping to halt totalitarianism,' Reynal wrote. Hoover declined – but placed the request in a file he had created on Orwell.

According to the citations in the FBI dossier, Orwell's books appealed to activists of all kinds. On the last page of the file – a memo on the bombing of the US Air Force Academy's officer's mess by a group calling itself 'Americong' – there follows an excerpt from *Nineteen Eighty-Four*: '[I]n a physical sense war involves very small numbers of people, mostly highly trained specialists. The fighting ... takes place on the vague frontiers whose whereabouts the average man can only guess.'

Perhaps more intriguingly still, William J. Donovan, head of OSS during the final years of the Second World War, met Orwell during a visit to London. Richard Dunlop, in his biography of Donovan (1982: 214), reports them talking about 'how British institutions were standing up under the strain of war'. Orwell fails to record this meeting in any of his diaries.

Orwell and that 'Little List' of 'Crypto-Communists'
Speculation about Orwell's links with the secret services intensified after Shelden reported in his biography of Orwell (1991: 467-469) that he had drawn up a 'little list' of 38 people, briefly (and somewhat crudely) identifying their politics, religious affiliations, sexual preferences and possible communist sympathies (see also Saunders 1999: 298-301). Orwell's original list contained 105 names. Intriguingly, the British government still refuses to open up the notebook to public view (Lucas 2003: 106). The 'known' suspects include Labour MPs, the future Poet Laureate, Cecil Day-Lewis, authors J. P. Priestley and John Steinbeck, journalist Richard Crossman, actors Michael Redgrave, Charlie Chaplin and Paul Robeson, actor and director Orson Welles, and the historians A. J. P. Taylor and Isaac Deutscher.

According to Lashmar and Oliver (1998: 97) Orwell supplied the list to his friend, the sister in law of the author Arthur Koestler, Celia Kirwan (née Paget) in 1949 when she was working as Robert Conquest's assistant for the secret state's propaganda unit, the Information Research Department (IRD), recently established by the Labour government. However, Newsinger notes (1999: 36-37): 'It is most unlikely that Orwell realised the real nature of IRD at the time.' Kirwan denied that the list ever reached the Foreign Office.[12] D. J. Taylor (2002) suggests that both Orwell at the time and Kirwan,[13] when it was finally published, were concerned to downplay its significance, though quietly emphasising the need for such items.

> Orwell thought it 'not very sensational'. This, after all was the height of the Cold War. And indeed, many IRD contacts were later revealed to have had communist sympathies (ibid).

Scott Lucas (op cit: 110), however, is unforgiving: 'Far from being a one-off indiscretion, Orwell's list is the culmination of his response to the left from the 1930s onwards. Not only could he not co-operate with many fellow writers and activists, not only did he denigrate them publicly and privately, but he maintained a watch on them as possible subversives.' James Smith, in his history of British writers and MI5 surveillance between 1930 and 1960, is equally scathing. He comments (2013: 145): 'There can be little doubt that Orwell's choice to provide this information to the IRD was a gross miscalculation, whatever excuses are made about physical sickness clouding his judgment or the sincerity of his belief regarding the necessity of opposing totalitarian communism.' Smith continues (ibid): '... given Orwell's wartime fears about the secret files being kept by police, it was hypocritical in the extreme for Orwell to then swell the secret files held by other agencies.'

The release of Public Record Office documents in 1995 finally threw some light on the IRD. It 'ran' dozens of Fleet Street journalists and a vast array of news agencies across the globe until (according to the official record) it was closed down by foreign secretary David Owen in 1977. It was funded, like MI6, by the 'secret vote' and was thus beyond parliamentary scrutiny. John Rennie, its second head between 1953 and 1958, was later appointed head of MI6.

IRD distributed across the globe 'white' (true), 'grey' (partially true) and 'black' (false) propaganda, planting smears, lies, false rumours and forged official reports in the media. As Phillip Deery comments: 'IRD worked hard to ensure that its propagandists – speechwriters, broadcasters, journalists and politicians – used the most effective words and phrases in their articles and speeches.'[14] And according to John Pilger (1998: 495-496):

> In the anti-colonial struggles in Kenya, Malaya and Cyprus, IRD was so successful that the journalism served up as a record of those episodes was a cocktail of the distorted and false, in which the real aims and often atrocious behaviour of the British were suppressed. Thus the bloodshed in Malaya was and still is misrepresented as a 'model' of counter-insurgency; the anti-imperial uprising in Kenya was and still is distorted as a Mau Mau terror campaign against whites; and the struggle for basic human rights in Northern Ireland became and remains a noble defence of order and stability against IRA terror.

Paul Lashmar and James Oliver (1998) argue:

> The vast IRD enterprise had one sole aim: to spread its ceaseless propaganda output (i.e. a mixture of outright lies and distorted facts) among top-ranking journalists who worked for major agencies, papers and magazines, including Reuters and the BBC, as well as every other available channel. It worked abroad to discredit communist parties in Western Europe which might gain a share of power by entirely democratic means, and at home to discredit the British Left.[15]

By 1960, IRD was the largest and fastest-growing department of the post-war Foreign Office though the official *Diplomatic List* for the year would have given no such indication (Aldrich 1998: 2-3). But under Harold Wilson, the Labour Party cut funding to IRD when it took office in 1964, again in 1968 and 'slashed' funding in 1970 (Dorril and Ramsay 1991: 110). The CIA's expansion in 1965 of the London-based propaganda unit, Forum World Features (FWF), with the knowledge and co-operation of British intelligence, was probably a response to the political and financial pressures on IRD (ibid). Nick Davies suggests (2008: 227) that FWF supplied reports to 140 newspapers around the world.

Conclusion
Intriguingly, the intelligence file on Orwell continued right up until his death. A note saying simply 'George Orwell @ Eric Arthur BLAIR died on the 21st, January, 1950' was made on 17 November 1952 (file number PF 62.162). Other items in the file include a copy of his application for a passport (just before he headed off to Spain), dated 8 December 1936. He writes

> Height: 6 ft 2 and a half inches
>
> Colour of eyes: Grey
>
> Colour of hair: Brown
>
> Visible distinguishing marks: Tattoo marks on backs of hands.

There are also photographs (catalogue reference kv/2/2699) and a copy of one of his 'As I Please' columns he wrote while literary editor of the leftist journal, *Tribune*, from 1943-1947 (see Keeble 2007; Anderson 2006). In the column, Orwell talks about being 'an industrious collector of pamphlets, and a fairly steady reader of political literature of all kinds'. He continues:

> When I look through my collection of pamphlets – Conservative, Communist, Catholic, Trotskyist, Pacifist, Anarchist or what-have-you – it seems to me that almost all of them have the same mental atmosphere, though the points of emphasis vary. Nobody is searching for the truth, everybody is putting forward a 'case' with complete disregard for fairness and accuracy, and the most plainly obvious facts can be ignored by those who don't want to see them.

Orwell goes on in the second section of the column to concentrate on pacifists, refusing to condemn them all. He adds:

> In my opinion a few pacifists are inwardly pro-Nazi, and extremist Left-wing parties will inevitably contain Fascist spies. The important thing is to discover which individuals are honest and which are not and the usual blanket accusation merely makes this more difficult.

It was possibly these comments on pacifism which particularly attracted the attention of Special Branch. Other sections of the column (on the prominence of men with Irish names in American history and on a long letter from Mr Martin Walter, controller of the British Institute of Fiction-Writing Science Ltd complaining that Orwell had 'traduced' him) were significantly cut away as unwanted (see Anderson op cit: 214-216).

There is, then, a paradox at the heart of Orwell's relationship to the intelligence services. For while he had, through his friendship with David Astor, probably joined the spooks in some capacity, he was still the subject of close Special Branch surveillance begun during his time as a journalist in Paris in the late 1920s. Moreover, while his submission of the 'little list' of 'crypto-communists' is often seen as an out-of-character behaviour, it is perhaps best seen as consistent with the acts of a man already caught up for a number years of with intelligence – and author of the most chilling warnings of the threat of the emergent secret state: *Nineteen Eighty-Four*.

Notes

[1] All the transcriptions from the intelligence files will follow the style of writing (punctuation, use of capital letters etc) of the original

[2] Ethel Mannin (1900-1984) is vastly underrated today. The author of 91 works (according to a list on Wikipedia) and six autobiographies, she was a friend of Orwell, a member of the Independent Labour Party in the 1930s and later moved towards anarchism (see Newsinger 2017)

[3] Cabell (2008: 40-52) also reports that Fleming may well have played a central role in luring Rudolf Hess to Scotland in May 1941. SOE was established by PM Winston Churchill and Hugh Dalton in July 1940 'to facilitate espionage and sabotage behind enemy lines' and serve as the nucleus of a resistance movement if Britain were invaded by the Axis Powers (ibid: 45)

[4] In an interview with the author, London, November 1999

[5] In a letter to the author dated 7 December 1999

[6] Wodehouse's note to MI5 was released on 25 August 2011. He said: 'I never had any intention of assisting the enemy and I have suffered a great deal of mental pain as the result of my action.' MI5 decided against taking any action. But in 1946, the case was re-evaluated and it was decided that if ever Wodehouse returned to the UK he would be prosecuted. Wodehouse moved to the US in 1945 and lived there until his death in 1975

[7] From October 1941 to March 1943, Ayer worked as a Special Operations Executive agent within British Security Co-ordination with cover symbol G.246, in the Political and Minorities Section. He worked on intelligence relating to Latin America, particularly Argentina and Chile. In 1950, he attended the Berlin Congress for Cultural Freedom as a member of the British delegation, which was funded by the Foreign Office through the Information Research Department. See http://www.spinprofiles.org/index.php/A.J._Ayer, accessed on 6 August 2009

[8] Email to author, 22 July 2011

[9] ibid

[10] See http://www.mail-archive.com/ctrl@listserv.aol.com/msg26142.html, accessed on 1 April 2012

[11] I would like to thank Tim Sasaki for alerting me to the existence of the FBI file on Orwell

[12] In a letter to the author from Peter Davison, dated 24 February 1999 (see http://www.mi5.gov.uk/output/former-dgs.html, accessed on 14 April 2009)

[13] In 1954, Celia married her second husband, the diplomat Arthur Goodman. They had two children but the marriage was cut short by his death in a shooting accident in 1964 (see Taylor 2002)

[14] The terminology of terrorism: Malaya 1948-52, *Journal of South East Asian Studies*, June, 2003. Available online at http://www.accessmylibrary.com/coms2/summary_0286-4205179_ITM, accessed on 11 June 2008

[15] See http://www.spinprofiles.org/index.php/Information_Research_Department, accessed on 14 February 2010

References

Aldrich, Richard (1998) *Espionage, Security and Intelligence in Britain 1945-1970*, Manchester, New York: Manchester University Press

Anderson, Paul (2006) *Orwell in Tribune*, London: Politico's

Ayer, A. J. 'Freddie' (1977) *A Part of My Life*, Oxford: Oxford Paperbacks

Baker, Carlos (1972 [1969]) *Ernest Hemingway: A Life Story*, Harmondsworth, Middlesex: Penguin Books

Bowker, Gordon (2003) *George Orwell*, London: Little, Brown

Cabell, Craig (2008) *Ian Fleming's Secret War*, Barnsley, South Yorkshire: Pen and Sword Books

Crick, Bernard (1980) *George Orwell: A Life*, Harmondsworth, Middlesex: Penguin Books

Cockett, Richard (1991) *David Astor and the Observer*, London: Deutsch

Davies, Nick (2008) *Flat Earth News*, London: Chatto and Windus

Donaldson, Frances (2005 [1982]) *P. G. Wodehouse: A Biography*, London: Carlton Publishing Group

Dorril, Stephen (2000) *MI6: Fifty Years of Special Operations*, London: Fourth Estate.

Dorril, Stephen and Ramsay, Robin (1991) *Smear*, London: Fourth Estate

Dunlop, Richard (1982) *Donovan: America's Master Spy*, New York: Rand McNally and Company

Fenton, Ben (2006) Orwell's comrade in Spain 'was a double agent', *Daily Telegraph*, 30 May

Keeble, Richard (2001) Orwell as war correspondent: A reassessment, *Journalism Studies*, Vol. 2, No. 3 pp 393-406

Keeble, Richard (2007) The lasting in the ephemeral: Assessing George Orwell's 'As I Please' columns, Keeble, Richard and Wheeler, Sharon (eds) *The Journalistic Imagination: Literary Journalists from Defoe to Capote and Carter*, London and New York: Routledge pp 100-115

Lashmar, Paul and Oliver, James (1998) *Britain's Secret Propaganda War 1948-1977*, Stroud: Sutton

Lucas, Scott (2003) *Orwell*, London: Haus Publishing

Masters, Anthony (1984) *The Man who was 'M': The Life of Maxwell Knight*, Oxford: Blackwell

Muggeridge, Malcolm (1975) *Chronicles of Wasted Time, Vol. 2: The Infernal Grove*, London: Fontana

Newsinger, John (1999) The American connection: George Orwell, 'Literary Trotskyism' and the New York intellectuals, *Labour History Review*, Vol. 64, No. 1 pp 23-43

Newsinger, John (2017) Ethel Mannin: Hidden from history, *Socialist Review*, October. Available online at http://socialistreview.org.uk/428/ethel-mannin-hidden-history

Pilger, John (1998) *Hidden Agendas*, London: VIntage

Rogers, Ben (1999) *A. J. Ayer: A Life*, London: Chatto and Windus

Saunders, Frances Stonor (1999) *Who Paid the Piper? The CIA and the Cultural Cold War*, Cambridge: Granta

Shelden, Michael (1991) *Orwell: The Authorised Biography*, London: Heinemann

Smith, James (2013) *British Writers and MI5 Surveillance 1930-1960*, Cambridge: Cambridge University Press

Taylor, D. J. (2002) Celia Goodman: Sensitive presence in the literary worlds of Connolly, Koestler and Orwell (obituary), *Guardian*, 6 November

Taylor, D. J. (2003) *Orwell: The Life*, London: Chatto and Windus

West, W. J. (1992) *The Larger Evils:* Nineteen Eight-Four*: The Truth behind the Satire*, Edinburgh: Canongate

Whiting, Charles (1999) *Hemingway Goes to War*, Stroud, Gloucestershire: Alan Sutton Publishing

Wolfe, Gregory (1995) *Malcolm Muggeridge: A Biography*, London: Hodder and Stoughton

- This essay was originally published in *Orwell Today*, edited by Richard Lance Keeble, Bury St Edmunds: Abramis, 2012 pp 151-163.

Chapter 3

Orwell – by his Great Friend David Astor

In 2000, Richard Lance Keeble interviewed David Astor, the legendary editor of the Observer *and the great friend of George Orwell, in his London home – close to the Lord's Cricket Ground. Since then, he has used snippets from the interview in articles he has written on Orwell. This is the full transcript of that interview. It was to be the last interview given by Astor: he died a year later on 7 December 2001*

How did Orwell strike you when you first met him in 1942?

I felt I had known him all my life: he was so straightforward. We met in the bar of the Langham Hotel, near the BBC in London. At that time, I was looking for writers to contribute to a new 'Forum' opinion column in the *Observer* ... I had asked Cyril Connolly [editor of the literary magazine, *Horizon*] 'Who's good on politics?' and he said at once 'Orwell'. I'd read 'The Lion and the Unicorn' and was much impressed. As Connolly said, Orwell was the first of the left-wing writers of that time to have discovered the English. He had a very strong feeling for English culture. Who else did? Most other English intellectuals were more at home admiring Soviet or French culture.

Did the stress on the need for a socialist and even violent revolution in 'The Lion and the Unicorn' frighten you?

No. I would have accepted any revolution he would have made as he was such a champion of liberty. He was also a social democrat, never a Marxist. His Spanish experience [fighting alongside the Republicans 1936-1937] was fundamental to his political development as that was when he discovered there wasn't any moral difference between communism and fascism. He was one of the first people to say so.

Did you subsequently read more of Orwell's works? Which were your favourites and what do you consider his strengths as a writer?

I went on to read everything he'd written. I particularly liked the critical essays he wrote for *Horizon*. And what appealed? Everything. He had that wonderful clear, open, simple style. He didn't talk down. He wasn't malicious but he was always strong. I liked his standard of judgment and the way he assessed people; for instance, his essay on Dickens. I don't think of him as a journalist. The best things he did for journalism were book reviews. He was a political writer, a literary critic but not a journalist. *The Road to Wigan Pier*, for instance, is a form of reportage that goes much deeper than news.

Do you think he felt uneasy working for a mainstream Fleet Street newspaper [when, for instance, Orwell travelled to the Continent as a war correspondent in 1945 for the Observer *and* Manchester Evening News*] given the strong criticisms he voices about them – as being propaganda for their proprietors – throughout his writings?*

He certainly did not write for hostile publishers. For instance, he chose to write for the *Partisan Review* in the States because it was an outlet he trusted. He wrote mainly book reviews for the *Observer* on his own terms. His first dealings were with Ivor Brown [*Observer* editor] who accepted him at my suggestion but didn't particularly like him. Eventually, he fell out with Brown. When I became editor in 1948, I made E. J. B. Rose literary editor. He failed to use two of Orwell's reviews. So I replaced him with Terence Kilmartin. He also showed hesitation over some of Orwell's reviews. As I did not want to force him on my colleagues, when he said he had received an offer from *Tribune* [in 1943] of a regular column, I agreed that he should take it. This never affected our friendship.

Did you ever talk about your times at Eton with Orwell?

Towards the end of his life, I had a son and had to decide which school to send him to. I asked George: 'What do you think of Eton as a school?' And he said: 'I've got nothing against the education. I think it's very good. But they will have to change the school dress. I wouldn't let my son have to wear a tailcoat and make a fool of him.' Orwell had apparently treated Eton as a kind of university. He got himself very well read but not by following the syllabus. Surprisingly, he became friends with the then-Provost, Monty James, an outstanding scholar who also wrote ghost stories. Ivor Brown, who disliked Eton, once gave Orwell a book on the school to review expecting him to slate it. Instead, Orwell wrote that Eton was the only 'public school' which was not reformed in the 19th century by Dr Arnold. It was, therefore, left with a certain amount of 'medieval class' and that enabled you to take the education you wanted. This approach may explain why he did not excel at Eton and also why he never felt his lack of university education.

You visited Orwell at his homes in London. How did they strike you?

I remember his basement flat in Belsize. It was run with characteristic simplicity and a nice, homely atmosphere. It had a small garden which he used as a chicken run. I spent the night there once. And I remember in the morning hearing the clanking of a bucket – as if he was a part-time farmer.

Orwell and his first wife, Eileen, adopted a son, Richard Horatio, just before Eileen's tragic death in 1945. What kind of father was he?

I saw him bath Richard with the greatest care but with a cigarette in his mouth. I asked him if he might return Richard to the adoption society now that he had no wife to help him. He answered: 'Certainly not.'

The only time Orwell worked as a straight reporter was as a war correspondent on the Continent in 1945 for the Observer *and* Manchester Evening News. *How did you rate his performance?*

This reporting was not particularly exciting because he went under a misapprehension. He hoped to pick up the atmosphere of a dictatorship but by the time he arrived in Germany it had largely disappeared.

During this assignment in Paris, Orwell met Malcolm Muggeridge and the philosopher A. J. Ayer who were both working for the intelligence services at the time. He also met Ernest Hemingway who had close links with OSS, the forerunner of the CIA. Could Orwell have been on an intelligence mission?

I feel certain that he had no link with intelligence.

What impact did Orwell have on the general development of the Observer?

He only gave me one piece of advice – at the end of the war when I went back to the *Observer*. He said the paper should get interested in Africa – particularly South Africa – and should see we didn't make the same mistakes as we'd made in India. As a result, the *Observer* became the first paper to take a serious interest in what was then a non-subject. We campaigned against apartheid before anyone else and I appointed writers – such as Colin Legum – specialising in Africa. Also when I became editor in 1948 I made Orwell's essay 'Politics and the English Language' the newspaper's style book.

You played an important role in Orwell's move to the remote Scottish island of Jura. How did that happen?

I gather he always had the idea to go to the Western Isles but I didn't know that. All I knew was that at the end of the war he was extremely tired and not well. And I thought that Jura was a lonely place he would like. He didn't go as my guest. My family had an estate in the centre of the island and I knew a family who lived in the extreme north at Kinuachdrachd. I wrote to them suggesting they take in Orwell as a paying guest. They had never had such a request and I had to use much persuasion to get him in. I thought he would simply take one holiday there. But he saw this empty house, Barnhill, nearby and to my amazement decided to try to rent it and live there. I certainly didn't think it was a suitable place for an unwell person to live. For instance, you had to travel 16 miles simply to pick up the post. However, I knew the Fletcher family who owned the north part of the island and I wrote to them supporting his application. I never visited him on the island as I felt it might be an imposition. He spent one night at our house half way up the island where my father happened to be. Both took to each other which I would quite have expected.

You helped Orwell a lot in his final illnesses.

Through family connections in America I was able to get the drug streptomycin sent to him in hospital. Nye Bevan [Minister of Health], who was a great admirer of Orwell, when asked for permission to import the drug agreed at once to do so.

How do you account for Orwell, towards the end of his life, supplying a list of 'crypto-communists' to his friend Celia Kirwan who was working for the Information Research Department, the propaganda unit of the Foreign Office, recently set up by the Labour government?

These people were working for the British government while being active sympathisers of 'fellow travellers' with the Soviet Union. The government would not have wanted to employ them if this affiliation had been known to them. I don't think Orwell was doing anything wrong in exposing them.

Sonia Brownell was to marry Orwell near the end of his life. What did you make of her?

He knew her as a strikingly good-looking member of the staff of *Horizon*. Later I imagined she was the model for Julia in *Nineteen Eighty-Four*. When she married him [on 13 October 1949] she certainly did not expect him to die. They were planning to take a holiday in Switzerland together with Lucian Freud, the artist. I, rightly or wrongly, took Sonia to be somebody who looked sexually active but wasn't. I imagined this must be the case when she married someone who was plainly an invalid. But I don't think she married him because he had money as his great success wasn't yet evident. Strangely, I don't think she understood him as an original thinker. After he died, she had had a quarrel with Arthur Koestler who thought she had not understood Orwell's real importance. However, I certainly think she came to respect him after he died and showed great loyalty to his memory and behaved extremely well as his literary executor. I cannot pretend to have understood her and did not keep in touch with her after his death.

You helped arrange the funeral. Did Orwell ever talk to you about any religious feelings?

It was a complete surprise to me that he had wanted to be buried in a church yard. As he could not have been buried in a London church yard, not being a parishioner, I persuaded the vicar of my local church [in the village of Sutton Courtenay, Oxfordshire, where the Astors had an estate] to bury him. But he had a funeral service in London. I came to it in a taxi with Avril, his sister, and I asked her: 'Who did Orwell most admire?' I was meaning what individuals he admired. But she took it to mean something else and answered: 'I can tell you that very easily: he admired the working class mother of ten.'

- This was first published in the Orwell Society *Journal* of June 2014, No. 4 pp 8-10 under the title: 'Exclusive: Orwell by his Great Friend David Astor'.

Chapter 4

Beyond Big Brother: The Story of Surveillance in Britain and America

A review of *We Know All About You: The Story of Surveillance in Britain and America*, by Rhodri Jeffreys-Jones, Oxford University Press, Oxford, 2017 pp 290 (ISBN 978 0 19 874966 0)

Orwell's *Nineteen Eighty-Four*, though first published in 1949, still stands as probably the most influential depiction of a Big Brother society in which state-controlled surveillance intrudes into the most intimate aspects of citizens' lives. As Peter Marks comments (2015: 14): 'The disembodied emblem of the Party (never seen in the flesh and only ever viewed in posters "plastered everywhere"), Big Brother, remains a potent symbol of totalitarian power and of invasive monitoring.'

In this outstanding, brief overview of the history of surveillance and debates surrounding it in the UK and US, University of Edinburgh academic Rhodri Jeffreys-Jones challenges head-on Orwell's representation of the secret state in his celebrated dystopian novel. According to Jeffreys-Jones, Orwell concentrated exclusively on state surveillance thus ignoring the crucial role of private snooping. Moreover, spying on working people has been the dominant feature in the history of surveillance – yet too often ignored by historians.

For Jeffreys-Jones, the rise of Europe's nation states, the growth of military organisation, urbanisation and of capitalism all contributed to the development of surveillance. He continues (pp 12-13): 'The United States, however, took the lead. Contrary to the assumptions of those who have concentrated on the role of the organized state, it was the distinctively American combination of weak government and strong business that underpinned the rise of surveillance.' An early example of private surveillance occurred on the slave plantations of rural America. But the world's first major surveillance operation resulted from the development of the credit rating industry. Agents 'made local inquiries into merchants' credit-worthiness, often equating it with moral characteristics. Under instruction from their boss, they would look for signs of sexual licence, slothfulness and drunkenness as well, of course, dishonesty. In building the profiles of potential clients, they paid heed to factors like ethnicity, age and business history. The credit reporters also checked tax assessments, lawsuits, bankruptcy proceedings and financial statements' (p. 15).

While in the 19th century no government activity remotely approached the scale of credit surveillance, however, at federal level there were developments: in 1790 Congress supplied President George Washington a 'contingency fund' to pay for spies – and the privilege of not having to account for how he spent it. Later, the Office of Naval Intelligence (formed in 1882) and the Military Information Division (1885) would not engage in domestic surveillance until the twentieth century. In the UK around this time, numerous police spies operated in an attempt to frustrate the franchise movement (p. 19). Then, in 1873, the Intelligence Branch of the War Office was formed – while a decade later the Irish Special Branch was formed within Scotland Yard to combat the rise of violent Irish nationalism and the Naval Intelligence Department came into being.

By the early twentieth century, private detectives (immortalised in Arthur Conan Doyle's Sherlock Holmes) in both the UK and US constituted a substantial industry (p. 20). In the UK, Admiral Reginald 'Blinker' Hall set up the Economic League in 1926, providing blacklists of radical trade unionists to employers (p. 27). Meanwhile, in the States, corporate surveillance of workers intensified. Col. Ralph Van Deman compiled lists of trade union activists nationwide. 'When he circulated his data to potential employers, they served as a blacklist. If you were on that blacklist, you did not get a job' (p. 26). Jeffreys-Jones argues (p. 28): 'Aimed as it was against working people and not the articulate middle classes [and I guess we can include Orwell in this group], blacklisting has not figured in the traditional litany of surveillance excesses.'

By the 1930s, the Pinkerton National Detective Agency, founded in 1850, was conducting massive snooping on workers – as revealed during hearings of the La Follete Civil Liberties Committee of the Senate (p. 72). General Motors could not conceal the fact that it had spent around $1 million on informers within the United Automobile Workers Union (ibid). At the state level, close watch was held on radical intellectuals. By the end of the 1930s there were FBI files on Clifford Odets, Ernest Hemingway, John Steinbeck, Pearl Buck, William Faulkner and Upton Sinclair, the Atlantic solo flyer Charles Lindbergh and the historian Harry Elmer Barnes (pp 82-89).

Even as Orwell was penning his dystopian masterpiece on his Scottish island refuge, 'Vansittartism' was creeping into the core of British life. Named after its architect, the senior diplomat, Sir Robert, later Lord Vansittart,

Jeffreys-Jones describes it as a silent (and, therefore, more insidious) form of McCarthyism – involving the blacklisting of BBC employees and the hounding of Church of England vicars (p. 30).

By the 21st century, private enterprises continued to play crucial roles in the security state. In the US for instance, the Office of the Director of National Intelligence reported in 2007 that more than 37,000 private contractors worked for the federal government on covert operations and security matters (p. 33). In the UK, a focus here is on the Hackgate controversy (highlighted in the Leveson Inquiry in 2011) – and the snooping conducted by the corporate press (pp 185-186). Later chapters take in a wide variety of subjects including:

- the surveillance of Communist Party and Socialist Workers Party members;
- the surveillance of black civil rights campaigners, feminists and pacifists in the US;
- Special Branch snooping on Jeremy Corbyn (later to be leader of the Labour Party);
- evidence that almost 75 per cent of American companies monitor worker communication,
- and the intensification of the activities of the secret state post 9/11 in both the US and UK (pp 187-219).

Jeffreys-Jones concludes that, in terms of harm done to people on a daily basis, private surveillance (ignored by Orwell) outperforms its public counterpart (p. 243). Yet some of Jeffreys-Jones's conclusions are distinctly off-target. For instance, he says (p. 244): 'The surveillance branches of the US and UK intelligence communities have in recent years behaved relatively well, to the best of our knowledge.' Moreover, the book is lacking a theoretical edge that could highlight the private sector not as autonomous from the state in advanced capitalist societies but economically, politically and ideologically closely tied to it.

However, overall, the author has presented a convincing critique of Orwellian statism – directing our attention to the (too often marginalised) role of private surveillance in the security state.

Reference
Marks, Peter (2015) George Orwell and the history of surveillance studies, Keeble, Richard Lance (ed.) *George Orwell Now!*, Bury St Edmunds: Abramis pp 13-29

• This review was first published in *George Orwell Studies*, Vol. 2, No. 1 pp 143-146.

Chapter 5

Two Wonderful Ways to Celebrate *Nineteen Eighty-Four*'s Anniversary

A review of two literary biographies marking the 70 years since Orwell's great dystopian novel was published – to global acclaim

You may well think that everything possible to say about Orwell's masterpiece, *Nineteen Eighty-Four*, has already been said – by the biographers, literary critics, bloggers and journalist commentators. Yet Dorian Lynskey (in *The Ministry of Truth: A Biography of George Orwell's* 1984, Picador) and D. J. Taylor (in *On* Nineteen Eighty-Four: *A Biography*, Abrams Press) both manage to offer new insights and information.

Lynskey's is the longer and more ambitious book (355 pages compared to Taylor's 194). It is split into two parts: the first begins in 1936 with Orwell on his way to fight alongside the Republicans in the Spanish civil war and follows the biographical chronology until the publication of *Nineteen Eighty-Four* and his death – just 227 days later. The second section traces the 'biography' of the novel – from 1954 and the first BBC production (afterwards, hundreds of viewers complained to the corporation about its excessive amounts of violence and sexuality) up to the era of President Donald Trump and all the controversies over 'fake news' and 'alternative facts' (which have helped send it roaring back on to the best-seller lists). In a spirited 'Afterword', Lynskey reminds us of Orwell's final comments: 'The moral to be drawn from this dangerous nightmare situation is a simple one: *Don't let it happen. It depends on you.*' And, clearly with a student market in mind, it ends with an 'Appendix' summarising the novel, chapter by chapter.

The utopian/dystopian tradition is explored in detail with insightful sections on H. G. Wells, Aldous Huxley, Jack London and Yevgeny Zamyatin. One writer new to me is Edward Bellamy (1850-1898), an American journalist and author of the utopian *Looking Backward 2000-1887*. Published in 1888, it won praise from Anton Chekhov, Leo Tolstoy, Jack London, Upton Sinclair, Mark Twain and William Morris and became the most popular novel in the US since *Uncle Tom's Cabin* (1852) and the most imitated since *Jane Eyre* (1847). It was still so well-known in the US in 1949 that the president of the Book of the Month Club described *Nineteen Eighty-Four* as 'Bellamy's *Looking Backward* in reverse'. But, as Lynskey acknowledges, Orwell made no reference to Bellamy anywhere in his writings.

In the biographical opening section, Lynskey does more than simply travel over well-trodden paths but incorporates his own, often incisive and original insights into Orwell – the man and his writings. For instance, he reports that in June 1940, the Nazis began compiling a list of 3,000 British nationals and European exiles to be arrested following a successful invasion. The list, discovered by British soldiers in 1945, included H. G. Wells, Aldous Huxley, Franz Borkenau, Kingsley Martin and Victor Gollancz but not Orwell. Lynskey adds: 'It was a kind of snub that the Nazis did not yet consider him worth arresting.'

Progressive, anti-capitalist novels of the early 1930s which Orwell overlooked (such as *Between Two Men*, by Frederik le Gros Clark, *Purple Plague*, by ILP leader Fenner Brockway, and *Tell the Truth*, by John Strachey's sister Amabel William-Ellis, which, intriguingly, included minor characters called Big Brother and Julia) are acknowledged. Perceptive comments about Orwell's personality pepper the prose throughout. For instance, he writes: 'Orwell did not like London at the best of times, but he bonded with it at the worst of times. The Blitz began on September 7, 1940, and the truth is Orwell found it rather exciting. The puritan in him appreciated the hardship; the socialist savoured the enforced solidarity; the man of action thrilled to the thunder of bombs...'

But Lynskey is most impressive when he moves to consider the novel's 'afterlife'. As he comments: 'The writer who didn't merit an entry in *Who's Who* until the year of his death and won only one award (a $1,000 literary prize from *Partisan Review*) quickly became a byword for honesty and decency.' David Bowie's longstanding obsession with the novel is detailed; its influence on writers such as Martin Amis, Anthony Burgess, Margaret Atwood, Milan Simecka, Neil Postman and film directors including Michael Radford, Terry Gilliam and Michael Moore is explored in depth. In a chapter titled 'Orwellmania', Lynskey tells the story of Apple's extraordinary *1984* advertisement, directed by Ridley Scott and broadcast at the Super Bowl – the biggest US television event of the year. As he observes: 'The commercial was a brilliant example of anti-corporate marketing, twisting Orwell's warning into an upbeat fable for the information age.'

Moreover, for those obsessed with Orwellian trivia, Lynskey has clearly done the counting – and can offer definite delights. For instance, in the novel where the manipulation of the past has become an elaborate industrial process, the word *remember* appears 110 times, *memory* 47 and *forget* or *forgotten* 46; the word *telescreen* is mentioned 119 times, while *rats* are mentioned in all but one of Orwell's nine books.

In contrast, the strength of Taylor's text lies in the way he traces the plot lines, characters, major themes and literary style of *Nineteen Eighty-Four* in Orwell's early life and writings. Lurking in the book is a connection to every other novel Orwell had written – and Taylor carefully teases out these links. For instance, each of his first four novels 'turns out to be quietly prefigurative of the nightmare landscapes of *Nineteen Eighty-Four*': Flory, in *Burmese Days* (1934), Dorothy Hare, in *A Clergyman's Daughter* (1935), Gordon Comstock, in *Keep the Aspidistra Flying* (1936), and George Bowling, in *Coming Up for Air* (1939), are all 'alone or relatively friendless, at the centre of a hostile world from which they cannot escape and where their every movement is subject to constant surveillance'.

Moreover, each of the central characters of these novels 'rebels against the agencies that are out to bring them down and each is eventually forced to retreat, capitulate or at any rate reach some accommodation with the forces that, either directly or indirectly, control their lives'. The sections in the novel where Winston dreams of the Golden Country (linking his love of nature with his love of women) echo the celebrations of the natural world in his earlier novels 'born out of a deep longing for the reflective, slow-moving rural life that Orwell had relished as a child'. And note the detail in Taylor's research: while Winston waits to be summoned to Room 101 he is joined by 'a mean looking man'. Suddenly there is a furious roar on the telescreen: 'Bumstead 2713. Bumstead J! Let fall that piece of bread.' Taylor adds: 'This turns out to be a reference to a man named Jack Bumstead, the son of a Southwold grocer with whom the Blairs had dealt in the 1930s ...'

Taylor is brief but can be insightful when examining the origins of the political ideas embedded in *Nineteen Eighty-Four*. Fighting in Spain, he saw the first warning signs of a phenomenon that would oppress him until the end of his life: the suspicion that the notion of objective truth was 'falling out of the world'. The influences of previous dystopian novels – by Jack London, H. G. Wells, Aldous Huxley and (the lesser known) Ernest Bramagh – are dissected; so too the impact of his two years (1941-1943) working for the BBC on the creation of the Ministry of Truth and Room 101 where Winston is tortured.

Part II of the biography, titled 'During (1943-1949)', considers the publication of *Animal Farm* (1945), his journalism over this period, the sudden death of his wife, his exile to the remote Scottish island of Jura with his recently adopted son, Richard, and sister Avril – and the extraordinary memoir about his years at St Cyprian's prep school, the ironically titled 'Such, Such Were the Joys'. Here Taylor highlights the similarities in the psychological atmosphere between the essay and the dystopian masterpiece. The school is a kind of police state while the young Eric Blair 'sneered at by his teachers for his parents' lack of money and constantly being told that he will never amount to anything', is an early version of Winston Smith.

The links between Sonia Brownell (whom Orwell is to marry in hospital – just days before his untimely death) and Julia (with whom Winston conducts a secret, passionate affair) are explored. And Taylor even wonders if Julia is the willing accomplice of friend-turned-torturer O'Brien: '... the honeytrap expressly set in place with the aim of luring Winston into danger and throwing him into the hands of the Thought Police'. Later in the book, Taylor is even more emphatic about Julia, describing her 'very probably an agent provocateur'.

The final section, 'After (1949 ad infinitum)', examines the novel critically and its 'afterlife' following publication: the international reception, its inspiration for other dystopian novels (by Anthony Burgess and Kingsley Amis, for example) rock songs and radio and film adaptations. In the novel's 12-page Appendix, Taylor detects one of its 'occasional glances at the prospect of a better world'. 'The conclusions of the piece are tantalising in their ambiguity, and the reader is perfectly entitled to assume that when the anonymous author writes that "It was expected that Newspeak would have finally superseded Oldspeak (or Standard English, as we should call it) by about the year 2050", the author is implying that this moment never occurred, that Newspeak has been, gone, and is now regarded as an historical curiosity.'

Michael Radford's 1984 feature film is carefully considered: the director's 'first wife, Czechoslovakian by birth, had been enrolled as a Young Pioneer. Parson's daughter, standing vigilantly by the door of her apartment in her Junior Spy uniform as Winston crawls home from the Ministry of Truth, is clearly modelled on this template'. But the performance by Suzanna Hamilton as Julia (her full-frontal nakedness during the sex scenes making it particularly popular in Japan where such explicitness had never before been allowed) is not commented on.

Both Taylor and Lynskey, then, offer distinct riches. But both, I feel, fail to acknowledge properly the central position of David Astor in the final years of Orwell's life – and his impact on the creation of *Nineteen Eighty-Four*. For it was Astor who introduced Orwell to the world of intelligence. He served in the early part of the Second World War in naval intelligence alongside Ian Fleming (author of the James Bond spy novels) and later with the covert Special Operations Executive (SOE). Thereafter, he maintained close links with intelligence. Astor also introduced Orwell to other intelligence friends through the Shanghai dining group (named after the Soho restaurant where they met) which he had created with his friend and old-Harrovian Edward Hulton.

There were clearly many influences on Orwell in the making of *Nineteen Eighty-Four*. Yet, given Orwell's introduction to the world of spooks by his friend Astor, is it not surprising then that his last great novel should describe a world of Big Brother, of endless warfare, child spies and telescreens – and where the state's surveillance intrudes into the individual's innermost private life? Orwell's ambivalent attitude to just about everything was reflected in his responses to the secret state. On the one hand, he supported it and became friends with some of its operators. But he also saw the secret state's growing powers and was horrified. So he dedicated all his energy (in what proved to be his final years) in his remote house on Jura to composing the crucial warning.

- This review originally appeared in the Orwell Society *Journal*, No. 15, autumn 2019 pp 31-34.

Chapter 6

Barnhill: Missing the Crucial Astor Link

A review of *Barnill: A Novel*, by Norman Bissell, Luarth Press, Edinburgh, 2019 pp 255

The Orwellian *oeuvre* is forever expanding. Only recently, David Dwan offered his scintillating, philosophical reflections on Orwell's political ideas, D. J. Taylor and Dorian Lynskey have had fascinating 'biographies' of *Nineteen Eighty-Four* published to coincide with the novel's 70th anniversary. Now, Norman Bissell contributes an affectionate portrait of Orwell, the man, writer, lover, recluse and caring father in *Barnhill: A Novel*.

As Bissell acknowledges in his fascinating Afterword 'Writing *Barnhill*' (pp 245-251), the Australian author, Dennis Glover, had a similar idea – publishing a novel about Orwell's final years, *The Last Man in Europe*, in 2017. But Bissell is very different, adopting an original and engaging approach by imaging the inner-most thoughts of both Orwell (no simple task since he was a man full of contradictions) and his second wife, Sonia Brownell. These musings appear alongside a more conventional narrative that, in general, follows the historical record closely.

Bissell has clearly done his homework and read widely. His bibliography at the end (p. 255), for instance, includes the major biographies – by Crick, D. J. Taylor, Bowker and Colls – the slim portrait of Sonia by her friend Hilary Spurling; memoirs by T. R. Fyvel and George Woodcock; memories of the man collected by Stephen Wadhams, Audrey Coppard and Bernard Crick; studies of the writings by W. J. West and, of course, Orwell's own writings. And there is a useful timeline (pp 241-244) from November 1943 when Orwell resigns his post at the BBC and becomes literary editor at the leftist journal, *Tribune*, until his death at University College Hospital, London, on 21 January 1950, aged just 46.

The novel begins in May 1944 with Orwell lying awake in his flat on Mortimer Crescent, London, alongside Eileen O'Shaughnessy, whom he had married in 1936. He muses: 'It must be about three o'clock. In the morning. I can't sleep for all these thoughts of my Hebridean island. And Eileen's snoring. ... We're winning the war now and all the little fascists will crawl back into their holes when we do. Until next time. But we've adopted some of their methods so we can win it. Like tapping phones and letter opening and lying on the radio' (p. 11).

The narrative then shifts to an argument between Orwell and Eileen over his continuing affair with his *Tribune* secretary, Sally McEwan. Eileen is deeply distressed. 'She grabbed the dinner plate and threw it at him' (p. 14). This explosion serves to jolt Orwell's conscience – and he decides to stop the affair and concentrate on Eileen and their plans to adopt a baby son. After their Mortimer Crescent flat is destroyed by a Nazi bomb, the scene shifts to the Orwells' new apartment in Canonbury Square where a party of friends is celebrating both the arrival of the adopted son Richard and the publication of *Animal Farm*.

And so the narrative moves on: through an imagined fishing expedition with his eccentric friend Paul Potts; Orwell's departure for the Continent to cover the final months of the Second World War for the *Observer*, his meeting at Hotel Scribe (or was it the Ritz?), in Paris, with Ernest Hemingway who lends him a gun. In Cologne, he is admitted to hospital but soon afterwards the terrible news comes by telegram: his wife has died in an operating theatre in Newcastle. So begins Orwell's search for a woman to help look after Richard.

Once Orwell settled in the remote house, Barnhill, on the Scottish island of Jura, Bissell carefully follows the record – showing him juggling domestic hassles with his attempts to launch into what was to be his last novel, *Nineteen Eighty-Four* (originally titled *The Last Man in Europe*). So the incident in which Paul Potts storms off after Orwell's sister Avril burns his manuscript in the fire is recalled; so too his suspicions that David Holbrook, the friend of child-minder Susan Watson, is a communist spying on him.

The dialogue can at times sound somewhat unconvincing and over-contrived – as can, indeed, be Sonia's interior monologue. For instance, Chapter 6 begins with her pondering Orwell's invitation: 'He gave me detailed instructions of how to get to Barnhill, but I had other plans. You see, that was a very special summer for me. I'd met Maurice Merleau-Ponty in Nice in May and we seemed to get on like a proverbial house on fire. Of course, he had a wife and a young daughter, but that's never stopped a Frenchman' (p. 125).

Some of the most enjoyable scenes are when Bissell lets his imagination run completely free: as for instance, when George misses his train connection in Glasgow and spends the evening in the city. In Montrose Street, he passes a large group of women. He asks them about their work and their foreman, Robert, what it was like in the city during the war. Everyone is surprisingly friendly towards him. Later that evening he buys black pudding from a fish and chip shop: 'It was certainly different from anything else he'd ever tasted, but he reckoned he could grow to like this Glasgow Italian speciality' (p. 142). He sees children playing amongst the filth in the Gorbals. On Stockwell Street, the sound of a fiddle and accordion at the Scotia Bar tempts him inside. Here he meets Robert and Johnny, who has actually heard of *Animal Farm* and read his 'As I Please' columns in *Tribune*. Bissell, enjoying a Creative Scotland grant to help research the novel, revels in capturing the city's patter:

> 'Look, let me get ye a dram tae go wi yer pint,' Johnny said. George tried to say no, but Johnny wasn't having it. 'Jist you move up wan so ye can talk tae yer freen' (p. 147).

And he follows up with this wonderful celebration of Glasgow as Orwell ponders: 'Still, it was a truly proletarian city. If there was one place where the revolution would break out, it would be Glasgow. It nearly had after the First World War when Lloyd George's government sent tanks into the city after police scattered the huge crowd of men with their red flags who were demanding a forty-hour week to create jobs for returning soldiers' (p. 151).

The drama of the near-death experience in the Corryvreckan whirlpool for Orwell, Richard and cousins Henry and Lucy is captured effectively. Amidst it all, Orwell is shown remaining stubbornly cool and nonchalant:

> 'Well, we must find something to eat. I'll see if I can find any birds' eggs and wood for a fire. I won't be long,' George announced as he trooped off (p. 175).

As Orwell continues bashing out his novel his health deteriorates: first he's admitted to Hairmyres Hospital near Glasgow – then to Cranham Sanatorium in the Cotswolds. With his novel delivered to the publishers, Orwell spends all his time reading:

> … everything from D. H. Lawrence to Edgar Allan Poe, *Jude the Obscure* to *New Grub Street*. He got through about three books a week since he was allowed to do little else. As time passed he read more and more of Joseph Conrad and Evelyn Waugh's work and decided to make notes on them in his notebook with the intention of writing extended essays about them. As his mood became blacker he even began reading Dante's *Divine Comedy*. He wanted to see what might lie in store for him, whether it be Heaven or Hell – or somewhere in-between (p. 204).

Finally admitted to University College Hospital, London, and just before his death, Orwell is visited by his old-Etonian classics teacher Andrew Gow. This ties into a theme Bissell has developed through the novel highlighting the (usually marginalised) role of spooks in Orwell's life. At the end of the novel, Sonia ponders (perhaps improbably) the possible links between Gow and the Cambridge Soviet Spy Ring of Burgess, Maclean, Philby and Blunt (p. 234).

The close ties with intelligence of Orwell's friends David Astor, the *Observer* editor, and 'Freddie' Ayer, the celebrated philosopher, are highlighted in the novel. But Orwell's own probable involvement with intelligence is never really exploited. Thus Orwell's trip to the Continent in 1945 to report the final days of the Second World War for the *Observer* is covered, but the fact that all the men he met in Paris – Ayer, Muggeridge, Hemingway and Harold Acton – were, in some way, connected with the security services is ignored. In 1944, Astor was transferred to a unit liaising between the Special Operations Executive and the Resistance in France, helping the French underground in London spread the word to groups throughout Europe. And Orwell, perhaps inspired by Astor, actually attended in Paris the first conference of the Committee for European Federation, bringing together Resistance groups from around Europe. The celebrated French novelist and editor of *Combat*, Albert Camus, was present but fell ill just before he was due to meet Orwell. If only Bissell had imagined that meeting actually going ahead – what fun he could have had!

- This review was first published in *George Orwell Studies*, No. 7, 2019 pp 123-126.

Section 2

Orwell and the Journalistic Imagination

Chapter 7

'The Art of Donald McGill': Orwell and the Pleasures of Sex

The centrality of sex in the writings of George Orwell has been largely missed by critics and biographers. Feminist critics such as Daphne Patai (1984) and Beatrix Campbell (1984) have accused Orwell of misogyny: rightly so. But as so often with Orwell (his character so complex and contradictory) there is another side to his personality which this chapter attempts to outline. So it aims to highlight briefly the place of sex in a selection of his works (*Down and Out in Paris and London, Homage to Catalonia* and 'Such, Such were the Joys'). In particular, it focuses on Orwell's (largely unacknowledged) explicit homoeroticism and his almost New Mannish frankness about his own sexual history. The chapter moves on to consider Orwell's remarkable 1941 *Horizon* essay on McGill's sexy seaside postcards. Like Orwell's essays and journalism on turned-up trouser legs, the common toad, cups of tea, boys' weeklies, pubs, Woolworth's roses, handwriting, common lodging houses and trashy American crime novels, this one is brilliantly original in challenging the expectations of his readers: directing his critical gaze at a manifestation of popular culture normally ignored. Orwell mixes attitudes of pleasure (captured, above all, in the humour of the sexy cartoons and his own writing) and *faux* shame. In the process, he explores with a lightness of touch such issues as the essential purpose of jokes, the notion of goodness, gender stereotypes – and the complexities of the human condition, no less.

> *Susan Watson recalled that when Orwell invited Aunt Nellie Limouzin – wrapped in black satin and adorned with jet beads – to tea in Canonbury Square, he'd amuse her with his collection of postcards by Donald McGill. He told her not to serve tea until Nellie had finished laughing at the jokes*
> (Meyers 2000: 268)

The Feminist Critique

The feminist critique of Orwell is, in many respects, persuasive. On his first novel, Urmila Seshagiri (2001: 111) argues: 'The life narratives of women in *Burmese Days* demonstrate that Orwell not only naturalizes but actively deploys misogyny to increase his critique of imperialism' (see also Bluemel 2012: 24; Beddoe 1984). According to Daphne Patai, author of the seminal

The Orwell Mystique: A Study in Male Ideology (1984), Orwell cultivated 'a traditional notion of masculinity, complemented by a generalized misogyny' (ibid: 15). He 'polarizes human beings according to sex roles and gender identity and legitimizes male displays of dominance and aggression' (ibid: 17). In his journalism, he repeatedly displays his misogyny. For instance, in a review of a novel by Joseph Conrad, he comments: 'One of the surest signs of his genius is that women dislike his books' (ibid: 18). In *Down and Out in Paris and London* (1933), Orwell tends 'to treat men as individuals and women as mere representatives of the inferior female sex' (ibid: 65). In *The Road to Wigan Pier* (1937), his homophobia is manifest 'in the ease with which he attached the label of "pansy" or "Nancy boy" to men he perceived as opponents' (ibid: 85). On *A Clergyman's Daughter* (1935), Patai comments:

> The very title of Orwell's second novel at once induces the reader to take a particular perspective on his protagonist. She is to be viewed not as an individual in her own right but rather in terms of her relationship to a man, a clergyman, her father (ibid: 96).

In *Homage to Catalonia* (1938), his account of his experiences fighting with the Republican militia in Spain, war is represented essentially as a 'masculine initiation rite' (ibid: 140-153).

According to Beatrix Campbell (1984: 129), women simply 'do not appear as protagonists in Orwell's working class'. On *Nineteen Eighty-Four*, she comments: 'Julia is Winston's sleeping partner in sedition. Her rebellion is essentially sexual. She's promiscuous, she's had hundreds of men and her subversion is sealed in an equation between corruption and sexuality.' This reduction of Julia to her corrupt biology renders her rebellion 'as something seething below the threshold of political consciousness' (ibid). For Christopher Hitchens, hardly noted as a feminist, (2002: 105): 'Every one of the female characters [in his novels] is practically devoid of the least trace of intellectual or reflective capacity.' And in his study of Orwell and religion, Michael G. Brennan highlights the way in which he generally ignores the many thousands of middle class and working class Catholic women in England, concentrating, rather, his 'anti-Church ire upon an unrepresentative metropolitan male elite of (often convert) Roman Catholics whose writings and public utterances so irritated him' (2017: xvii-xviii).

Along with Orwell's representation of gender issues, his behaviour, sadly, could also at times be described as misogynistic. In a letter to a relative in 1972, Jacintha Buddicom, a childhood friend of the then-Eric Blair, wrote: 'How I wish I had been ready for betrothal when Eric asked me to marry him on his return from Burma [in 1927]. He had ruined what had been such a close and fulfilling relationship since childhood by trying to take us the whole way before I was anywhere near ready for that' (Davison 2010: 9, cited in Bluemel 2012: 19). Bluemel (ibid) suggests that this substantiates the claim by Dione Venables, in a 'Postscript' to the reprint of Buddicom's memoir *Eric and US: A Remembrance of George Orwell* (2006 [1974]: 182), that he had come close to raping Buddicom. Biographer Bernard Crick also tells of the occasion in 1944 when Orwell accompanied a former BBC acquaintance home late one night after a party at William and Hetta Empson's house in Hampstead, north London, and while crossing the Heath, tried 'to make love to her far too persistently, somewhat violently even' (Crick 1980: 465). A few months later, Orwell made a 'vigorous pass' at Anne Popham (later to wed the art historian, Quentin Bell) while he sat beside her on a bed in an Islington flat. Crick reports (ibid: 485) that Orwell 'said that he was very attracted to her, kissed her and asked if she would consider marrying him. Touched and flattered, though embarrassed and a little shocked by his dispassionate precipitancy, she disengaged herself...'. Later, he sent Popham two letters, not apologising but trying to explain his actions. In the first he wrote: 'It is only that I feel so desperately alone sometimes...' (ibid).[1]

In his biography of Orwell, Robert Colls lists his possible sexual relationships (2013: 292):

> As well as the prostitutes of Burma, Paris, London and Marrakech there is a leading group of other contenders including Jacintha Buddicom, Brenda Salkeld, Eleanor Jaques [Colls has her incorrectly as Jacques], Mabel Fierz [Colls has her incorrectly as Friez], Rosalind Obermeyer. Kay Walton, Sally Jerome, Stevie Smith, Lydia Jackson, Inez Holden, Celia Paget, Ruth Graves, Anne Popham, Audrey Jones, Sally McEwan and Orwell's second wife Sonia Brownell. From what we know of these women and their relationship with Orwell, if they were sexual partners we can be sure they were not only sexual partners.

Colls goes on to suggest that, while it was said Eileen had her flings, 'if she did they seem not to have been nearly so numerous nor so speculative as his' (ibid: 199). John Newsinger is also very critical of Orwell's attitudes to women. He writes (2018: 154): 'He regularly dismissed both "feminists" and "feminism". He was unfortunately one of those male socialists who were opposed to every oppression, except that of women.'

But Then: The Other Side of Orwell
Orwell was a complex man with many sides to his personality. And one was distinctly 'un-misogynistic'. This is perhaps not surprising: his mother, Ida (née Limouzin) was a feminist and his aunt Nellie (with whom he stayed

occasionally while investigating the plight of the poor in London in the late 1920s and in the early 1930s when she moved to Paris) was to marry Eugène Adam, an ex-anarchist, Esperantist and founder member of the French Communist Party (Brennan 2017: 25). As Brennan comments (ibid: 5):

> Ida and Nellie, and sometimes their eldest sister Norah who had also returned to England, attended Suffragette meetings, concerts and theatres in London. They moved within Fabian circles, mixing with H. G. Wells, G. K. Chesterton and E. E. Nesbit, the author of *The Ballads and Lyrics of Socialism* as well as *The Railway Children*. The radical Christian socialist Conrad le Despenser Roden Noel, the 'Red Vicar' of Thaxted, was at that time the curate of Nellie's local parish in Paddington.

Many of the women Orwell was later to be associated with (Jacintha Buddicom, Stevie Smith, Inez Holden, Mabel Fierz, Celia Kirwan – not to mention his two wives Eileen O'Shaughnessy and Sonia Brownell) were forceful characters who would hardly have tolerated a misogynist. Yet, as Bluemel points out, in the writings of many of them 'there is hardly a mention of feminism, even as these same writings often show sensitivity to women's sexual dependency and their consequently diminished access to well-paid work, accumulated wealth, and assured comfort' (Bluemel 2012: 21).

As a father to Richard Horatio, whom he and Eileen adopted in June 1944, Orwell certainly confounded the expectations of his day, displaying considerable affection for the child, taking him for walks in the pram – and even changing his nappies (though with a cigarette in his mouth) (see Chapter 3). As Crick records on a visit to Arthur and Mamaime Koestler's house near Blaenau Ffestiniog in Merionethshire, Wales, in late December 1945:

> There were long walks that Christmas. Orwell would carry Richard along on his hip and Celia [Kirwan, Mamaime's twin sister] noticed how competently he coped with the little boy, bathing him and changing him as if to the manner born, relaxed and unanxious about him – practical activities very unusual in fathers of his generation (Crick 1980: 483).

And his son, Richard, comments: 'My father was totally devoted to me after Eileen died, in a way which was rare at that time: he fed me; he changed my nappies and clothes; he helped me take a bath. Most men didn't do that sort of thing then.'[2]

In the field of domestic politics, Orwell also displayed distinctly progressive (almost New Mannish!) attitudes. For instance, while engaged in his researches into poverty in the north of England (later published in *The Road to Wigan Pier*, in 1937), he stayed in Sheffield with the Searles family. In his diary for 5 March 1936, he records (Orwell and Angus 1970 Vol. 1: 222):

> We had an argument one evening in the Searles' house because I helped Mrs S. with the washing up. Both of the men disapproved of this, of course. Mrs S. seemed doubtful. She said that in the North working class men never offered any courtesies to women (women are allowed to do all the housework unaided, even when the man is unemployed and it is always the man who sits in the comfortable chair) and she took this state of things for granted, but did not see why it should not be changed.

Orwell goes on to identify the gender politics at work in the kitchen and how simply doing the washing up while unemployed could damage a man's sense of his own masculinity – and how, paradoxically, this was accepted by women: 'I think it is instinctively felt by both sexes that the man would lose his manhood if, merely because he was out of work, he became a "Mary Ann"' (ibid).

Sexuality and *Down and Out*

In *Slumming: Sexual and Social Politics in Victorian London* (2004), Seth Koven examines how a wide range of clergymen, journalists, novelists, philanthropists, social investigators and reformists in late nineteenth century Britain ventured into poor areas – particularly in London. Koven argues that 'the widely shared imperative among well-to-do men and women to traverse class boundaries and befriend their outcast brothers and sisters in the slums was somehow bound up in their insistent eroticization of poverty and their quest to understand their own sexual subjectivities' (ibid: 4). Orwell was following a long line of socially-concerned writers (such as Jack London, James Greenwood, Charles Booth, Beatrice Potter) when between 1928 and 1931 he went 'down and out' and lived alongside the beggars and hop pickers. Significantly, his celebrated account of his experiences, the part fiction/part memoir *Down and Out in Paris and London* (1933) features sexuality prominently. The account begins with Charlie, a fellow Parisian down-and-out, boasting (somewhat offensively) of his sexual exploits, raping a prostitute in a brothel: 'Without another word I pulled her off the bed and threw her onto the floor. And then I fell upon her like a tiger! ... More and more savagely I renewed the attack. Again and again the girl tried to escape, she cried out for mercy anew, but I laughed at her' (Orwell 1980 [1933]: 19).

One of the most remarkable aspects of the book, somewhat underplayed in critiques of the text to date, is the way in which homosexuality is treated so openly: this at a time when it was illegal and taboos hindered any serious discussion of the subject. While staying overnight at a spike in London, Orwell describes how a man began making 'homosexual attempts' upon him (ibid: 86). Orwell adds: 'He was a feeble creature and I could manage him easily, but of course it was impossible to go to sleep again. For the rest of the night we stayed awake, smoking and talking. ... Homosexuality is general among tramps of long standing, he said' (ibid). Later, when reflecting on his experiences, Orwell argues that one of the 'great evils' of the tramp's life is that he is cut off entirely from contact with women (ibid: 115). He continues:

> It is obvious what results of this must be: homosexuality, for instance, and occasional rape cases. ...The sexual impulse, not to put it any higher, is a fundamental impulse, and starvation of it can be almost as demoralizing as physical hunger (ibid: 116).

Homage to Catalonia and Homoeroticism

Traditionally warfare is often seen as a site for male bonding (Keeble 2015a). Indeed, *Homage to Catalonia* (1962 [1938]), Orwell's account of his time spent fighting alongside Republican militiamen during the Spanish civil war in 1937, begins with a description of a meeting at the Lenin barracks in Barcelona with an Italian soldier which, it could be argued, has a remarkably overt homoerotic element (Keeble 2015b: 213). As he looks intensely at the man, Orwell is fascinated by his violence: he was 'a tough-looking youth of twenty-five or six, with reddish-yellow hair and powerful shoulders. His peaked leather cap was pulled fiercely over one eye ... Something in his face deeply moved me' (op cit: 7). The dramatic narrative then shifts to greater intimacy: first they engage in awkward, clipped dialogue – and then the scene comes to a sort of climax as the men's hands touch: 'As we went out he stepped across the room and gripped my hand very hard' (ibid). Orwell reflects: 'Queer, the affection you can feel for a stranger!' This generalisation serves two purposes (Keeble 2015b: 213). From the isolated incident, Orwell is able to draw out an observation about the human predicament and at the same time avoid the personal voice. Perhaps Orwell felt a certain embarrassment/shame about the intensity of feelings for the stranger. He goes on to say, somewhat sadly, that he was never to see the Italian militiaman again. And moving on to an impersonal, generalised 'one' voice (as if to protect himself from pain), while stressing how much that kind of male bonding was a constant feature of life fighting, he comments: 'One was always making contacts of that kind in Spain' (op cit: 7). Indeed, the intensity of the feeling for the Italian was so strong for Orwell that he later in 1939 celebrated the meeting in a poem, 'The Italian soldier shook my hand', which ends movingly: 'But the thing that I saw in your face/No power can disinherit:/No bomb that ever burst/Shatters the crystal spirit.'[3] Earlier, while serving with the Imperial Police in Burma (from 1922-1927), attractive boys had been of sexual interest to Eric Blair, according to John Sutherland (2016: 98-99):

He was, he recalled later, attracted by the androgynous beauty of the dominant Burmese race – the 'Burman'. He came to relish the attentions of his young native servants ('boys') when they handled his naked body 'intimately' while bathing and dressing him. Their male bodies, golden, not boiled-beef red, were not disfigured by pubic hair (how did he know that?).

Orwell's ambivalent attitudes towards homosexuality appear in his response to Oscar Wilde. Kristian Williams points out how Orwell expressed in his writings and letters his disdain for 'Nancy poets', 'pious sodomites' and the 'pansy left' (2017: 41). Yet, throughout his life, Orwell had a high opinion of Wilde's writings. Among the last books he read while confined to a sanatorium were two accounts of Wilde's trials and his prison letter, 'De Profundis' (ibid: 42). Williams comments astutely: 'Chief among the commonalities between Orwell and Wilde are their recognition of the value of aesthetics and their opposition to all forms of Puritanism' (ibid: 43).

'Such, Such Were the Joys' (and Sorrows) of Sex

Orwell's (partly fictionalised) memoir of his time at St Cyprian's prep school, near Eastbourne, between 1911 and 1917, 'Such, Such Were the Joys' (1970 [1952]), is remarkable for the explicitness of the sexual content (Keeble 2018; Chapter 9). At the start of Section IV, for instance, there is a lengthy discussion of sex and homosexuality in particular. Sex becomes linked with secrecy, betrayal, ignorance, confusion and shame. Earlier, he had reported how he had 'sneaked' to his favourite teacher, Brown 'a suspected case of homosexuality' (1970 [1952]: 401). He continues: 'I did not know very well what homosexuality was, but I knew that it happened and was bad, and this was one of the contexts in which it was proper to sneak. Brown told me I was a "good fellow" – which made me feel horribly ashamed' (ibid: 401-402). All this leads to a remarkably frank account (how true, how fictional?) of his own sex life and of the sexual development of youths in general. Orwell was never much impressed by psychoanalysis, as biographer Gordon Bowker stresses (Bowker 2003: 48). Yet, if being open about one's feelings and sexuality (making the personal political) is another mark of today's New Man, then Orwell was well ahead of his times (Keeble 2018: 85). Here, he admits to being 'in an almost sexless state, which is normal or at any rate common in boys of that age' (1970 [1952]: 402). Carefully, he teases out the chronology of his sexual awakening. At five or six 'like many children' (so aiming to generalise from the personal), he moves through a period of sexuality.

> My friends were the plumber's children up the road and we used sometimes to play games of a vaguely erotic kind. One was called 'playing

at doctors' and I remember getting a faint but definitely pleasant thrill from holding a toy trumpet, which was supposed to be a stethoscope, against a little girl's belly (ibid: 403).

Next, he falls deeply in love with a girl named Elsie. And he goes on to dwell on his boyhood sexual confusions with what appears compelling honesty (though it may well be all fiction). Most of the Facts of Life (those capital letters indicating their Importance and Severity) are learned through watching animals. The section climaxes with him noticing his penis sometimes standing of its own accord – and his feeling shame (ibid).

Orwell's Changing Attitudes Towards Women

Orwell was a complex man, full of contradictions. Newsinger even detects a shift in his attitudes towards women during the Second World War (2018: 154). For instance, in August 1945, he writes a sympathetic review of Virginia Woolf's *A Room of One's Own* in which she explores some of the reasons why women have not produced 'literature of the first order'. And he concludes with the comment that 'almost anyone of the male sex could read it with advantage' (ibid: 125).

Orwell's whole life can be considered an educational project. He had an enormous appetite and curiosity about life – a deep desire to understand himself and the times he was living in. And through his wonderfully original and often witty writings he is seeking to encourage us all to join him on his journey (Keeble 2016). As a result, he is constantly surprising us. For instance, in one of the 'As I Please' columns (28 July 1944) he writes for the leftist weekly *Tribune* between 1943 and 1947, he even comments perceptively on the appeal of women's magazines such as *Lucky Star*, the *Golden Star*, *Peg's Paper*, *Secrets* and the *Oracle*. A woman has written to him pointing out that while stories in these mags often highlighted unemployment, in contrast, trade unions and socialism were never mentioned (Anderson 2006: 167). In response, Orwell suggests that such mags deal essentially in fantasies that sublimate the class struggle and aim to make a lot of money for the publishers. He continues:

> But, curiously enough, reality does enter into these women's magazines, not through the stories but through the correspondence columns, especially in those papers that give free medical advice. Here you can read harrowing tales of 'bad legs' and haemorrhoids written by middle-aged women who give themselves such pseudonyms as 'A Sufferer'. 'Mother of Nine' and 'Always Constipated'. To compare these letters with the love stories that lie cheek by jowl with them is to see how vast a part mere day-dreaming plays in modern life (ibid: 168).

In another column on 28 April 1944, he considers the right of women to wear make-up after a juvenile magistrate in London's East End has complained about girls of 14 dressing and talking like those of 18 and 19 and putting 'the same filth and muck on their faces' (ibid: 132). In reply, Orwell says that 'one of the big failures in human history has been the agelong attempt to stop women painting their faces'. Then, he even provides a potted history of women's make-up, no less:

> The philosophers of the Roman empire denounced the frivolity of the modern woman in almost the same terms as she is denounced today. In the fifteenth century the church denounced the damnable habit of plucking the eyebrows. The English puritans, the Bolsheviks and the Nazis all attempted to discourage cosmetics, without success. In Victorian England rouge was considered so disgraceful that it was usually sold under some other name, but it continued to be used (ibid).

And on 8 November 1944, Orwell devoted the first section of his 'As I Please' column to examining in some considerable detail an American fashion magazine (ibid: 317). He takes care to list the content of the pictures: ball dresses, mink coats, step-ins, panties, brassieres, silk stockings, slippers, perfumes, lipsticks, nail varnish 'and, of course, women, unbelievably beautiful, who wear them or make use of them' (ibid). He next observes 'the striking prose style of the advertisements': 'an extraordinary mixture of sheer lushness with clipped and sometimes very expressive technical jargon'. And with a typically Orwellian flourish, he focuses on what's missing:

> A fairly diligent search through the magazine reveals two discreet allusions to grey hair, but if there is anywhere a direct mention of fatness or middle age I have not found it. Birth and death are not mentioned either: nor is work, except that a few recipes for breakfast dishes are given. The male sex enters directly or indirectly into perhaps one advertisement in twenty and photographs of dogs or kittens appear here and there. In only two pictures, out of about three hundred, is a child represented (ibid: 318).

Orwell is said to have virtually invented the discipline of Cultural Studies with his entirely original examinations of everyday things such as boys' weeklies, cups of tea, the common toad, trashy American crime novels, pubs, common lodging houses and handwriting (Keeble 2016; Chapter 24). In addition, he comments on women's fashion magazines, make-up and journals such as *Lucky Star* and *Peg's Paper*. All this certainly reveals another side of Orwell's character that feminist critics have significantly ignored.

Drawing Conclusions from McGill's Postcards

One of Orwell's most original studies of popular culture focuses on the sexy seaside postcards of Donald McGill – published in Cyril Connolly's literary journal *Horizon* in September 1941.[4] According to John Sutherland, Orwell began collecting these postcards at about the age of twelve (2016: 77). 'They were available at newsagents in seaside Eastbourne (not Henley). Not all newsagents would let children buy them, but some would, particularly stands around the pier' (ibid; see also Crick 1980: 91). In her memoir, *Eric and Us* (2006 [1974]) Jacintha Buddicom remembers him showing her a selection of his 'less naughty McGill items' (ibid). Many considered the cartoons pornographic. In fact, some years after Orwell died, in May 1954, McGill was held in a police cell for an hour while awaiting trial over the allegedly obscene representation of a stick of rock – appearing in a cartoon like a giant penis. He was fined £50, had costs of £25 to pay plus his own, higher legal costs. While he had prepared a defence, he pleaded guilty on legal advice (Kennedy 2004; Barrell 2012).

These were, then, highly controversial cartoons 'with their endless succession of fat women in tight bathing dresses and their crude drawing and unbearable colours' (Orwell 1965 [1941]: 142). Biographer Robert Colls describes them as 'dirty' and 'smutty-humorous' (2013: 155). Yet Orwell relishes in the sexuality of the images – and their humour.

The wording of the title of the essay is profoundly important. For Orwell deliberately subverts all traditional notions about cultural values – which rate the plays of Shakespeare and the novels of Jane Austen, say, as Art and sexy seaside postcards as non-Art. So the title emphasises Orwell's central point – that McGill's cartoons were to be taken seriously as Art – with a capital 'A'. Irony is defined by John Sutherland as 'saying one thing and meaning another' (2011: 93) The etymological origin of the word – the Greek *eironeia* – translates as 'deception', 'hypocrisy' or 'lie'. In literature, irony makes simple things more slippery – but by doing so, truer to life. The title 'Such, Such Were the Joys' is ironic. But there is nothing ironic about 'The Art of Donald McGill.'

The Subtle Deployment of *Faux* Shame

Orwell uses a number of subtle strategies to win over the somewhat highbrow readers of *Horizon* whom he presumes in the text will not be acquainted with the postcards (though many of the male readers may well have secretly acquired their own store – like Orwell...). He begins by providing an explanatory overview: 'They are a *genre* of their own, specializing in very "low" humour, the mother-in-law, baby's nappy, policemen's-boot type of joke and distinguishable from all the other kinds by having no artistic pretensions' (ibid, italics in the original). Next, he expresses *faux* shame:

> Your first impression is of overpowering vulgarity. This is quite apart from the ever-present obscenity and apart also from the hideousness of the colours. They have an utter lowness of mental atmosphere which comes not only in the nature of the jokes but, even more, in the grotesque, staring blatant quality of the drawings (ibid: 143).

But none of this outrage prevents Orwell from pressing on to analyse the content. First, he identifies the main subject areas: sex, home life, drunkenness, WC jokes, inter-working class snobbery and stock figures. He highlights both the visible and (equally interesting) the invisible (see Keeble 2015c: 18). 'Foreigners seldom never appear. The chief locality joke is the Scotsman, who is almost inexhaustible. The lawyer is always a swindler, the clergyman always a nervous idiot who says the wrong thing' (op cit: 146). He also links the postcards' 'low' form of comedy with the music hall ribaldry of Max Miller. As Peter Marks stresses (2011: 123): 'Both the postcards and music hall, of course, primarily are working class forms of entertainment, expressing an earthy and open attitude to life's hardships.'

Endorsing the 'Sancho Panza View of Life'

Having set the scene, attempting to win over his readers with his *faux* shame and serious analysis, Orwell moves on to translate the real pleasure he derives from the sexy images and jokes into a profound discussion of the deeper social, class, moral and psychological aspects of the postcards. Their particular kind of humour only has meaning, he argues, in the context of a 'fairly strict moral code' (ibid: 148). And he reassures his highbrow readers that jokes about nagging wives and over-bearing mothers-in-law 'do at least imply a stable society in which marriage is indissoluble and family loyalty taken for granted' (ibid: 149). 'The postcards,' he suggests, 'give expression to the Sancho Panza view of life' – which Orwell goes on to endorse unreservedly.

> The Don Quixote-Sancho Panza combination ... is simply the ancient dualism of body and soul in fiction form ... Evidently, it corresponds to something enduring in our civilization, not in the sense that either character is to be found in a 'pure' state in real life, but in the sense that the two principles, noble folly and base wisdom, exist side by side in nearly every human being. If you look into your own mind, which are you, Don Quixote or Sancho Panza? Almost certainly you are both. There is one part of you that wishes to be a hero or a saint, but another part of you is a little fat man who seeks very clearly the advantages of staying alive with a white skin. He is your unofficial self, the voice of the belly protesting against the soul (ibid: 151-152).

For Crick (1980: 436), this amounts to nothing less than a profound comment about 'the uncrushable life-force of the common people' while Colls (2013: 156) suggests it reflects his 'devotion to a politics of actually existing ordinariness'.

Orwell's imagined audience is clearly male here – as he addresses his reader as 'he' and being 'unfaithful to your wife' (op cit: 152). But by now he is relishing in the raw sexuality of the cartoons – so his writing shifts to pronouncing (with tremendous *éclat*) on the complexities of the human condition and the social function of jokes. 'Codes of law and morals, or religious systems never have much room in them for the humorous view of life. Whatever is funny is subversive, every joke is ultimately a custard pie' (ibid). Is Orwell right here? In stressing the subversive role of humour, he is revelling in being the dissident, the controversialist, the maverick. But not all jokes play this role. For instance, the wit and mockery of the court jester in the Middle Ages essentially served the interests of the court, while today sexist, racist, ageist jokes merely reinforce dominant prejudices (Keeble 2015c: 18-19).

Orwell ends the essay in a droll, witty, aphoristic sort of way: 'On the whole, human beings want to be good, but not too good, and not quite all the time' (op cit: 154).

Conclusion

Orwell's representations of gender have long interested academics. His treatment of sexuality, in contrast, has been little covered by Orwellian commentators. Yet this chapter argues that sex lies at the core of much of Orwell's writings. The gloomy, dystopian vision of *Nineteen Eighty-Four*, his most celebrated novel, has probably helped create a public image of Orwell as a gloomy, pessimistic, humourless and – in the context of this chapter – a rather unsexual man.[5] In fact, the opposite is the case. For his times, Orwell is remarkably open about sexual matters, even his homoerotic tendencies – and the development of his own sexuality. In *Down and Out in Paris and London* and the essay 'Such, Such Were the Joys' he confronts issues around homosexuality quite bravely – since it was then illegal and gays faced awful discrimination.

Feminist critics are right to point to the largely negative representations of women in his writings. But this chapter has highlighted writings – often ignored – that reveal a very different side to Orwell: happy to deconstruct in detail a women's fashion magazine or outline, in brief, the history of women's make-up. Moreover, Orwell's *Horizon* essay on Donald McGill's postcards amounts to a joyful affirmation of the hedonistic, Sancho Panza attitude to life – and a celebration, nothing less, of the pleasures of sex.

Notes

[1] See also Levy, Paul (2016) How does the last surviving member of the Bloomsbury set celebrate her 100th birthday? *Guardian*, 17 June. Available online at https://www.telegraph.co.uk/women/life/how-does-the-last-surviving-member-of-the-bloomsbury-set-celebra/, accessed on 13 August 2018

[2] See https://www.franceculture.fr/emissions/linvite-des-matins/george-orwell-au-present. Translations from the French by the author

[3] See https://www.orwellfoundation.com/the-orwell-foundation/orwell/poetry/the-italian-soldier-shook-my-hand/

[4] A Donald McGill Museum has opened in Ryde, Isle of Wight. See https://saucyseasidepostcards.com/

[5] For instance, biographer Jeffrey Meyers (2000: 376-377), in his index, lists 37 characteristics (from 'attitude to animals', 'austerity' and 'cockiness' to 'violent temper' and 'working class persona'). But there is no mention of sexuality. Similarly, biographer D. J. Taylor (2003:) also has 37 entries under 'Attitudes, habits and characteristics' in his Index (from 'Animals, love of' to 'Working classes, attitude to') but there is no mention of sex or sexuality. Bernard Crick (1980: 653-654) lists 'sadism, accusations of GO's', 'self-pity', 'smoking habits' and 'sterility' but there is no category for 'sexuality'. In contrast, Gordon Bowker has 25 entries under 'sex and sexuality' in his Index (2003: 491)

References

Anderson, Paul (ed.) (2006) *Orwell in Tribune: 'As I Please' and Other Writings 1943-7*, London: Politico's

Barrell, Tony (2012) May the sauce be with you, *Sunday Times Magazine*, 20 February pp 52-55

Beddoe, Deirdre (1984) Hindrances and help-meets: Women in the writings of George Orwell, Norris, Christopher (ed.) *Inside the Myth: Orwell: Views from the Left*, London: Lawrence and Wishart pp 139-154

Bluemel, Kristin (2012) The intimate Orwell: Women's production, feminist consumption, Keeble, Richard Lance (ed.) *Orwell Today*, Bury St Edmunds: Abramis pp 15-29

Bowker, Gordon (2003) *George Orwell*, London: Little, Brown

Brennan, Michael G. (2017) *George Orwell and Religion*, London and New York: Bloomsbury

Buddicom, Jacintha (2006 [1974]) *Eric and US: A Remembrance of George Orwell,* UK: Finlay Publishers, revised edition edited by Venables, Dione

Campbell, Beatrix (1984) Orwell: Paterfamilias or Big Brother?, Norris, Christopher (ed.) *Inside the Myth: Orwell: Views from the Left*, London: Lawrence and Wishart pp 128-136

Colls, Robert (2013) *George Orwell: English Rebel*, Oxford: Oxford University Press

Crick, Bernard (1980) *George Orwell: A Life*, Harmondsworth, Middlesex: Penguin

Davison, Peter (ed.) (2010) *George Orwell: A Life in Letters*, London and New York: Penguin

Hitchens, Christopher (2002) *Orwell's Victory*, London: Allen Lane, the Penguin Press

Keeble, Richard Lance (2015a) Homage to literary journalism, *orwellsocietyblog*, 24 November. Available online at https://orwellsoc1ietyblog.wordpress.com/2015/11/24/homage-to-literary-journalism-in-homage/, accessed on 15 August 2018

Keeble, Richard Lance (2015b) Orwell and the war reporter's imagination, Keeble, Richard Lance (ed.) *George Orwell Now!*, New York: Peter Lang pp 209-224

Keeble, Richard Lance (2015c) 'There is always room for one more custard pie': Orwell's humour, Keeble, Richard Lance and Swick, David (eds) *Pleasures of the Prose: Journalism and Humour*, Bury St Edmunds: Abramis pp 10-25

Keeble, Richard Lance (2016) Orwell, the university and the university of life. Keynote talk at Orwell symposium, Goldsmiths, University of London, 10 January. Available online at https://orwellsocietyblog.wordpress.com/2016/01/10/orwell-the-university-and-the-university-of-life/

Keeble, Richard Lance (2018) 'Such, Such Were the Joys' and the journalistic imagination, *George Orwell Studies*, Vol. 2, No. 2 pp 69-90

Kennedy, Maev (2004) Exhibition marks 50 years of holding back the sauce, *Guardian*, 22 May

Koven, Seth (2006) *Slumming: Sexual and Social Politics in Victorian London*, Princeton and Oxford: Princeton University Press

Marks, Peter (2011) *George Orwell the Essayist: Literature, Politics and the Periodical Culture*, London and New York: Continuum

Meyers, Jeffrey (2000) *Orwell: Wintry Conscience of a Generation*, New York and London: W. W. Norton and Company

Newsinger, John (2018) *Hope Lies in the Proles: George Orwell and the Left*, London: Pluto Press

Orwell, George (1980 [1933]) *Down and Out in Paris and London, George Orwell: Complete and Unabridged*, London: Secker and Warburg/Octopus pp 15-120

Orwell, George (1962 [1941]) The Art of Donald McGill, *Decline of the English Murder and Other Essays*, Harmondsworth, Middlesex: Penguin pp 142-154

Orwell, George (1970 [1952]) Such, Such Were the Joys, Orwell, Sonia and Angus, Ian (eds) *The Collected Essays, Journalism and Letters, Vol. 4: In Front of Your Nose 1945-1950*, Harmondsworth, Middlesex: Penguin Books pp 379-422

Orwell, Sonia and Angus, Ian (eds) (1970) *The Collected Essays, Journalism and Letters of George Orwell, Vol. 1: An Age Like This*, Harmondsworth: Middlesex: Penguin

Patai, Daphne (1984) *The Orwell Mystique: A Study in Male Ideology*, Amherst: University of Massachusetts Press

Seshagiri, Urmila (2001) Misogyny and anti-imperialism in George Orwell's *Burmese Days*, Lázaro, Alberto (ed.) *The Road from George Orwell*, Bern: Peter Lang pp 105-119

Sutherland, John (2011) *50 Literature Ideas You Really Need to Know,* London: Quercus

Sutherland, John (2016) *Orwell's Nose: A Pathological Biography*, London: Reaktion Books

Taylor, D. J. (2003) *Orwell: The Life*, London: Chatto and Windus

Williams, Kristian (2017) *Between the Bullet and the Lie: Essays on Orwell*, Chico, Oakland, Edinburgh, Baltimore: AK Press

- This essay was first published in *George Orwell Studies*, Vol 3, No. 1, 2018 pp 21-36.

Chapter 8

'There is Always Room for One More Custard Pie': Orwell's Humour

Introduction: Failure but also Fun

George Orwell was a very complex character full (like most of us) of contradictions. Critics of his life and works have often associated him with failure, pessimism, guilt and the terror of torture. The very word 'Orwellian' has come to be associated, in part, with the gloom, authoritarianism and oppressiveness of the Big Brother society as described in his celebrated dystopian novel, *Nineteen Eighty-Four* (1949) where the state invades the most private aspects of the individual's life.

According to his life-long friend Richard Rees, Orwell sought refuge in 'failure, failure, failure' (cited in Davison 2011: x). And significantly, of his schooldays at St Cyprian's, Eastbourne (1911-1916), which he revisited later in life in the ironically titled 'Such, Such Were the Joys' (2001 [1960]), he wrote: 'Failure, failure, failure – failure before me, failure ahead of me – that was by far the deepest conviction that I carried away' (ibid: 400). His novels certainly tend to end rather gloomily. As Alok Rai comments in his significantly titled text, *Orwell and the Politics of Despair* (1998: 148): 'It is of course remarkable that every single one of Orwell's novels is about failed rebellions, secessions.' Indeed, Flory, in *Burmese Days* (1934), ends up disgraced and committing suicide. Dorothy, the anti-heroine of *A Clergyman's Daughter* (1935), escapes from her prison to a new dawn only to find herself back in the soul-destroying routine from which she thought she had freed herself. George Bowling, in *Coming up for Air* (1939), ends his trip down memory lane finding the pond where he used to fish built over – and the site of a rubbish dump. The narrative of *Nineteen Eighty-Four* (1949) ends with the terrible rat torture scene and with Winston Smith meekly submitting to his torturer, O'Brien, and these grim words: 'He loved Big Brother.'

Géraldine Muhlmann even highlights the way in which *Down and Out in Paris and London* (1933) ends in the failure of his remarkable exercise in participant observation: 'I should like to know people like Mario and Paddy and Bill the moocher, not from casual encounters, but intimately; I should like to understand what really goes on in the souls of the *plongeurs* and tramps and Embankment sleepers. At present I do not feel that I have seen more than the fringe of poverty' (2008: 201). D. J. Taylor, in his award-winning biography, has a whole chapter devoted to 'Orwell's failure' (2003: 318-321) which begins: 'Orwell was obsessed by the idea of failure. Life, he once wrote, was on balance a succession of defeats, and only the very young or the very foolish believed otherwise.'

This chapter examines the other side of Orwell. It will seek to explore his character as revealed in his writings and described by his biographers – and identify the lighter aspects of his personality. It looks at his profound fascination with wit as a subject to explore – and the humorous elements in his writings.

The Lighter Side of Orwell's Personality

A number of Orwell's biographers have tended to downplay his humorous side. Christopher Hitchens (2002: 127) says of Orwell's first published novel *Burmese Days*: 'As is customary with Orwell, there are very few jokes and they are extremely dry.' Lucas (2003: 76) has five entries on his pessimism and talks of him being in 1945 'lost in his pessimism'. Indeed, he is rather dismissive about his sense of irony, commenting: 'Orwell had a sense of irony, even if it was no more than naming his dog Marx.' D. J. Taylor (2003: 461), under 'characteristics', highlights his love of animals, sense of failure, love of nature, paranoia, self-pity and unworldliness – but there is no mention of humour. Bowker (2003: 489) lists his misogyny and sadism – but likewise ignores his humour.

Other commentators, however, have seen a different Orwell. In his 'Introduction' to *George Orwell: A Life in Letters*, Peter Davison (2011: xiv) recalls how David Astor, Orwell's great friend and editor of the *Observer*, had told him how he would telephone Orwell when he felt depressed and ask to meet him in a local pub because he knew he would make him laugh and cheer him up. Jeffrey Meyers (2000: 34) talks of Orwell having a 'sophisticated sense of humour' and that he 'relished the absurd'. At Eton:

> One of his star turns was to go around inquiring about the religions of new boys and naming a series of extinct creeds. 'Are you Cyrenaic, Sceptic, Epicurean, Cynic, Neoplatonist, Confucian or Zoroastrian?' he would ask a bewildered youngster. 'I'm a Christian.' 'Oh,' said Eric, 'we haven't had that before.'

Meyers (ibid: 267) also shows how Orwell ('the old colonial policeman'), in a review of *The Hamlet* in 1940, wittily puts down the American novelist William Faulkner by describing characters as if they were a primitive tribe in a remote corner of the earth: '...people with supremely hideous names

– names like Flem Snopes and Eck Snopes – sit about on the steps of village stores, chewing tobacco, swindling one another in small business deals, and from time to time committing a rape or a murder.'

Bernard Crick throughout his biography is deeply sensitive towards Orwell's lighter side. For instance, he reports (1980: 222) one of the boys at the Hawthorns High School for Boys, in Hayes, Middlesex, where Orwell taught in the early 1930s remembering his 'inward laughter'. While fighting with the Trotskyist POUM militia against General Franco's fascists in Spain 1936-1937, his friendship with Georges Kopp grew 'because they had a similar sardonic humour' which 'helped to pass the time away' (ibid: 322). Later (ibid: 359), a fellow patient at Preston Hall sanatorium, Aylesford, Kent, in 1938 is quoted remembering Orwell in 'fits of laughter. Catching my eye, he beckoned me over, having been amused by two large caterpillars performing antics on the long stems of grass'. Crick adds: 'He appears like some Buddhist monk laughing at the aptness of the small things of creation.'

And Malcolm Muggeridge (ibid: 420) remembers speaking to Orwell about his time at the BBC 1941-1943 – with authors reading their 'gems of Western culture' with a view to enthusing folk in India and South-East Asia for the Allied cause. 'When I delicately suggested that this may well have failed to hit its target, the absurdity of the enterprise struck him anew and he began to chuckle, deep in his throat, very characteristic of him and very endearing.' In 1945 (ibid: 505), Orwell's friend Celia Kirwan enjoyed reading 'Old George's Almanac' in the Christmas number of *Tribune* as an example of his comic self-mockery. The article predicts a whole series of appalling disasters for 1946: 'Gazing into my crystal, I see trouble in China, Greece, Palestine, Iraq, Egypt, Abyssinia, Argentine and a few dozen other places. I see civil wars, bomb outrages, public executions, famines, epidemics and religious revivals. An exhaustive search for something cheerful reveals that there will be a slight improvement in the regimes of Spain and Portugal and that things will not go too badly in a few countries too small or remote to be worth conquering.' But he ends sardonically: '1946 will still be appreciably better than the last six years' (Anderson 2006: 271).

Not surprisingly then, Orwell's diaries are full of witty observations, humorous anecdotes and high spirits. While down-and-out with the hop-pickers in Kent in September 1931, he records with clear delight the 'uproarious scenes' on Saturdays 'for the people who had money used to get well drunk and it needed the police to get them out of the pub. I have no doubt the residents thought us a nasty vulgar lot, but I could not help feeling that it was rather good for a dull village to have this invasion of cockneys once a year' (Orwell 2009: 17).

In March 1936, while researching the condition of the northern English working class for his book, *The Road to Wigan Pier* (1937), Orwell stayed with the Grey family at 4 Agnes Terrace, Barnsley. He records 'Mr G.' talking about his war experiences especially the malingering he witnessed when he was invalided with an injury to his leg. One man feigned insanity and got away with it: 'For days he was going around with a bent pin on a bit of string, pretending to be catching fish. Finally he was discharged and on parting with G. he held up his discharge papers and said: "This is what I was fishing for"' (ibid: 58).

The Humour in *Homage*

Homage to Catalonia (1962 [1938]) is celebrated as a vivid, deeply personal account of his time on the frontlines in the Spanish civil war of 1936-1937 (though it actually sold only 700 copies during his lifetime) (see Hunter 1984). Orwell wrote the book in a state of 'white hot anger' during the second half of 1937 and this helps account partly for the extraordinary freedom of his writing, its flair, outspokenness, its creative, imaginative, literary richness – and its use of an eclectic range of literary techniques (see Keeble and Tulloch 2012 and 2014). It is reportage – but it also amounts to art. As Orwell commented in 'Why I write' (1970 [1946]): 'What I have most wanted to do throughout the past ten years is to make political writing into an art.' Indeed, drawing on the work of Max Saunders (2010), Nick Hubble (2012: 36) argues that *Homage* amounts to a 'prime example' of the genre of autobiografiction, cleverly blending two well-established forms - autobiography and fiction. Orwell actually had rather a low opinion of journalism – considering it 'mere pamphleteering' – and a horror of the 'subworld of freelance hackery' (Keeble 2007: 6). And yet, as Peter Davison stresses in the 'Introduction' to the collection of Orwell's journalism (2014: 2): 'Although Orwell continued to the end of his days to strive for success as a novelist, three of his nine "books" are the product of his journalism in a form in which he excelled: documentary reportage: *Down and Out in Paris and London*, *The Road to Wigan Pier* – and *Homage to Catalonia*.'

One of the book's most striking aspects is the range of literary genres and tones Orwell incorporates into the text. For instance, there are profiles (of individuals, cities, groups), sections of very direct, personal, emotional writing (conveying an earnestness to convey authentic/real experience); elements of background description, generalising comment and concrete experience; and personal commentary, eye-witness reportage informed by a social political awareness. In addition, there is a journalistic emphasis on the extraordinary and the contradictory; confessional writing; a practical, down-to-earth awareness/sensibility; press content analysis/critique; political analysis (however reluctant). Amidst all this flowering of the journalistic imagination, it's easy to marginalise the important role humour plays in the book.

Throughout the reportage is infused with a droll, self-deprecating wit: military cynicism mixed with military know-how. Of his time on the frontline fighting for the Trotskyite POUM militia against Franco's forces, he writes: 'It is curious, but I dreaded the cold much more than I dreaded the enemy' (op cit: 21). On the Russian gun he comments: 'Its great shells whistled over so slowly that you felt certain you could run beside them and keep up with them' (ibid: 83). Of the fat Russian agent, he says: 'I watched him with some interest for it was the first time that I had seen a person whose profession was telling lies – unless one counts journalists' (ibid: 135). And notice his brilliantly down-beat, anti-heroic description of being shot through the neck on 20 May 1937, a model of journalistic clarity and conciseness drawn from personal experience:

> The whole experience of being hit by a bullet is very interesting and I think it is worth describing in detail. ... Roughly speaking it was the sensation of being at the centre of an explosion. ... Not being in pain I felt a vague satisfaction. This ought to please my wife, I thought, she had always wanted me wounded which would save me from being killed when the great battle came (ibid: 177).

He assumes he is about to die and continues: 'It is very interesting to know what your thoughts would be at such a time. My first thought, conventionally enough, was for my wife. My second was a violent resentment at having to leave this world which, when all is said and done, suits me so well' (ibid: 178). He adds: 'No one I met at this time ... failed to assure me that a man who is hit through the neck and survives is the luckiest creature alive. I could not help thinking that it would be even luckier not to be hit at all' (ibid). He describes a cathedral as 'one of the most hideous buildings in the world'. 'I think the Anarchists showed bad faith in not blowing it up when they had the chance' (ibid: 214).

Chapter 11 includes a detailed account of the fighting in Barcelona in May 1937 (after the government ordered the anarchists to surrender their arms) which he viewed from a roof overlooking the main avenue, the Ramblas – and the distorted coverage of the events in the Spanish and British press. But notice his dead-pan debunking of the lofty claims of history:

> When you are taking part in events like these you are, I suppose, in a small way, making history and you ought by rights to feel like a historical

character. But you never do because at such times the physical details always outweigh everything else. Throughout the fighting I never made the correct 'analysis' of the situation that was so glibly made by journalists hundreds of miles away. What I was chiefly thinking about was not the rights and wrongs of this miserable internecine scrap but simply the discomfort and boredom of sitting day and night on that intolerable roof and the hunger which was growing worse and worse. ... If this was history it did not feel like it... (ibid: 134).

Amidst all the horror of trench warfare (when it flares up), Orwell also manages to inject some humour into his narrative. For instance, Orwell is involved in a rare attack on the fascist lines and he sees 'a shadowy figure in the half-light' (ibid: 90). He continues:

I gripped my rifle by the small of the butt and lunged at the man's back. He was just out of my reach. Another lunge: still out of reach. And for a little distance we proceeded like this, he rushing up to the trench and I after him on the ground above, prodding at his shoulder-blades and never quite getting there – a comic memory for me to look back upon, though I suppose it seemed less comic to him (ibid).

Pleasure of Reading 'As I Please' Columns

I personally cannot read the eighty wonderful 'As I Please' columns Orwell contributed to *Tribune*, the leftist journal, between 1943 and 1947 without constantly smiling at his wit and high spirits. Through the columns Orwell was, in effect, defining a new kind of radical politics:

It involved reducing the power of the press barons, facing up to racial intolerance, defending civil liberties. Yet it also incorporated an awareness of the power of language and propaganda, a celebration of the joys of nature and an acknowledgement of the cultural power of Christianity. Above all, it recognized the extraordinary richness of the individual's experience ... (Keeble 2007: 113).

Humour and high spirits are the constant ingredients of the columns. For instance, on 24 December 1943, he critiques 'the pessimists': there is Pétain (French 'chief of state' in the Vichy regime, 1940-1944) preaching 'the discipline of defeat', Sorel (the French philosopher, supporter of the far-right) denouncing liberalism, Berdyaev (the Russian theologian) 'shaking his head over the Russian revolution'; Beachcomber (the columnist) 'delivering side-kicks at Beveridge in the *Express*'. Above all, he denounces 'their refusal to believe that human society can be fundamentally improved' (Anderson 2006: 73). His tone is constantly shifting – from ironic self-effacement to de-mystification and debunking. In his 7 January 1944 column (ibid: 80), he mocks the ruling classes in this way:

> Looking through the photographs in the New Years Honours List I am struck (as usual) by the quite exceptional ugliness and vulgarity of the faces displayed there. It seems to be almost the rule that the kind of person who earns the right to call himself Lord Percy de Falcontowers should look at best like an overfed publican and at worst a tax-collector with a duodenal ulcer ... What I like best is the careful grading by which honours are always dished out in direct proportion to the amount of mischief done – baronies for Big Business, baronetcies for fashionable surgeons, knighthoods for tame professors.

On 4 February 1944, in typical idiosyncratic style, he chose to link a comment on trouser ends (of all things) to the war effort in this highly original way (Anderson op cit: 94):

> Announcing that the Board of Trade is about to remove the ban on turn-up trouser ends, a tailor's advertisement hails this as 'a first instalment of the freedom for which we are fighting'. If we are really fighting for turned-up trouser ends I should be inclined to be pro-Axis. Turn-ups have no function except to collect dust and no virtue except that when you clean them out you occasionally find a sixpence there ... I would like to see clothes rationing continue until the moths have devoured the last dinner jacket and even the undertakers have shed their top hats. I would not mind seeing the whole nation in dyed battledress for five years if by that means one of the main breeding points of snobbery and envy could be eliminated.

Humour Amidst Dystopian Gloom of *Nineteen Eighty-Four*

Ironic and satiric humour runs all through Orwell's gloomy dystopian masterpiece, *Nineteen Eighty-Four* (1949). Bernard Crick, in one of the most perceptive analyses of the novel, talks of it as being inspired by 'satiric rage' (2007: 147). He identifies seven broad satiric themes:

- The division of the world at Tehran by Stalin, Roosevelt and Churchill.
- The mass media and proletarisation (now termed 'dumbing down').
- Power-hunger and totalitarianism – particularly in the depiction of the torturer O'Brien who is shown driven mad by power-hunger.
- The corruption of language in the drive towards Newspeak.
- The destruction of any objective history and truth by the Ministry of Truth.

- The view (well-known at Orwell's time) of James Burnham (1941) that capitalism and communism will converge through managerialism.

Crick argues convincingly (ibid: 148-149) that the novel is 'plainly a satire on hierarchical societies in general'. 'Orwell's satire is so consistent that the dictator is actually called "Big Brother". "Big Brother is watching you," but not watching over you as a brother should.' Moreover, Crick suggests that a positive finale can be seen to the otherwise darkly pessimistic text if the end is considered not with the anti-hero Winston Smith loving Big Brother but at the conclusion of the appendix titled 'The Principles of Newspeak'. Here we are told that translations into Newspeak of writers such as Shakespeare, Milton, Swift, Byron and Dickens were going slowly so the 'final adoption of Newspeak had been fixed for late a date as 2010'. Crick concludes (ibid: 158): 'If we read *Nineteen Eighty-Four* as Swiftian satire, this is as good to say "this year, next year, sometimes, never". Colloquial language, the common people and common sense will survive the most resolute attempts at total control.'

There is also satiric humour in Orwell's decision to give the room where Winston is tortured the number 101 – after his office at 55 Portland Place, London where he worked for the BBC's Eastern Service from 1941-1943 (Meyers 2000: 214). Bowker (2003) also reflects on the fact that the name of O'Brien happened to be the codename of Hugh O'Donnell, the KGB handler of David Crook who was keeping a close eye on Orwell in Spain (Keeble 2012: 154). He concludes that Orwell was oblivious to this and so 'the fact that the character in *Nineteen Eighty-Four* who first wins the confidence of Winston Smith and then betrays him is given the name O'Brien must be one of the strangest coincidences in literature' (op cit: 219). But Orwell had close connections with the spooks and probably went to the Continent in 1945 as part of some kind of intelligence mission for David Astor (Keeble 2012). So he may well have found out this information about O'Donnell through his contacts. If so – what a wonderful satiric jibe!

Sexy, Seaside Postcards, Sancho Panza and the Subversive Role of Humour
Moreover, humour was a constant subject in Orwell's writings. Orwell virtually invented the discipline of Cultural Studies with his commentaries on so many of the manifestations of popular culture (usually considered too trivial and unworthy of attention by the intellectual and cultural elite) which fascinated him – crime novels, boys' weeklies, women's magazines, cups of tea, Woolworth's roses, common lodging houses and handwriting. In one of his most celebrated essays – published in Cyril Connolly's *Horizon* in September 1941 – he examines the seaside postcards of Donald McGill 'with their endless succession of fat women in tight bathing-dresses and their

crude drawing and unbearable colours' (Orwell 1965 [1941: 142).[1] As Peter Marks observes (2011: 122):

> Orwell treats the postcards seriously, as valuable sociological evidence of ideas and cultural forces at work in society. The postcards reflect and reinforce certain stereotypes and conventions (marriage only benefits the woman; all drunken men have optical illusions) that individually might be dismissed as crass, but that collectively, especially given how popular they are, suggest unconsciously accepted customs and attitudes embedded in national culture.

The presumption is that highbrow *Horizon* readers will not be acquainted with the postcards so he begins by providing an explanatory overview: 'They are a *genre* of their own, specializing in very "low" humour, the mother-in-law, baby's nappy, policemen's-boot type of joke and distinguishable from all the other kinds by having no artistic pretensions' (op cit: 142, italics in the original). Just as physically Orwell adventured into 'low' life with his stint as a hotel *plongeur* in Paris and travels with tramps and hop-pickers (as narrated in *Down and Out in Paris and London*) here he is exploring 'low' culture.

He lists three of their typical 'Max Millerish', music hall-type jokes. For instance: 'I like seeing experienced girls home.' 'But I'm not experienced,' 'You're not home yet!' and then provides a 'rough analysis of their habitual subject-matter'. Theoretical abstraction was never part of Orwell's repertoire; his essays are never buried in endless references which encumber so much of academic writing: but they are bursting with original, lively, clearly expressed ideas.[2] So the subjects of sex, home life, drunkenness, WC jokes, inter-working class snobbery and stock figures are covered in some detail. He observes both the visible – and (equally interesting) the invisible: 'Foreigners seldom or never appear. The chief locality joke is the Scotsman, who is almost inexhaustible. The lawyer is always a swindler, the clergyman always a nervous idiot who says the wrong thing' (ibid: 146).

Orwell moves on from the specifics to discuss the broader social and class aspects of the postcards. Their particular brand of humour can only have meaning, he argues, in relation to a 'fairly strict moral code' (ibid: 148). And he is able to reassure his highbrow readers that jokes about nagging wives and tyrannous mothers-in-law 'do at least imply a stable society in which marriage is indissoluble and family loyalty taken for granted' (ibid: 149).

Orwell's brilliant, inventive coda uses the 'vulgar' postcards as platform on which to pronounce, quite profoundly, on the complexities of the human condition and the social function of jokes. The postcards 'give expression to the Sancho Panza view of life' (ibid: 151). And he concludes, somewhat aphoristically: 'Codes of law and morals, or religious system, never have much room in them for the humorous view of life. Whatever is funny is subversive, every joke is ultimately a custard pie' (ibid).

'Every Joke is a Tiny Revolution': Orwell on Writers' Humour

Orwell's fascination with humour was also reflected in his book reviewing and essays on writers such as Charles Dickens, Rudyard Kipling, Jonathan Swift, Mark Twain and P. G. Wodehouse. Significantly, in 'Lear, Tolstoy and the Fool' (1947), Orwell celebrates Shakespeare's exuberance, his vitality and love of life, bawdy jokes and riddles – comparing all that with Tolstoy's dull puritanism. In his celebrated essay on Dickens (1962 [1940]: 137), which combines a detailed study of an essentially literary subject with a critique of contemporary political attitudes (Marks 2011: 94), he returns to his theme of the 'subversive' role of humour, suggesting that his constant wish to preach a sermon was 'the final secret of his inventiveness':

> For you can only create if you can *care*. Types like Squeers and Micawber could not have been produced by a hack writer looking for something to be funny about. A joke worth laughing at always has an idea behind it, and usually a subversive idea. Dickens is able to go on being funny because he is in revolt against authority, and authority is always there to be laughed at. There is always room for one more custard pie (emphasis in the original).

In his study of Rudyard Kipling (1965 [1942]: 45-62), Orwell is keen to highlight his comic style. He suggests that in his soldier poems, especially Barrack-Room Ballads, there is an 'underlying air of patronage' (ibid: 51). 'Kipling idealizes the army officer, especially the junior officer, and that to an idiotic extent, but the private soldier, though lovable and romantic, has to be comic. He is always made to speak in a sort of stylized Cockney, not very broad but with all the aitches and final "g's" carefully omitted' (ibid).

Orwell is even able to display his polymathic knowledge of (and highly opinionated views on) English humorous writing in his 1,884-word essay 'Funny not vulgar' (first published in the *Leader*, on 28 July 1945). Notice the striking, rhetorical opening and the massive build-up of data:

> The Great Age of English humorous writing – not witty and not satirical, but simply humorous – was the first three quarters of the nineteenth century. Within that period lie Dickens's enormous output of comic writings, Thackeray's brilliant burlesques and short stories, such as 'The Fatal Boots', ... Surtees's *Handley Cross*, Lewis Carroll's *Alice in Wonderland*, Douglas Jerrold's *Mrs. Caudle's Curtain Lectures*, and a

> considerable body of humorous verse by R. H. Barham, Thomas Hood, Edward Lear, Arthur Hugh Clough, Charles Stuart Calverley and others. Two other comic masterpieces, F. Anstey's *Vice Versa* and the two Grossmiths' *Diary of a Nobody*, lie only just outside the period I have named. And, at any rate until 1860 or thereabouts, there was still such a thing as comic draughtsmanship, witness Cruikshank's illustrations to Dickens, Leech's illustrations to Surtees and even Thackeray's illustrations of his own work (Orwell 1970 [1945]: 324).

With typical provocation, he next argues that Britain has produced no writing of any value in the current century while comic verse has lost all its vitality (ibid: 324-325). For a laugh, people are more likely to go to a music hall or a Disney film or buy a few Donald McGill postcards than resort to a book or periodical. But Orwell is concerned to understand what causes laughter (so drawing his readers into this educational process) but without resorting to any obscure theoretical abstractions. And so he returns to his favourite theme of the subversive role of humour:

> A thing is funny when – in some way that is not actually offensive or frightening – it upsets the established order. Every joke is a tiny revolution. If you had to define humour, you might define it as dignity sitting on a tin-tack. Whatever destroys dignity, and brings down the mighty from their seats, preferably with a bump, is funny. And the bigger the fall, the bigger the joke (ibid: 325).

Today, he suggests, humorists are 'too genteel, too kind hearted and too consciously lowbrow'. 'P. G. Wodehouse's novels or A. P. Herbert's verses seem always to be aimed at prosperous stockbrokers whiling away an odd half hour in the lounge of some suburban golf course. They and all their kind are dominated by an anxiety not to stir up mud, either moral, religious, political or intellectual' (ibid). Yet, significantly, Stefan Collini has taken particular offence at Orwell's constant critique of British intellectuals (as in this essay) and intellectual theorising. He writes (2007: 350):

> Orwell probably did more than any other single writer in the middle of the twentieth century to shape and harden attitudes towards intellectuals in Britain. His iconic status both as the courageous truth-teller and as the champion of the individual in the face of totalitarian tendencies of modern states has meant that his writings have helped shape a semantic field in which freedom, honesty, and plain speech are contrasted with tyranny, ideological fashion and pretension and in which the term 'intellectuals' is strongly associated with the latter of these two poles.

Orwell's interests in politics, humour and the broader social impacts of literature come together in his essay 'In defence of P. G. Wodehouse' (first published in the journal *Windmill*, then being edited by Kay Dick and Reginald Moore, in 1945). The famous comic writer, and creator of Bertie Wooster and Jeeves, had been captured by the Germans while living in Belgium in 1940, and taken to Germany where he had made a series of broadcasts. He was promptly damned as a traitor in the British press, libraries withdrew his books, the BBC banned his lyrics (Marks 2011: 137). And he was then moved to Paris 'under some kind of house arrest' (Bowker 2003: 324). Orwell had been introduced to Wodehouse by Malcolm Muggeridge – who was keeping his eye on him for British intelligence – while in Paris during his stint reporting on the closing months of World War Two for David Astor's *Observer* and *Manchester Evening Post* (Keeble 2001 and 2012).[3] Orwell states his defence of the writer near the opening, suggesting that 'the events of 1941 do not convict Wodehouse of anything other than stupidity' (Orwell 1998 [1945]: 53). Some were arguing that Wodehouse was mocking the British aristocracy. Nonsense, says Orwell:

> On the contrary, a harmless old-fashioned snobbishness is perceptible all through his work. Just as an intelligent Catholic is able to see that the blasphemies of Baudelaire or James Joyce are not seriously damaging to the Catholic faith, so an English reader can see that in creating such characters as Hildebrand Spencer Poyns de Burgh John Hanneyside Coombe-Crombie, 12th Earl of Dreever, Wodehouse is not really attacking the social hierarchy. Indeed, no one who genuinely despised titles would write of them so much. Wodehouse's attitude towards the English social system is the same as his attitude towards the public-school moral code – a mild facetiousness covering an unthinking acceptance (ibid: 57).

As Marks summarises Orwell's argument, Wodehouse essentially remained 'a comedian foolishly playing for laughs in a time of grave danger, a political naïf, a puppet for the cynically manipulating German propaganda machine' (op cit: 138).

Wit and the Common Toad
One of my favourite pieces of Orwellian journalism, which never fails to amuse me, is his essay 'Some thoughts on the common toad' (Orwell 1980 [1946]: 744-746). It shares many of the characteristics of the numerous 'As I Please' columns he wrote for the leftist journal *Tribune*, where he was literary editor between 1943 and 1947, which feature surprisingly idiosyncratic, 'ordinary' subject matter (Keeble 2007: 103). These are all deliberately distant in tone and style from the heavy diet of political polemic and policy analysis that

filled the rest of the journal's pages (Anderson 2006: 26). For instance, he expands on a passing comment of a barmaid, responds to a Board of Trade announcement announcing a ban on turned-up trouser ends, answers a reader's query or set a brain-teaser. But his 'common toad' column captures Orwell's love of animals, the changing of the seasons and the extraordinarily intense way in which he observed nature. As Meyers comments, he combined 'close observation and unusual facts with tenderness for a repulsive creative' (2000: 225). He starts the column with a gentle, witty dig at Anglo-Catholics, saying that 'after his long fast, the toad has a spiritual look, like a strict Anglo-Catholic towards the end of Lent' (Orwell 1980 [1946]: 744). He continues:

> I mention the spawning of the toads because it is one of the phenomena of spring which most deeply appeal to me, and because the toad, unlike the skylark and the primrose, has never had much of a boost from the poets.[4]

So here is the ever maverick Orwell delighting in speaking out for one of the forgottens of the animal kingdom. From this unlikely source his prose then flows on to a critique of capitalism no less – and a celebration of life and the pleasure principle. He writes:

> Is it wicked to take a pleasure in spring and other seasonal changes? To put it more precisely, is it politically reprehensible, while we are groaning, or at any rate ought to be groaning, under the shackles of the capitalist system, to point out that life is frequently more worth living because of a blackbird's song, a yellow elm tree in October, or some natural phenomenon which does not cost money and does not have what editors of left-wing newspapers call a class angle (ibid: 745-746).

And he ends on an elegiac note – his prose soaring almost into a form of poetry:

> The atom bombs are piling up in the factories, the police are prowling through the cities, the lies are streaming from the loudspeakers, but the earth is still going round the sun, and neither the dictators nor the bureaucrats, deeply as they disapprove of the process, are able to prevent it (ibid: 746).

Conclusion

At the start of this chapter, I noted how Orwell's novels tended to end rather gloomily. Yet Orwell knew that stories which conclude on a down-note are far more likely to provoke thought than those which end up-beat. Stories with happy endings (as Hollywood knows only too well) so often leave you feeling OK with the world, the *status quo*. Orwell constantly challenges and questions the *status quo*. And he knew instinctively that society was largely built on narratives of success, finding it difficult to confront and speak about failure. For Orwell failure is an intrinsic, important part of life (see Keeble 2012: 6).

Failure, as Terry Eagleton says, was Orwell's forte (see Davison 2011: ix). But then, as this chapter has argued, so too was fun.

Notes

[1] Donald McGill was to be held in a police cell in Lincoln in May 1954 (for an hour) while awaiting trial over the obscene publication of a stick of rock (appearing in a cartoon like a ginormous penis). He was fined £50, had costs of £25 plus his own higher legal costs. While he had prepared a defence, he pleaded guilty on legal advice. See Kennedy, Maev (2004) Exhibition marks 50 years of holding back the sauce, *Guardian*, 22 May. Available online at http://www.theguardian.com/uk/2004/may/22/arts.artsnews, accessed on 21 February 2015. See also Barrell, Tony (2012) May the sauce be with you, 26 February, *Sunday Times Magazine* pp 52-55

[2] This absence of references and footnotes may be due to the fact that Orwell neither enjoyed nor endured a conventional university education

[3] Muggeridge later became a close friend of Orwell, attended his funeral and became editor of *Punch* (1953-1957), broadcaster and Christian convert. He wrote on the Wodehouse saga (1968: 92): 'The Germans, in their literal way, took his works as a guide to English manners and actually dropped an agent in the Fen country wearing spats. This unaccustomed article of attire led to his speedy apprehension. Had he not been caught, he would, presumably, have gone on to London in search of the Drones Club, and have thought to escape notice in restaurants by throwing bread about in the manner of Bertie'

[4] Orwell had a certain fascination for copulating creatures. In his diary entry for 2 February 1936, he writes: 'For the first time in my life saw rooks copulating. On the ground, not in a tree. The manner of courtship was peculiar. The female stood with her beak open and the male walked round her and it appeared as though he was feeding her' (Orwell 2009: 48). Interestingly, Davison records that Orwell had originally written 'copulating' in *Road to Wigan Pier*: but being considered too explicit it was first changed to 'courting' and finally to 'treading' (ibid: 49)

References

Anderson, Paul (2006) *Orwell in* Tribune*: 'As I Please' and Other Writings 1943-7*, London: Politico's

Burnham, James (1941) *The Managerial Revolution: What is Happening in the World*, New York: John Day Co.

Bowker, Gordon (2003) *George Orwell*, London: Little, Brown

Campbell, Beatrix (1984) *Wigan Pier Revisited: Poverty and Politics in the 80s*, London: Virago Press

Collini, Stefan (2007) *Absent Minds: Intellectuals in Britain*, Oxford: Oxford University Press

Crick, Bernard (1980) *George Orwell: A Life*, Harmondsworth, Middlesex: Penguin Books

Crick, Bernard (2007) *Nineteen Eighty-Four*: Context and controversy, Rodden, John (ed.) *The Cambridge Companion to George Orwell*, Cambridge: Cambridge University Press pp 146-159

Davison, Peter (ed.) (2011) *Orwell: A Life in Letters*, London: Penguin

Hitchens, Christopher (2002) *Orwell's Victory*, London: Allen Lane and the Penguin Press

Hubble, Nick (2012) Orwell and the English working class: Lessons in autobiografiction for the Twenty-First Century, Keeble, Richard Lance (ed.) *Orwell Today*, Bury St Edmunds: Abramis pp 30-45

Hunter, Lynette (1984) *George Orwell: The Search for a Voice*, Milton Keynes: Open University Press

Keeble, Richard (2001) Orwell as war correspondent: A reassessment, *Journalism Studies*, Vol. 2, No. 3 pp 393-406

Keeble, Richard (2007) Introduction: On journalism, creativity and the imagination, Keeble, Richard and Wheeler, Sharon (eds) *The Journalistic Imagination: Literary Journalists from Defoe to Capote and Carter*, London: Routledge pp 1-14

Keeble, Richard (2007) The lasting in the ephemeral: Assessing George Orwell's 'As I Please' columns, Keeble, Richard and Wheeler, Sharon (eds) *The Journalistic Imagination: Literary Journalists from Defoe to Capote and Carter*, London: Routledge pp 100-115

Keeble, Richard Lance (2012) Orwell, *Nineteen Eighty-Four* and the spooks, Keeble, Richard Lance (ed.) *Orwell Today*, Bury St Edmunds: Abramis pp 151-163

Keeble, Richard Lance and Tulloch, John (2012) *Global Literary Journalism: Exploring the Journalistic Imagination, Vol. 1*, New York: Peter Lang

Keeble, Richard Lance and Tulloch, John (2014) *Global Literary Journalism: Exploring the Journalistic Imagination, Vol. 2*, New York: Peter Lang

Lucas, Scott (2003) *Orwell*, London: Haus Publishing

Meyers, Jeffrey (2000) *Orwell: Wintry Conscience of a Generation*, New York and London: W. W. Norton and Company

Muggeridge, Malcolm (1968) *Tread Softly for you Tread on My Jokes*, London: Fontana

Muhlmann, Géraldine (2008) *A Political History of Journalism*, Cambridge: Polity Press

Orwell, George (1962 [1938]) *Homage to Catalonia*, Harmondsworth, Middlesex: Penguin

Orwell, George (1962 [1940]) Charles Dickens, *Inside the Whale and Other Essays*, Harmondsworth, Middlesex: Penguin Books pp 80-141

Orwell, George (1962 [1941]) The Art of Donald McGill, *Decline of the English Murder and Other Essays*, Harmondsworth: Penguin pp 142-154. First published in *Horizon*, September

Orwell, George (1965 [1942]) Rudyard Kipling, *Decline of English Murder and Other Essays*, Harmondsworth: Penguin pp 45-62. First published in *Horizon*, February

Orwell, George (1970 [1945]) Funny not vulgar, Orwell, Sonia and Angus, Ian (eds) *The Collected Essays, Journalism and Letters, Vol. 3: As I Please*, Harmondsworth: Penguin Books pp 324-329. First published in the *Leader*, 28 July

Orwell, George (1998 [1945]) In defence of P. G. Wodehouse, Davison, Peter (ed.) *The Complete Works of George Orwell*, Vol. XVII pp 53-61. First published in *Windmill*, No. 2, July

Orwell, George (1970 [1946]) Why I write, *Collected Essays, Journalism and Letters*, Vol. 1, Harmondsworth, Middlesex: Penguin Books 1970 pp 23-30. First published in *Gangrel*, No 4

Orwell, George (1980 [1947]) Lear, Tolstoy and the fool, George Orwell Complete and Unabridged, London: Secker and Warburg pp 792-803; *Polemic*, No. 7, March

Orwell, George (2001 [1960]) Such, Such Were the Joys, *Orwell's England* (texts selected by Davison, Peter), London: Penguin Books pp 362-408. First published, posthumously, in *London Magazine*

Orwell, George (2009) *The Orwell Diaries* (edited by Davison, Peter), London: Penguin Books

Orwell, George (2010) *A Life in Letters* (selected by Davison, Peter), London: Penguin Books

Orwell, George (2014) *Seeing Things As They Are: Selected Journalism and Other Writings* (selected by Davison, Peter), London: Harvill Secker

Patai, Daphne (1984) *The Orwell Mystique: A Study in Male Ideology*, Amherst: University of Massachusetts Press

Rai, Alok (1988) *Orwell and the Politics of Despair*, Cambridge: Cambridge University Press

Saunders, Max (2010) *Self-Impression: Life Writing, Autobiografiction, and the Forms of Modern Literature*, Oxford: Oxford University Press

Taylor, D. J. (2003) *Orwell: The Life*, London: Chatto and Windus

- This essay was first published in *The Pleasures of the Prose*, edited by Richard Lance Keeble and David Swick, Bury St Edmunds: Abramis, 2015 pp 10-25.

Chapter 9

'Such, Such Were the Joys' (and Pains)

Introduction

Much of the debate over Orwell's essay 'Such, Such Were the Joys', about his years at St Cyprian's prep school, concentrates on the extent to which his recollections are truthful or imagined. Little attention has been directed at the literary elements of the essay. This chapter examines in detail the literary devices Orwell uses: such as dramatic narratives, verbatim dialogue, the balancing of tones and attitudes, the sexually explicit, the polemical, confessional and intimate voices, historical generalisations, the journalistic style and social/cultural analysis.

Orwell also uses the memoir to explore a vast range of issues: personal identify, fact, fiction, education, sexuality, morality, religion, education and private education in particular, the psychology of children, the baffling incomprehensibility of the world to the child's mind. In addition, it explores such issues as the importance of the critical, historical imagination, literary genres, the need to confound expectations and speak the unspeakable, memory, polemic, self-revelation and the powers of the reflective mind. Above all, the chapter examines the complexities of Orwell's seemingly 'plain style'.

Beyond the Fact/Fiction Binary

Much of the debate over Orwell's long, 15,000-word essay 'Such, Such Were the Joys', about his years (1911-1917) at St Cyprian's prep school near Eastbourne, East Sussex, concentrates on the extent to which Orwell's memoir is truthful or imagined. As Peter Marks summarises (2011: 185), Orwell (or Eric Blair as he was then) finds himself 'regularly in a state of apprehension and abasement: humiliated by the headmaster and (especially) the headmaster's wife, nicknamed Sambo and Flip respectively, degraded by teachers; bullied and sneered at by those of a supposedly superior class; forced to endure mindless teaching, physical privations and filth'.

Significantly, biographer D. J. Taylor (2003) concludes: 'A trawl through the reminiscences of several old boys supplies evidence to rebut, or at any rate to call into serious question, nearly all of Orwell's allegations. Far from being a sadistic flogger, Mr Wilkes was remembered as a shy and notably unaggressive character. ... As for the supposed squalor of the school, this, for nearly half the duration of Eric's stay, was the Great War, when food was scarce and comfort at a premium.'

On the other hand, refuting this, Gordon Bowker (2003: 29) quotes Cecil Beaton, a contemporary at St Cyprian's, suggesting that Orwell had, despite some exaggeration, 'seen through all the layers of snobbery and pretence' of the couple who ran it and 'captured them both perfectly'.

Yet this approach tends to miss the essential purpose of the essay – which was to raise serious questions through various literary devices (which have gone largely unexplored) about a vast range of subjects: personal identify, fact, fiction, education, sexuality, morality, religion, education and private education in particular, the psychology of children, the baffling incomprehensibility of the world to the child's mind. In addition, it explores such issues as the importance of the critical, historical imagination, literary genres, the need to confound expectations and speak the unspeakable, the unreliability of memory, self-revelation and the powers of the reflective mind. Jeffrey Meyers (2000: 17) describes it as 'a masterpiece of polemical autobiography ... one of the best essays in English'.

Alex Woloch (2016: 54) highlights Orwell's 'persistent confusion of fiction and nonfiction' and argues that the 'nonfictional' text 'is always in danger of being most deceptive (because we take it too easily at face value)'. In a similar mode, Orwell's biographer Bernard Crick (1980: 35) usefully comments that 'Such, Such' is 'the most puzzling of all his works to locate accurately between fiction and non-fiction'.

> Do we think of documentaries as necessarily conveying the literal truth about the 'I' who pretends to be what the author must know he never can be, 'a camera'? Should we rather not try to gain some critical distance from the documentary technique by exploring the author's intentions biographically as well as by examining the literary result (ibid).

This paper, following Crick, will attempt to identify the literary elements which make it so 'brilliant' (ibid).

The Complexity of Orwell's Plain Style
Orwell is famous for his clear prose, his 'plain style' (Woloch 2016). At the end of his essay, 'Why I write' (1946 [1970: 30]), he summed up this approach this way: 'Good prose is like a window pane.' But contradictions/complexities/paradoxes even accompany this seemingly clear statement. It comes after he has written: '...yet it is also true that one can write nothing readable unless one constantly struggles to efface one's own personality.' In a sense,

all of Orwell's writing (his novels, non-fiction, essays, poetry, journalism) is autobiographical in that it is overtly drawing from his own subjective experiences and political/ethical/literary preoccupations. As Gordon Bowker comments astutely (2003: 145): 'The autobiographical element was a means by which he tried always to relate what he wrote to his own life, continually to reveal himself within the mental landscape through which he was passing. It lent his writing a quality of pilgrimage.'

Lynette Hunter (1984: 1) is right, then, to stress the complexity of his literary strategy. She comments:

> From the beginning he recognizes that the distinction between form and content, subject and object, fiction and documentary, are all versions of the fundamental separation between fact and value that has dominated rationalist humanism since the seventeenth century. And for Orwell, the final question is indeed one of value and morality; his writing career is concerned with a search for a valid voice with which to persuade others and express opinion.

Indeed, for Woloch (2016: 44), Orwell's plain style 'always expresses the *hope* that an idea will come across directly, fully actualized in one specific event of writing. But Orwell's prodigious, formally shifting work sweeps up all such actualized moments into a much larger, and thus less finalized, textual field' (italics in the original).

Most literature is written with a clear audience in mind, and, in some respects, this can serve as a constraint on the creative process. Orwell, in contrast, composed 'Such Such' with no real expectation of it ever being published in his lifetime. It libelled the headmaster and his wife – and, as he acknowledged, it was too long for a periodical (*CWGO* 19: 149). Alex Woloch (2016: 330) describes it as 'an intentionally posthumous publication'. As a result, a feeling of intense creative freedom appears to propel the writing throughout.

If Orwell did have any sense of an 'imaginary audience' it would have been his friend Cyril Connolly who was at the school when Blair arrived and who would later, as editor of *Horizon*, publish many of Orwell's most celebrated essays. Significantly, his *Enemies of Promise* (1961 [1938]) carries an autobiographical section, 'A Georgian Boyhood', in which he remembers his time at St Cyprian's (called St Wulfric's – also to avoid any libel hassles) somewhat more approvingly than Orwell. He even describes Flip as a 'warm-hearted and inspired teacher' (ibid: 174). Orwell may well have conceived 'Such, Such Were the Joys' as a riposte to Connolly. Yet, in *Enemies*, Orwell is mentioned by name – and very positively:

> I was a stage rebel, Orwell a true one. Tall, pale, with his flaccid cheeks, large spatulate fingers and supercilious voice, he was one of those boys who seem born old. ... He saw through St Wulfric's, despised Sambo and hated Flip but was invaluable to them as scholarship fodder. ... The remarkable thing about Orwell was that alone among the boys he was intellectual and not a parrot for he thought for himself, read Shaw and Samuel Butler and rejected not only St Wulfric's but the war, the Empire, Kipling, Sussex and Character (ibid: 178; 179).

Jeremy Lewis, in his biography of Connolly (1998: 95), records how Orwell, in his earlier essay on the British intelligentsia, 'Inside the Whale' (1940), refers, 'somewhat scathingly', to the 'Theory of Permanent Adolescent' and continues:

> Cultured middle class life has reached a depth of softness at which a public school education – five years in a lukewarm bath of snobbery – can actually be looked upon as an eventful period. To nearly all the writers who have counted during the thirties, what more has ever happened than Mr Connolly records in *Enemies of Promise*? It is the same pattern all the time: public school, university, a few trips abroad, then London. Hunger, hardship, solitude, exile, war, prison, persecution, manual labour – hardly even words (ibid).

By the late 1940s, Orwell's views about the centrality of boyhood experiences to the formation of character had changed dramatically – and in 'Such, Such' he put the record straight. At the same time, he noticeably failed to celebrate any friendship with a fellow pupil (either Connolly or any other) at St Cyrprian's. Daphne Patai comments (1984: 7): 'As a writer, Orwell was primarily stimulated by negative impulses: he needed to write *against* something' (italics in the original).

The Title and Section I: Gender Politics and Literary Journalism

The Threat of Being Beaten

The title itself indicates that this is going to be a deliberately constructed literary/creative work. It is taken from 'The Echoing Green', one of Blake's *Songs of Innocence* poems (of 1789). Bowker comments (2003: 66): 'As the mature Orwell fully realized, an echoing green is a more complex metaphor for the relationship between artistic and literal truth. ... If he mocked myths of childhood joy unbounded, he was surely well aware that by using such a quotation as the title of his essay he was drawing attention to the fact that the author was the creator, not remembrancer. Echoes both repeat and distort.' The opening tone is ironic; and the essential message is: 'Don't take this as the literal truth.'

Interestingly, the essay is divided into six sections. It was clearly a structure that appealed to Orwell: his study of Dickens (1939) was similarly divided. The strategy serves a number of important purposes: each section, we can assume as readers, carries distinct ideas and themes; it helps the reading process by providing breaks (reading 'breathing spaces') through what otherwise will be an intimidating 15,000 words; and at the start of each section, the text assumes a new energy, a new rhythmic vitality, a new significance. In some respects this is drawing on the conventions of journalism in which various strategies are adopted (e.g. the insertion of space in the copy followed by a few words in capital letters, say) to indicate thematic changes and introduce rhythmic variety into the copy.

The most obvious feature of journalistic writing is the stress on the most important or the most dramatic in the opening section (known, in the jargon, as the 'intro'). This convention only emerged after decades of newspaper writing, driven largely by commercial imperatives and the need for concise writing (newspaper space, in effect, costing money). Distinguishing itself from fiction in the crowded marketplace of ideas, journalism succeeded on the basis of its claims to accuracy and authenticity with the most important and dramatic 'facts' being thrust at the top of stories to draw the attention of the reader (Keeble 2007: 9). Here, Orwell, in effect, gives play to his 'journalistic imagination', beginning with a particularly striking, shocking, highly personalised, confessional narrative ('I' appears six times in the first three sentences).

The writing, as in journalism, is concise. The sentences are short. He begins: 'Soon after I arrived at St Cyprian's (not immediately, but after a week or two, just when I seemed to be settling into the routine of school life) I began wetting my bed.' The words in the parenthesis delay slightly the full impact of the revelation but when it appears at the end of the sentence ('I began wetting my bed.') it carries all the more weight. Perhaps in no other way could Eric Blair (as Orwell then was) more offend the manly ethos of the school than through this overt display of effeminacy: as in the second par, Orwell writes: '... it was looked on as a disgusting crime which the child committed on purpose and for which the proper cure was a beating' (1970 4 [1952]: 379). The opening dramatic narrative then moves through a series of happenings which culminate (inevitably) in a beating for Blair.

Intriguingly, the manly ethos is enforced in the first instance by two women: indeed, the tensions surrounding gender and sexuality are to run through the text. We are first introduced to Mrs W., the headmaster's wife (her real name, Cicely Wilkes, obscured to avoid libel), only very briefly: originally attention is focused on the lady she is chatting with: 'She was an intimidating, masculine-looking person wearing a riding habit, or something I took to be a riding habit' (ibid). The description of Mrs W. is slightly delayed – so when it does appear it carries more impact. She is nicknamed Flip: there is a lightness and a certain sexual daring about the name – chosen because of her 'flippy-floppy bosom', according to John Sutherland (2016: 61). There is even a warm intimacy in her official name, Mum, that also contrasts with the heaviness of the threat she poses for Blair. Like the other lady, she is described as rather manly: 'She was a stocky square-built woman with hard red cheeks, a flat top to her head, prominent brows and deep-set, suspicious eyes.'

Orwell cleverly conveys the impressions of a sensitive boy alongside the insights of the elderly man looking back on the past.[1] Continuing the manly theme and ever aware of people's speech patterns and rhythms, here Mrs W. is described as 'jollying one along with mannish slang ("Buck up, old chap! And so forth")'. But the elderly narrator, looking back, sees all the 'false heartiness' behind the 'jollying' (1970 4 [1952]: 320). 'It was very difficult to look her in the face without feeling guilty, even at moments when one was not guilty of anything in particular' (ibid). So this early section of the essay culminates with Flip shaming Blair in front of the stranger by revealing how he 'wets his bed every night' and threatening to get the Sixth Form to beat him if he wets again. Along with guilt and shame comes terror and the freezing of the senses: 'I could not speak.' He mis-hears the phrase 'the Sixth Form' as 'Mrs Form' and assumes this is the strange lady who is to do the beating.

The Beating: The Fiction/Non-Fiction Continuum

From focusing on the nightmarish fear of being beaten by a strange woman in the essay's opening, the narrative in the second part of the first section culminates in an actual beating – by a man. It begins with a woman, the 'grim statuesque matron', one morning pulling back his bed clothes to reveal the clammy sheets. Orwell captures the terror evoked by her thunderous order by capitalising the first two words of the phrase: 'REPORT YOURSELF to the headmaster after breakfast.' And by making that short sentence a single paragraph, Orwell is using all the literary devices available to highlight the 'dreaded words' (ibid: 381).

Compared to the women involved in the drama – all of whom are described in manly, menacing terms – the man who is to administer the beating (the headmaster, Lewis Chitty Vaughan Wilkes, nicknamed Sambo) is portrayed in precisely the opposite way: he is 'curiously oafish' 'with a chubby face which was like that of an overgrown baby, and which was capable of good humour'. Indeed, throughout the essay Orwell is concerned to show the complex gender politics at play: here the women's violence is manifested in their looks and spiteful words; the man may be a grown-up baby but he does the violent deed. Since the beating culminates this part of the essay, Orwell describes it in some detail. Blair begins by admitting his offence:

> When I had said my say, he read me a short but pompous lecture, then seized me by the scruff of the neck, twisted me over and began beating me with the riding crop. He had a habit of continuing his lecture while he flogged you, and I remember the words 'you dir-ty lit-tle boy' keeping time with the blows (ibid).

The tension at the heart of the narrative slackens a little when Blair reports that the beating did not hurt. This was 'a sort of victory and partially wiped out the shame of the bed-wetting'. Some boys are hanging about in the passage outside and a section of dialogue follows:

'D'you get the cane?'

'It didn't hurt,' I said proudly.

Flip had heard everything. Instantly her voice came screaming after me:

'Come here! Come here this instant! What was that you said?'

'I said it didn't hurt,' I faltered out.

'How dare you say a thing like that? Do you think that is a proper thing to say? Go in and REPORT YOURSELF AGAIN!' (ibid: 382).

From a literary point of view this (apparently verbatim) dialogue is intriguing. It is tied up with all the other detail of the narrative: it is, in part, a rhetorical strategy to convince the reader of its authenticity and 'truthfulness' (just as the use of direct speech in journalism serves to support its claims for veracity). Trust is crucial in the relationship between the author of non-fiction and the reader: how can we be assured that these are the 'facts' and not fiction? Here, the detail of the remembered dialogue aims to convince us of the narrative's truthfulness. As Marks comments (2011: 186): 'The relatively long account gathers some of its persuasive power simply from the quantity of detail supplied, itself a tactic Orwell uses to substantiate the veracity of his testimony.' Yet, paradoxically, that very detail tempts us to doubt its 'truthfulness'. For how can anyone remember events from so long ago with such clarity and in such detail? It could be mainly fiction. Orwell, thus, is deliberately placing his narrative in the space between non-fiction and fiction. As Lynette Hunter (1984: 5) comments on Orwell's experiments with genre:

> ...commentators come to the writing with critical expectations that lie within the framework that Orwell came to challenge. The most common

expectation is that fiction and non-fiction, the novel and the documentary are always significantly divided from each other and this prevents the reader from appreciating Orwell's own suggestion that they can be viewed fruitfully as part of a continuum.

The drama continues as Sambo lays into Blair, seemingly for about five minutes, ending up breaking the riding crop. 'The bone handle went flying across the room' (ibid). As John Sutherland comments (2016: 64), this final whipping 'has something orgasmic about it – a lachrymose, and unusual, ejaculation of a kind'. Sambo certainly ends up sounding totally absurd, pathetically blaming Blair:

> 'Look what you've made me do!' he said furiously, holding up the broken crop.

Reflections on the Beating

In the final part of the first section, Orwell reflects back on the ordeal – both from a personal perspective and more generally. He cries – and the feelings are complex, extremely powerful, multi-layered and difficult to capture.

> I was crying partly because I felt this was expected of me, partly from genuine repentance, but partly also because of a deeper grief which is peculiar to childhood and not easy to convey: a sense of desolate loneliness and helplessness, of being locked up not only in a hostile world but in a world of good and evil where the rules were such that it was actually not possible for me to keep them (ibid).

It's not surprising the outburst of crying is examined in such detail: after all, like bed-wetting, it was considered sissy and effeminate: an act that was completely out of keeping with the public school ethos of manly service for the empire (see Grant 2004).

A number of commentators have also seen links between the depiction of young Blair in the desolate, lonely and oppressive world of St Cyprian's and the fate of anti-hero Winston Smith in the grim, dystopian novel, *Nineteen Eighty-Four* (1949) which Orwell was working on at the same time. As Bowker argues (2003: 29):

> Orwell's notorious memoir of the school, 'Such, Such Were the Joys', the product of over thirty years of brooding, is his own anatomy of melancholy, complemented only by *Nineteen Eighty-Four*. It is the recollection of a place and period viewed through a highly sensitive and complex mind, filtered through time and coloured by ideology, the account of a closed and oppressive world from the alter ego of Winston Smith, the last apostle of free thought. It is as much a polemic aimed at the English private school system as a piece of reflective self-analysis…

As Orwell continues his self-analysis, he looks back on the experience with the benefit of hindsight. He remains determined to convince the reader of the authenticity of the account – but, at the same time, to surprise with his conclusions. He moves away from the subjective 'I' voice to comment more generally: '... it can also happen that one's memories grow sharper after a long lapse of time, because one is looking at the past with fresh eyes and can isolate and, as it were, notice facts which previously existed undifferentiated among a mass of others' (1970 4 [1952]: 383). He goes on to conclude, surprisingly, that 'the second beating seemed to me a just and reasonable punishment'. 'To get one beating, and then to get another and far fiercer on top of it, for being so unwise as to show that the first had not hurt – that was quite natural.' And from reflecting with the benefit of hindsight, he is suddenly able to capture more sharply a feeling he experienced at the time of the flogging: 'I accepted the broken riding crop as my own crime' (ibid).

Just as the section structure gives Orwell the opportunity to vary the intensity of the narrative: to open with a focus on intense drama and feelings and move on to calmer reflections so it allows him to end with a striking flourish. Here, Orwell completely confounds expectations. Having stressed the horror of the flogging, he writes:

> I did not wet my bed again – at least, I did wet it once again, and received another beating, after which the trouble stopped. So perhaps this barbarous remedy does work, though at a heavy price, I have no doubt (ibid 383-384).

D. J. Taylor (2003: 31) comments: 'There are one or two passages in "Such, Such Were the Joys" that indicate a striving for balance' and this may be one such example. But perhaps it is more typical of Orwell the controversialist, the maverick, the writer reflecting critically on his society and on his own experiences. Orwell the man was also constantly changing – both his styles of living (from Eton, to Imperial Police service in Burma, then down and out with the destitute in Paris and London; then teacher, freelance writer, Republican fighter in Spain, broadcaster, literary editor, war correspondent, through all of this a voracious reader) and styles of writing (essayist, novelist, polemicist, poet). Significantly, in his essay 'Why I write' (1970 [1946]: 29]), he commented: 'I find that by the time you have perfected any style of writing, you have outgrown it.' Just as his life was full of surprising turns, so his writing incorporated surprising twists: while the essay appears to be a damning critique of the public school system Orwell slips in reflections which cleverly modify that extreme view.

Section II: From the Personal to the Political

The School as Symbol

Following the intensely personal, dramatic narrative that fills the whole of Section I, in contrast, Section II is more reflective: the focus shifts from the personal to the social, cultural and political. The school – with its hierarchical organisation, the favouritism shown the sons of the wealthy, its obsession with the 'evil' of competition and success and, above all, its 'outrageous' sense of history (and lack of critical awareness of the imperial past) – is shown as a microcosm of the broader society beyond its walls:

> History was a series of unrelated, unintelligible but – in some way that was never explained to us – important facts with resounding phrases tied to them. Disraeli brought peace with honour. Clive was astonished at his moderation (ibid: 386).

History is, then, reduced to mere banal clichés.

The issue of corporal punishment returns – but this time the focus shifts away from the angst-ridden personal drama with the students, in general, shown as passive in the face of the school's bullying regime: 'Indeed, I doubt whether classical education ever has been or can be successfully carried on without corporal punishment. The boys themselves believed in its efficacy' (1970 4 [1952]: 388). The 'three castes' at the school are shown as reflecting the class divisions in the broader society, and significantly, Orwell identifies with the 'underlings'.

> There was the minority with an aristocratic or millionaire background, there were the children of the ordinary suburban rich, who made up the bulk of the school, and there were a few underlings like myself, the sons of clergymen, Indian civil servants, struggling widows and the like. These poorer ones were discouraged from going in for 'extras' such as shooting and carpentry, and were humiliated over clothes and petty possessions (ibid).

Orwell, in his writings, constantly confronts the difficulty of writing. As he put it in 'Why I write': 'The job is to reconcile my ingrained likes and dislikes with the essentially public, non-individual activities that this age forces upon all of us. It is not easy. It raises problems of construction and of language and it raises in a new way the problem of truthfulness' (op cit: 28). Earlier in 'Such, Such', he had written of 'the deeper grief which is peculiar to childhood and not easy to convey' (op cit: 382]). Here he again confronts the problem of capturing feelings from so many years ago – which are both highly intense and ambivalent. He says:

> It is not easy to convey to a grown-up person the sense of strain, of nerving oneself for some terrible, all-deciding combat, as the date of the examination crept nearer – eleven years old, twelve years old, then thirteen, the fatal year itself! (ibid: 390).

Clearly central here is the unspoken fear of failure. But the fear is followed 'by an almost irresistible impulse *not* to work' (ibid, italics in the original) so making failure difficult to avoid and so self-inflicted. Throughout his life, Orwell both feared and embraced failure as an important, intrinsic part of human existence (Keeble 2012: 6). Failure is commonly experienced by characters in his novels; and it is a subject for reflection in his nonfiction. So typically he comments in 'Why I write' (op cit: 29): '…every book is a failure,' Failure (and its opposite, success) was also the subject of a lengthy discussion in Connolly's *Enemies of Promise*. For instance, he writes (1961 [1938]: 129): 'Of all the enemies of literature, success is the most insidious.' To some extent, then, Orwell used 'Such, Such' to continue his dialogue with Connolly about literature and the social standing of authors.

Poverty and St Cyprian's Big Brother

Poverty is another constant Orwellian preoccupation. His first published book *Down and Out in Paris and London* (1933) was his part memoir/part fictional account of his time with the tramps in London and Essex and the Parisian proletariat, *The Road to Wigan Pier* (1937) was his eye-witness, sociological investigation into poverty in Northern England – and so on. 'Probably the greatest cruelty one can inflict on a child is to send it to a school among children richer than itself,' says Gordon Comstock in his novel, *Keep the Aspidistra Flying* (1936). Here, the obsession with poverty focuses on his own, painful predicament which ties in with his fear of being constantly under surveillance. The annual fees of £180 were way beyond the Blairs' means since the salary of his father, an official in the Opium Department of the Indian Civil Service, was just £650 p.a., falling to less than £200 when he retired in 1912. But, as John Sutherland records (2016: 62), Ida, Orwell's mother, 'wangled half-fees for Eric'. 'She was helped by the fact that her brother Charles Limouzin lived in Eastbourne and, a hero on the local links, played golf with Lewis, captain of the club.' But Orwell writes:

> I did not at first understand that I was being taken at reduced fees: it was only when I was about eleven that Flip and Sambo began throwing the fact in my teeth. … Sambo, who did not aspire to be loved by his pupils, put it more brutally, though, as was usual with him in pompous language. 'You are living on my bounty' was his favourite phrase in this context (1970 4 [1952]: 392).

Next, to illustrate the pain of poverty, he tells the story of when he secretly went to a sweet shop a mile or more from the school to buy some chocolates. Opposite he sees a 'small sharp-faced man' (ibid). 'Instantly, a horrible fear went through me. There could be no doubt as to who the man was. He was a spy placed there by Sambo!' (ibid). Afterwards, he fears a summons to the head's office – but it never comes. The implication is that young Blair may well have imagined the 'spy'. He continues: 'It did not seem to me strange that the headmaster of a private school should dispose of an army of informers, and I did not even imagine that he would have to pay them. ... Sambo was all powerful: it was natural that his agents should be everywhere' (ibid: 392-393). Is Orwell here playing with the notion of the surveillance state dominated by an all-powerful Big Brother which he most creatively realised in his dystopian novel *Nineteen Eighty-Four* (1949)?

The second section comes to a climax with a detailed exploration of his feelings towards St Cyprian's own Big Brother and Big Sister: hate, guilt and shame are all mixed up in the young Blair. He conveys the intensity of the hatred by mentioning it twice: 'I hated Sambo and Flip with a sort of shamefaced remorseful hatred...' and later in the paragraph: 'I hated both of them. I could not control my subjective feeling and I could not conceal them from myself' (ibid). Perhaps worst of all is the sense of helplessness in the face of feelings he could not control. Orwell's whole career as an engaged intellectual, after all, was dedicated to understanding the personal and the political and thereby gain some degree of self-control and power to effect meaningful, progressive change in society.

Section III: Unsettling the Reader with Changing Moods and Attitudes
Part One: Oh the Joy of Those Occasional Expeditions!

This section is extraordinary for the way in which Orwell confounds expectations, constantly unsettling the reader with his changing moods and attitudes. He begins dramatically: 'No one can look back on his schooldays and say with truth that they were altogether unhappy' (ibid: 394). The sentence stands alone as a single paragraph so visually acquiring more impact. Having so far concentrated on the gloom, despair, fear and shame of his St Cyprian's ordeal, he now suddenly shifts tack and remembers some 'good memories ... among a horde of bad ones' (ibid). The next paragraph is bursting with positive words: 'wonderful', 'more wonderful', 'joy', 'pleasure', 'excitement' and 'fascinating'. Given the title of the essay, 'joy' is a particularly significant word and the writing appears to reach some kind of climax in the next paragraph when he remembers going butterfly-hunting with a teacher called Brown (presumably a pseudonym): 'and oh, the joy of those occasional expeditions!' (ibid: 395).

But such a positive mood cannot be sustained for long and so the attention quickly shifts back to Flip: 'From her point of view, natural history ("bug-hunting" she would probably have called it) was a babyish pursuit which a boy should be laughed out of as early as possible' (ibid). In other words, an interest in nature was not consistent with the aggressively masculinist ethos of the school – and so had to be mocked. Then the mood suddenly shifts again (even in the same paragraph) with the focus fixed on the teacher Brown. With an awareness of the complex dynamics of working relationships perhaps exceptional for a young boy, Blair sees that Brown, having been at the school from its early days, had built up a certain independence: 'If it ever happened that both of them [Flip and Sambo] were away, Brown acted as deputy headmaster, and on those occasions instead of reading the appointed lesson for the day at morning chapel, he would read us stories from the Apocrypha' (ibid).

The moods in the next paragraph constantly shift, too. For the adult Orwell looking back at the young Blair there appears to be some sort of conclusive finality about this opening short sentence: 'Most of the good memories of my childhood, and up to the age of about twenty, are in some way connected with animals' (ibid: 395-396). And he repeats that phrase 'good memories' in the follow-up sentence, 'goodness' being associated with warmth: 'So far as St Cyprian's goes, it also seems, when I look back, that all my good memories are of summer' (ibid: 396). But the summer joys cannot be sustained and immediately Orwell shifts to bad memories of cold winters: running nose, the daily nightmare of football and the torment of being blamed for his poor health.

Oh, the Squalor!

The rest of this section is devoted to a meticulous and highly detailed examination of the squalid conditions at the school. The writing is clearly fired by anger, hatred and disgust: at the same time, it's always colourful and highly literary. Orwell was throughout his life a voracious reader. Earlier in the essay, he had written: 'Ian Hay, Thackeray, Kipling and H. G. Wells were the favourite authors of my boyhood' (ibid: 394). Here, he deliberately places his depiction of the squalor in a literary context referring (subtly, in passing) to Thackeray, Dickens and Samuel Butler.

The poet and novelist William Makepeace Thackeray (1811-1863) had attended Charterhouse School but had hated it, later dubbing it in his fiction 'Slaughter House'.[2] Here, Orwell writes: 'Almost as in the days of Thackeray, it seemed natural that a little boy of eight or ten should be a miserable, snotty-nosed creature, his face almost permanently dirty, his hands chapped, his nails bitten, his handkerchief a sodden horror, his bottom frequently blue with bruises' (ibid: 396). To what extent is Orwell exaggerating? We will never know. But he clearly suspected readers may think so – and so he cleverly disarms this criticism with this reflection: 'Whoever writes about his childhood must beware of exaggeration and self pity' (ibid: 398). He continues, referencing the infamous school of Mr Wackford Squeers, in Dickens's *Nicholas Nickleby* (1839), where pupils are abused and neglected and where Nickleby goes to teach: 'I do not claim that I was a martyr or that St Cyprian's was a sort of Dotheboys Hall. But I should be falsifying my own memories if I did not record that they are largely memories of disgust' (ibid).

The reference to Samuel Butler (1835-1902) is fascinating. His *Erewhon* (of 1872) is an anti-utopian novel, 'part science-fiction, part social commentary, part adventure fantasy, part comic satire' which may well have influenced Orwell's *Nineteen Eighty-Four*.[3] Here, Orwell writes: 'Boys are Erewhonians: they think that misfortune is disgraceful and must be concealed at all costs' (ibid: 400). But perhaps more influential on the Orwell of 'Such, Such Were the Joys' was Butler's subtle representation of Erewhon, always avoiding blanket denunciations. As Tierle comments:

> Butler presents each aspect and institution in the novel from two angles, even while satirising the university (as the Colleges of Unreason) and the church (the worship of 'Mrs Grundy' in the form of Ydgrun). It's always weighed up from two sides. Thus *Erewhon* is strictly speaking, we might say, neither a utopia nor a dystopia but rather what we might call an *equitopia*, a world that is weighed in the balance and neither painted as a nightmare hell-on-earth (or elsewhere) nor depicted as a heavenly paradise.[4]

Food, Glorious Food!

Orwell's disgust first focuses on the meals: 'The food was not only bad, it was also insufficient' (ibid: 397). By the late 1940s, Orwell had developed a heightened awareness of the political/economic factors influencing the individual's psychology – politics, culture, the media and social institutions in general – and had come to see the school essentially as a commercial enterprise dedicated to snobbery. So looking back with the benefit of hindsight, he is able to write: 'As usual, I did not see the sound commercial reason for this underfeeding. On the whole, I accepted Sambo's view that a boy's appetite is a sort of morbid growth which should be kept in check as much as possible' (ibid).

Next, Orwell evokes the horrors of toilet facilities describing 'the slimy water of the plunge bath' and the murky seawater of the local baths which came straight in from the beach and 'on which I once saw floating a human turd' (ibid). He continues: 'It is not easy for me to think of my schooldays without seeming to breathe in a whiff of something cold and evil-smelling – a sort of compound of sweaty stockings, dirty towels, faecal smells blowing along corridors, forks with old food between the prongs, neck-of-mutton stew, and the banging of doors of the lavatories and the echoing chamber-pots in the dormitories' (ibid: 398-399). To a certain extent, the picture drawn here is reminiscent of Orwell's account of his time spent in a spike (1970 [1931]: 59-60):

> It was a disgusting sight, that bathroom. All the indecent secrets of our underwear were exposed: the grime, the rents and patches, the bits of string doing duty for buttons, the layers upon layers of fragmentary garments, some of them mere collections of holes, held together by dirt. The room became a press of steaming nudity, the sweaty odours of the tramps competing with the sickly, sub-faecal stench native to the spike.

Paradoxically, then, Orwell's prep school ordeals did not result in a life-long aversion to grime, rather the reverse: for four years, having returned from serving with the Indian Imperial Police in Burma in 1927, he determined to become a writer and voluntarily spent many months with the down and outs. After all, grime, the stench of the spikes and poverty, as he realised, could make great copy…

Flip the Focus, Again

For the final part of this section, Orwell focuses once again on Flip. In keeping with the overall approach of this section, even here Orwell moderates his animosity: 'Thus, although my memories of Flip are mostly hostile, I also remember considerable periods when I basked under her smiles, when she called me "old chap" and used my Christian name, and allowed me to frequent her private library, where I first made acquaintance with *Vanity Fair*' (1970 4 [1952]: 401). Significantly, reading – in this case Thackeray's celebrated novel of 1848 – is associated for Orwell with positive experiences. And it's Flip's special 'vocabulary of praise and abuse' which particularly draws his attention, Orwell carefully showing the syllables she emphasised through the use of italics:

> There was '*Buck* up, old chap!' which inspired one to paroxysms of energy; there was 'Don't *be* such a fool!' (or, It's path*etic*, isn't it), which made one feel a born idiot; and there was 'It isn't very straight of you, isn't it?' which always brought me to the brink of tears (ibid: 402).

The section ends on a powerful, emotional note. But instead of using the 'I' voice he distances himself slightly from the feeling (in keeping with the overall nuanced approach of this section) and talks of the impersonal 'one':

> And yet all the while, at the middle of one's heart, there seemed to stand an incorruptible inner self who knew that whatever one did – whether one laughed or snivelled or went into frenzies of gratitude for small favour – one's only true feeling was hatred (ibid).

Section IV: Confronting Taboos

Sex and Homosexuality

Connolly has devoted a whole chapter in *Enemies of Promise* (No. 14: 'The Charlock's Shade') to homosexuality amongst writers but in his chapter on his time at St Wulfric's there was no explicit mention of it. Significantly, the gay writer John Addington Symonds (1840-1893) had written about homosexuality during his time at Harrow – and an affair between a headmaster and pupil, no less – in his autobiography, *Memoirs*. But it was not to be published until 1984.[5] Orwell was clearly determined to confront the taboo – and explore his own sexuality in the process.

This was not first time Orwell had confronted homosexuality in his writings. For instance, even in his first published book, *Down and Out in Paris and London* (1980 [1933]), another complex mix of actuality and fiction (Bowker 3003: 144), he tells of the occasion when he is the victim of a homosexual assault in a spike: 'About midnight the other man began making homosexual attempts on me – a nasty experience in a locked, pitch-dark cell. He was a feeble creature and I could manage him easily, but of course it was impossible to go to sleep again' (op cit: 86). In the reflective section at the end of the book, he does not condemn but understands the prevalence of homosexuality amongst tramps in the context of the absence of women:

> It is obvious what the results of this must be: homosexuality, for instance, and occasional rape cases. But deeper than these there is the degradation worked in man who knows that he is not even considered fit for marriage. The sexual impulse, not to put it any higher, is a fundamental impulse, and starvation of it can be almost as demoralizing as physical hunger (ibid: 116).

The opening paragraph of this new section of 'Such, Such' sets the scene for a lengthy discussion about sex and homosexuality in particular: '... there was sex, which was always smouldering just under the surface and which suddenly blew up into a tremendous row when I was about twelve' (op cit: 402).

Orwell had actually anticipated the focus on homosexuality with a brief, passing mention of it towards the end of the previous section, confessing that he had 'sneaked' to his favourite teacher Brown 'a suspected case of homosexuality' (ibid: 401). Sex is immediately associated with secrecy, betrayal, ignorance, confusion and shame: 'I did not know very well what homosexuality was, but I knew that it happened and was bad, and that this one of the contexts in which it was proper to sneak. Brown told me I was "a good fellow", which made me feel horribly ashamed' (ibid: 401-402). Now the drama surrounding the 'tremendous row' is narrated. The general outlines are first sketched. Orwell claims he doesn't know precisely what went on, but he imagines it was a group masturbation involving some precocious South American boys (ibid: 402): 'There were summonses, interrogations, confessions, floggings, repentances, solemn lectures of which one understood nothing except some irredeemable sin known as "swinishness" or "beastliness" had been committed' (ibid). All the boys are made to feel implicated.

The spotlight suddenly then falls on Blair. There is mockery and irony when he writes: 'A solemn, black-haired imbecile of an assistant master, who was later to be a member of Parliament [a dig, then, at the political elite] took the older boys to a secluded room and delivered a talk on the Temple of the Body' (ibid: 403). Suddenly, he sets his 'cavernous black eyes' on Blair and adds sadly: '... you I hear are one of the very worst.' His guilt was confirmed and all the terrors surrounding sexuality come to haunt him. 'I too had done the dreadful thing, whatever it was, that wrecked you for life, body and soul, and ended in suicide or the lunatic asylum.'

All this leads Orwell into a remarkably frank account of his own sex life and commenting on the development of sexuality of youths in general when appropriate. Bowker highlights throughout his biography Orwell's predisposition to secrecy: 'While in many ways he could be brutally honest about himself, some aspects of him remained concealed behind a carefully constructed persona, secret sides of himself he seems to have feared and which he may have hoped would remain hidden, even beyond the grave' (op cit: 3). Perhaps the fact that Orwell knew 'Such, Such' was not to be published during his lifetime gave him the psychological space to open up – and perhaps fictionalise, too.

Orwell is often accused of being a misogynist.[6] In fact, Orwell's attitude to women is far more complex. In his handling of his son, Richard, for instance, he was in many ways a New Man, changing nappies (though admittedly with a cigarette in his mouth), showing him real affection and love.[7] Gordon Bowker comments (2003: 48): 'With the exception of an occasional attempt to interpret his dreams, Orwell was never much impressed by psychoanalysis.'

But if being open about one's feelings and sexuality (making the personal political) is another mark of today's New Man, then Orwell was well ahead of his times. Here, he admits to being 'in an almost sexless state, which is normal or at any rate common in boys of that age' (ibid). Carefully, he teases out the chronology of his sexual awakening. At five or six, 'like many children' (so deliberately generalising from the personal), he passes through a phase of sexuality.

> My friends were the plumber's children up the road, and we used sometimes to play games of a vaguely erotic kind. One was called 'playing at doctors' and I remember getting a faint but definitely pleasant thrill from holding a toy trumpet, which was supposed to be a stethoscope, against a little girl's belly (op cit: 403).

Again, he draws out the general reflection from the personal anecdote: he falls deeply in love with a girl named Elsie (significantly known only by her first name unlike the boys who are mostly known by their family names) at the convent school he attended: 'She seemed to me grown up, so I suppose she must have been fifteen. After that, as so often happens, all sexual feelings seemed to go out of me for many years' (ibid: 404). Orwell goes on to dwell on his boyhood sexual confusions with what appears to be a compelling honesty, which is all the more challenging for the reader given the deliberate positioning of the essay in the uncertain gap between fact and fiction. Most of the Facts of Life (those first letters capitalised to indicate their Importance and Severity) he learns from observing animals. 'I knew all the dirty words and in my bad moments I would repeat them to myself, but I did not know what the worst of them meant, nor want to know. They were abstractly wicked, a sort of verbal charm' (ibid). The paragraph climaxes with him noticing his penis sometimes standing of its own accord, and he comes to believe (or half believe) that the 'crime' that sparked the row was linked to that. 'At any rate, it was something to do with the penis – so much I understood. Many other boys, I have no doubt [that phrase adding extra rhetorical persuasiveness], were equally in the dark' (ibid).

Boys' Own Stories
Having attempted to link his own psychological exploration with the plight of boys in general, Orwell now introduces a 'human interest' element, switching the focus of the narrative to the plight of four boys who are all significantly named: Ronalds, Heath, Beacham and Horne (either pseudonyms to protect identities or all of them mere fictions). The sounds of Ronalds being flogged by Sambo are heard. But Flip's eyes settle on Blair. Confusion and guilt (the dominant feeling of the boy Blair) return. '"You see," she said. I will not swear that she said "You see what you have done," but that was the sense of it. We

were all bowed down with shame' (ibid: 405). Heath is forced to read from the Bible: 'Whoso shall offend one of these little ones that believe in me, it were better for him that a millstone were hanged about his neck, and that he were drowned in the depth of the sea' (ibid). Flip taunts Heath who breaks down into 'snivelling tears'. Beacham is 'similarly overwhelmed' after being accused of having black rings round his eyes'. Later, Orwell realises these were supposed to be symptoms by which masturbators could be detected. Without knowing this at the time, he accepts the black rings are a sign of depravity and gazes anxiously into glass 'looking for the first hint of that dreaded stigma, the confession, which the secret sinner writes upon his own face' (ibid: 406).

In contrast, the final story – about Horne who had been flogged and expelled – brings some light to an otherwise dark narrative. Horne is sent to Eastbourne College, which is despised by Sambo. 'You had no chance if you went to a school like that: at best your destiny would be a clerkship.' But in the following term he meets Horne in the street. He looks normal, not at all ashamed of being at the other college – and glad to have escaped St Cyprian's. But the dark swiftly returns: 'I still believed in the sexual mythology that had been taught me by Sambo and Flip. The mysterious, terrible dangers were still there' (ibid).

Section V: Contradictory Codes
Education into Snobbery

The opening part of this new section moves away from the intense narrative (involving the fates of the four boys) and reflects on broader social, cultural, sporting and class-based issues. The first sentence sets the scene: 'The various codes which were presented to you at St Cyprian's – religious, moral, social and intellectual – contradicted one another if you worked out their implications' (ibid: 407). He highlights the 'sheer vulgar fatness of wealth' in the years before 1914. And adds in a sweeping historical generalisation: 'After 1918 it was never quite the same again. Snobbishness and expensive habits came back, certainly, but they were self-conscious and on the defensive' (ibid: 409). Other intriguing features of the broader cultural scene he considers are the 'curious cult of Scotland' and the values associated with competitive sports.

> Virtue consisted in winning: it consisted in being bigger, stronger, handsomer, richer, more popular, more elegant, more unscrupulous than other people – in dominating them, bullying them, making them suffer pain, making them look foolish, getting the better of them in every way. Life was hierarchical and whatever happened was right (Ibid: 411).

The Instinct to Survive

In keeping with the overall intention in the essay to be 'even-handed' rather than dogmatically polemical, Orwell writes that his sense of guilt and inevitable failure 'was balanced by something else: that is, the instinct to survive' (ibid: 413). This instinct is dramatised in a confrontation with a boy named 'Johnny Hale' (unusual in being given a first name). After Hale picks on him for some reason, Orwell smashes his fist into his face (ibid: 414). How much is this Orwell, the intellectual – and later imperial policeman and Republican militiaman in the Spanish civil war (1936-1937) – still needing to prove his manliness in a conventional aggressive way?

This section ends following the chronological order with Blair/Orwell saying good-bye to Flip. The tension and hatred remain to the very end as does his sensitivity to language, its rhythms and the tone of expression:

> The tone in which she said good-bye was nearly the tone in which she had used to say *little butterflies* [italics in the original]. I had won two scholarships [to Wellington and Eton] but I was a failure, because success was measured not by what you did but by what you were. I was 'not a good type of boy' and could bring no credit on the school (ibid: 416).

Section VI: Reflections

The Only Certainty is Uncertainty

Orwell deliberately mixes the personal and political throughout this final section. First, he sets the scene, then asks a question: 'All this was thirty years ago and more. The question is: Does a child at school go through the same kind of experiences nowadays?' But he is determined to stress the impossibility of knowing. 'The only honest answer, I believe, is that we do not with certainty know' (ibid: 417). His over-emphatic assertiveness in the following sentence, in fact, paradoxically betrays his uncertainty: 'Of course, it is obvious that the present-day attitude towards education is enormously more humane and sensible than that of the past.' Later on he even qualifies that claim: 'The child and the adult live in different worlds. If that is so, we cannot be certain the school, at any rate boarding school, is not still for many children as dreadful an experience as it used to be' (ibid: 421).

Conclusion: Confronting Humbug

In 'Why I write', Orwell listed 'four great motives for writing' – putting aside the need to earn a living (1946 [1970, 1: 25-26]): aesthetic enthusiasm, historical impulse, political purpose. But for No 1 motive he said: 'Sheer egoism: Desire to seem clever, to be talked about, to be remembered after death, to get your own back on grown-ups who snubbed you in childhood, etc etc. It is humbug to pretend that this is not a motive and a strong one.' Certainly, in 'Such, Such Were the Joys' Orwell achieves enormous pleasure in crafting the memoir as a deliberately literary piece in the many ways identified in this chapter. At the same time, he is certainly getting his own back at Flip and Sambo.

In the essay's final, long paragraph, Orwell looks back in loathing at his time at St Cyprian's. Writing about it has, in any case, been cathartic: 'Now, however, the place is out of my system for good. Its magic [a strangely positive-sounding word] works no longer, and I have not even enough animosity left to make me hope that Flip and Sambo are dead or that the story of the school being burnt down was true' (ibid: 422).[8] That final word is the crucial one: Orwell wants to leave us wondering: how much do truth and fiction mix in his memoir – as indeed in all history.

Notes

[1] The exact year when Orwell composed the essay is not known. Crick devotes a whole Appendix in his biography (1980: 586-589) to the topic. He cites Ian Angus who, with Sonia Orwell, edited the *Collected Essays, Journalism and Letters*, who says it 'was written by May 1947' (1970 4: 330). Crick, in contrast, suggests that 'its uncertain pose between the autobiographical and the polemical, is far more consistent with his bitter and jagged writing of the 1938-43 period, with his mood of failure and frustration, indeed, than with the calm, composed and measured post-war essays' (op cit: 587).

[2] See http://spartacus-educational.com/Jthackeray.htm, accessed on 9 February 2018

[3] See Samuel Butler's *Erewhon*: Dystopia before dystopia, by Oliver Tearle. Available online at https://interestingliterature.com/2018/02/02/samuel-butlers-erewhon-dystopia-before-dystopia/, accessed on 8 February 2018

[4] Ibid

[5] See https://www.the-tls.co.uk/articles/public/locked-up-beyond-reach/, accessed on 9 February 2018

[6] Bowker quotes the poet Stephen Spender (2003: 128): 'Orwell was very misogynist. I don't know why. [He] was a strange sort of eccentric man full of strange ideas and stranger prejudices. One was that he thought that women were extremely inferior and stupid. ... He rather despised women.' See also Patai, Daphne (op cit) and Csaszar, Ivett (2010) Orwell and women's issues: A shadow over the champion of decency, *Eger Journal of English Studies*, Vol. 10 pp 39-56. Available online at http://anglisztika.ektf.hu/new/content/tudomany/ejes/ejesdokumentumok/2010/Csaszar_2010.pdf, accessed on 11 February 2018

[7] See Venables, Dione (n. d) George Orwell: Plain speaking and hidden agendas. Available online at https://www.orwellfoundation.com/the-orwell-foundation/orwell/resources/dione-venables-orwell-plain-speaking-and-hidden-agendas/, accessed on 11 February 2018

[8] The school actually did burn down in 1939: see Taylor, D. J. (op cit: 36)

References

Bowker, Gordon (2003) *George Orwell*, London: Little, Brown

Connolly, Cyril (1961 [1938]) *Enemies of Promise*, London: Routledge and Kegan Paul; Harmondsworth, Middlesex: Penguin Books

Crick, Bernard (1980) *George Orwell: A Life*, Harmondsworth, Middlesex: Penguin

CWGO (1998) *The Collected Works of George Orwell, Vols 1-20*, Davison, Peter (ed.) London: Secker and Warburg

Grant, Julia (2004) A real boy and not a sissy: Gender, childhood and masculinity, 1890-1940, *Journal of Social History*, Vol. 37, No. 4 pp 829-851

Keeble, Richard (2007) Introduction: On journalism, creativity and the imagination, Keeble, Richard and Wheeler, Sharon (eds) *The Journalistic Imagination: Literary Journalists from Defoe to Capote and Carter*, London and New York: Routledge pp 1-14

Keeble, Richard Lance (2012) Introduction: Orwell – the cultural icon of today, Keeble, Richard Lance (ed.) *Orwell Today*, Bury St Edmunds: Abramis pp 5-12

Lewis, Jeremy (1998) *Cyril Connolly: A Life*, London: Pimlico

Marks, Peter (2011) *George Orwell the Essayist: Literature, Politics and the Periodical Culture*, London and New York: Continuum

Meyers, Jeffrey (2000) *Orwell: Wintry Conscience of a Generation*, New York and London: W. W. Norton and Company

Orwell, George (1968 [1931]) The spike, Orwell, Sonia and Angus, Ian (eds) *The Collected Essays, Journalism and Letters, Vol. 1: An Age Like This, 1920-1940*, Harmondsworth, Middlesex: Penguin Books pp 58-66; *Adelphi*, April

Orwell, George (1980 [1933]) *Down and Out in Paris and London*, George Orwell, London: Secker and Warburg/Octopus pp 15-120

Orwell, George (1970 1 [1946]) Why I write, Orwell, Sonia and Angus, Ian (eds) *The Collected Essays, Journalism and Letters, Vol. 1: An Age Like This, 1920-1940*, Harmondsworth, Middlesex: Penguin Books pp 23-30; *Gangrel*, summer

Orwell, George (1970 4 [1952]) Such, Such Were the Joys, Orwell, Sonia and Angus, Ian (eds) *The Collected Essays, Journalism and Letters, Vol. 4: In Front of Your Nose 1945-1950*, Harmondsworth, Middlesex: Penguin Books pp 379-422; *Partisan Review*, September-October

Patai, Daphne (1984) *The Orwell Mystique: A Study in Male Ideology*, Amherst: University of Massachusetts Press

Sutherland, John (2016) *Orwell's Nose: A Pathological Biography*, London: Reaktion Books

Symonds, John Addington (1968) *The Memoirs of John Addington Symonds*, Grosskurth, Phyllis (ed.) London: Hutchinson

Taylor, D. J. (2003) *Orwell: The Life*, London: Chatto and Windus

Woloch, Alex (2016) *Or Orwell: Writing and Democratic Socialism*, Cambridge, Massachusetts and London: Harvard University Press

- This essay was first published in *George Orwell Studies*, Vol. 2, No. 2, 2018 pp 69-90.

Chapter 10

Orwell and Film Reviewing: Another Look

Orwell, in effect, invented the discipline of Cultural Studies with his brilliant pieces on such diverse subjects as boys' weeklies, sexy seaside postcards, pubs, turned-up trouser legs, cups of tea, junk shops and the common toad. But what was his attitude to films? The picture is mixed – perhaps not surprisingly given Orwell's complex and contradictory personality.

Interestingly, in his award-winning biography, *Orwell: The Life* (2003), D. J. Taylor records him as being 'keen' on Burmese cinema while serving as an Imperial Policeman there between 1922 and 1927 (p. 74). Later, in the early 1930s, joining his family in the Suffolk resort, Southwold, Orwell would accompany his father in one of the old man's favourite pastimes: watching films in the tiny local cinema in Duke of York's Road near the common (p. 137). 'A screening of *The Constant Nymph* [directed by Basil Dean, in 1933] took him back to his first reading of Margaret Kennedy's novel years before in Burma. Older and better read, Orwell cheerfully owned up to this lapse of judgement.'

In 1934, he wrote to his friend, Brenda Salkend: 'I went to the pictures last week and saw Jack Hulbert in *Jack Ahoy* which I thought very amusing & a week or two before that there was quite a good crook film which, however, my father ruined for me by insisting on telling me the plot beforehand' (*Complete Works of George Orwell* X: 346). And a letter to his friend Rayner Heppenstall in 1935 describes a visit with the anthropologist Geoffrey Gorer to see Greta Garbo in *Anna Karenina* (ibid: 399).

While in Spain, fighting on the Republican side during the civil war in 1937, Orwell even took a boy from the Barcelona slums to the cinema – and plied him with brandy and chocolate – in an attempt to make amends after he had been suspected (wrongly) of stealing from his fellow militiamen (Taylor 2003: 238-239). In Casablanca, on their way back home after a short visit to Morocco just before World War Two, Orwell and his wife, Eileen, took the time to go to the cinema where the film was accompanied by a cine-reel demonising Germany. 'Such propagandising in this out-of-the way corner of the French empire could only mean one thing, Orwell decided: war was certain' (ibid: 264). Later still, while the Orwells were living in London after he had been appointed literary editor of the leftist journal, *Tribune*, in 1943, his Dakin nieces and nephews would visit. One recalled that 'they went to see Chaplin in *The Gold Rush*, where Orwell laughed louder than anyone else in the cinema' (ibid: 329).

Intriguingly, this clear fascination for the cinema is not reflected in the early novels and works of reportage where film is only rarely mentioned. Gordon Comstock, in *Keep the Aspidistra Flying* (1936), tries to fight the money god but his inevitable final collapse is prefigured outside a cinema: 'Gordon halted outside a garish picture-house, under the weary eye of the commissionaire, to examine the photographs. Greta Garbo in *The Painted Veil*. He yearned to go inside, not for Greta's sake, but just for the warmth and the softness of the velvet seat. He hated the pictures, of course, seldom went there even when he could afford it. Why encourage the art that is destined to replace literature? But still, there is a kind of soggy attraction about it … after all, it's the kind of drug we need. The right drug for friendless people' (Chapter 4).

In *The Road to Wigan Pie* (1937), the cinema is seen as a 'favourite refuge' for the unemployed in the battle to keep warm and may even have helped reduce social unrest: 'Of course, the post-war development of cheap luxuries has been a very fortunate thing for our rulers. It is quite likely that fish and chips, art silk stockings, tinned salmon, cut-price chocolate … the movies, the radio and football pools have between them averted revolution' (Section 1: v).

Orwell actually did a stint as film and theatre reviewer for *Time and Tide* (the vaguely right-of-centre journal edited by Margaret, Lady Rhondda) between October 1940 and August 1941. But it has tended to draw little attention from his biographers. Bernard Crick, in *George Orwell: A Life* (1980) dismisses his film reviewing as 'with few exceptions, hasty, heavy-handed and banal' (pp 259-260).

It receives no mention at all in Robert Colls's *George Orwell: English Rebel* (2013). John Sutherland, in *Orwell's Nose: A Pathological Biography* (2016: 195) simply records: 'He landed a regular reviewing position with the eccentric Lady Rhondda's *Time and Tide* and churned out for the magazine's meagre readership low-grade pap on literature and film.' Gordon Bowker mentions his *Time and Tide* stint only *en passant* (2003: 268-269): 'Reviewing plays and films he felt was somehow demeaning and, rather than treating cinema as an art, he wrote about the sociology of the film industry deploring Hollywood escapism and glorification of sadistic violence and "the intellectual contempt which American film producers seem to feel for their audience". … His great exception was Chaplin, a one-time performer on the London music halls, for which he retained a minor passion, especially for the bawdy patter of performers such as Max Miller ...' D. J. Taylor (2003: 283, 291) also has little to say on Orwell's film reviewing.

Jeffrey Meyers (2000: 201-203), in *Orwell: Wintry Conscience of a Generation*, devotes three pages to the reviews. But he remains very critical of the output. Orwell, he says, was in 'no mood to appreciate the modest virtues of morale building escapist entertainment'. He loathed *One Night in Lisbon* (directed by Edward H. Griffith, 1941) and angrily exclaimed: 'What rot it all is! What sickly enervating rubbish! How dare anyone present the war in these colours when thousands of tanks are battling on the plains of Poland and tired aircraft workers are slinking into the tobacconist's shop to plead humbly for a small Woodbine.' According to Meyers, Orwell was 'not interested in film as an art form and rarely even mentioned the directors'. 'He was mainly concerned with the political, social and moral content of films, their propaganda value, the way they reflected the progress of the war and the difference between English and American cinema. Orwell mainly reviewed films of poor quality and his reviews were generally short and formulaic: an opening comment, discussion of the plot, snap judgement on the film and remarks on the cast with particular praise for veteran English character actors.'

Orwell was repelled by the gratuitous violence in American culture, which he later discussed in his essay on detective novels, 'Raffles and Miss Blandish'. And, according to Meyers, he failed to recognise a good movie when he saw one: Raoul Walsh's *High Sierra* (1941). But Charlie Chaplin's *The Great Dictator* (1940) 'challenged Orwell's prejudice against Hollywood and he was impressed by the way Chaplin presented serious ideas through absurd comedy'.

Michael Shelden, in *Orwell: The Authorised Biography* (1991: 353-354) devotes three paragraphs to the film reviewing and comments: 'Orwell liked *The Great Dictator* so much that he called for the government to subsidise showings of it so that it could be seen by people who could not afford seats in the "three West End picture houses" where the film had opened.'

Undoubtedly the best appreciation of Orwell's film reviews was penned by my late friend and University of Lincoln colleague, John Tulloch, in his essay 'Sceptic in the palace of dreams: Orwell as film reviewer'. It appeared in *Orwell Today* (pp 79-101) which I edited in 2012. John was an extraordinary polymath: a conversation with him was an education in itself. My tribute to him, 'John Tulloch: On the Importance of Mischief-Making' (*Ethical Space: The International Journal of Communication Ethics*, Vol 12, No. 1, 2015 pp 23-29) is included in *Journalism Beyond Orwell*, a collection of my essays published by Routledge (2020). John loved Orwell's writings and in the Introduction to

Global Literary Journalism: Exploring the Journalistic Imagination (2012: 10) which we jointly edited, he was at pains to highlight the veracity of Orwell's voice in his celebrated essay 'A Hanging' (1931): 'Trust in the veracity of the voice (thus eliminating any doubts that Orwell actually witnessed the hanging) derives from accurate, precise observation and an emotional response which remains completely appropriate in relation to the facts of the case. Honesty – and the trust we feel for this voice – is in those details.'

Of the 45 films reviewed by Orwell, Tulloch notes that 37 were produced in the US while eight were made in the UK (Meyers wrongly states that Orwell composed only 26 film reviews, 2000: 201). Every review is incorporated into a fact-packed, tabulated list taking in the film's title, director, main actors, date of publication, number of words and a brief comment.

For Orwell, US practice exposes British shortcomings: *Unholy War* and the *Heart of Britain* are 'terrible. What is the use, in the middle of a desperate war, in which propaganda is a major weapon, of wasting time and money on producing this kind of stuff?' In particular, he identifies 'the dreadful BBC voice … more valuable to Hitler than a dozen new submarines' (p. 95).

Orwell sees American film as representative of US civilisation. 'Apart from the cultural degradation of the masses, the US shared with Britain the weaknesses of capitalist democracy which Orwell diagnosed as an inability to create a willing consensus and rationally organise its resources to defeat Fascism' (ibid). US products for Orwell display greater production skills. But technique merely serves to conceal the persistent vices of escapism: 'a lack of realism, implausibility and a failure to engage with the needs of their audience' (p. 96). Also noteworthy is Hollywood's lack of respect for film-goers. 'Reviewing *The Lady in Question*, a Hollywood remake of a French movie and a vehicle for Rita Hayworth, Orwell discerns through the "coarse meshes of the American film … the intellectual contempt which American film producers seem to feel for their audience"' (ibid).

Tulloch goes on to argue that even where an American film is powerful, Orwell's 'judgement is heavily qualified by contempt for what he presents as its materialist values' (p. 97). *High Sierra* is dismissed as 'the *ne plus ultra* of sadism, bully-worship, gun-play, socks on the jaw and gangster atmosphere generally' although he concedes that 'the direction is competent and the acting distinctly good' (ibid). Orwell even begins to develop a theory about the western and the need for action-based, escapist yarns in the middle of a war, in his respectful review of Fritz Lang's *Western Union* (1941): 'The reason must be the fantasy of individual adventure – the lonely traveller on his horse, with no protection save his revolver and his skill in using it – supplies a psychological need in a world which grows constantly more dangerous but also more regimented' (ibid).

On a few occasions, Orwell reports audience reaction, in the form of 'allegedly' overheard conversations, such as during his mainly contemptuous review of *Waterloo Bridge* (starring Vivien Leigh and Robert Taylor, directed by Mervyn LeRoy, 1940) (p. 85).

Tulloch concludes even-handedly (p. 98): 'He shared in many of the standard prejudices of the Thirties intellectual against film – it was a mass art, machine-made by capitalism, producing low-grade rubbish for working class consumption. ... Nevertheless, the reviews contain some valuable insights and embody a developing vision of the possibilities of film, both in its degraded form as a mass-produced mechanism for propaganda and escapism and an agency through which contrary, humane perceptions can be articulated. Orwell made heroic efforts to overcome his inbuilt class prejudices, and cultivated a belief in the innate human values of ordinary people and their capacity to remake society.'

Yet Orwell professed a rather dim view of film reviewing. In his *Tribune* essay 'Confessions of a Book Reviewer' (of 3 May 1946), he damns book reviewing as a 'quite exceptionally thankless, irritating and exhausting job'. But there was one activity even worse: '.... I must say that the book reviewer is better off than the film critic who cannot even do his work at home but has to attend trade shows at eleven in the morning and, with one or two notable exceptions, is expected to sell his honour for a glass of inferior sherry.'

All that said, Orwell's undoubted fascination with film culminated in his representation of the Big Brother society in his dystopian masterpiece, *Nineteen Eighty-Four*, where screens and films are ever-present. Two-way surveillance telescreens follow the individual's every action while the Two Minute Hate (memorably captured in Michael Radford's film of *1984*) is conducted in front of massive screens displaying the ultimate Enemy of the People: Emmanuel Goldstein.

And near the start of the novel, the anti-hero Winston Smith begins his diary on 4 April 1984 with this entry: 'Last night to the flicks. All war films. One very good one of a ship full of refugees being bombed somewhere in the Mediterranean. Audience much amused by shots of a great huge fat man trying to swim away with a helicopter after him...'

Orwell is not well-known as a film reviewer. Yet this essay has attempted to highlight his personal fascination with the medium, the often original insights in his film reviews (as highlighted in John Tulloch's essay), his awareness of its possibilities as both an art form and propaganda tool – and its potential for remaking the way we understand the world. As Orwell wrote: 'Everyone must have noted the extraordinary powers that are latent in the film – the powers of distortion, of fantasy, in general of escaping the restrictions of the physical world. I suppose it is only from commercial necessity that the film has been used chiefly for silly imitations of stage plays, instead of concentrating as it ought on things that are beyond the stage. Properly used, the film is the one possible medium for conveying mental processes' (*Complete Works of George Orwell* XII: 134).

- This essay was first published at https://orwellsocietyblog.wordpress.com/2019/04/16/orwell-and-films-another-look/, in April 2019.

Chapter 11

Struggle with the Prose (Just About) Worth the Effort

A review of *Or Orwell: Writing and Democratic Socialism*, by Alex Woloch, Massachusetts, London: Harvard University Press, 2016; ISBN 978 0 674 282483

Is it not intriguing to note how writers over the centuries have tended to look down on their literary journalism? Indeed, since their emergence in the early seventeenth century in Europe's cities, particularly London, the 'news media' (variously known as corantos, diurnals, gazettes, proceedings and mercuries) have been associated with scandal, gossip and 'low' culture. While the term journalist emerged in France in the 1830s to refer to writers on periodicals (distinguishing them from writers of literature), the identification of journalism largely with newspapers and mass culture has had a profound impact on the sensibilities of men and women of letters. Typically George Orwell, considered by many as one of the greatest UK journalists of the last century, constantly looked down on his journalism as 'mere pamphleteering' and a lesser form of literature. On a basic level, journalism has provided writers with an income. Yet this very fact has reinforced journalism's position as a sub-literary genre. For while literature is often seen as the fruit of 'scholarship' and 'inspiration' – hence pure, disinterested and above market considerations – journalistic writing is viewed as distorted by the constraints of the market, tight deadlines or word limits.

Significantly, Orwell is best known as the author of *Animal Farm* (1945) and *Nineteen Eighty-Four* (1949) – and his journalism has been marginalised in the academy. But recently major studies by Paul Anderson (2006) and Peter Marks (2011) and the publication of Orwell's collected journalism (in *Seeing Things As They Are*, edited by Peter Davison, 2015) have helped place the spotlight on his 'pamphleteering'.

This new, strangely titled, text by Alex Woloch, Professor of English at Stanford University, continues this trend – and comes lauded with high praise. According to Aidan Wasley, of the University of Georgia: 'This is a fascinating and important work, probably the best and most original book on Orwell I have read. It is the first book on Orwell that truly attends to the complexities of Orwell's language, composition technique and poetics.' While Jed Esty, of the University of Pennsylvania, comments: 'Woloch turns his considerable ingenuity and superb ear to the task of a slow, close investigation of Orwell's writing. ... An accomplished and subtle book.'

The first half examines the non-fiction prose, including 'A Hanging' (1931), *The Road to Wigan Pier* (1937) and the three essays, 'Charles Dickens', 'Boys' Weeklies' and 'Inside the Whale' which together made up the collection *Inside the Whale and Other Stories* (1940). The second half focuses entirely on the 80 'As I Please' columns Orwell contributed to the leftist journal, *Tribune*, between 1943 and 1947.

Woloch's writing style throughout is dense and extremely challenging for the reader. He is very slow getting into first gear: he begins with an 11-page Prologue, subtitled 'Reagan and Theory' and then moves on to an Introduction of 57 pages. Once he launches into the main body of his text ('The Paradoxes of the Plain Style: The 1930s') his writing appears to be bursting over with complexity — with one idea piling over another. It's almost as if the simple sentence cannot contain the intensity of his analytical project. So hardly a sentence goes by without its flow being broken by the inclusion of text inside a bracket. Let me provide just one example: on page 140, he writes:

> While reflection takes place by 'stop[ping],' it also (perhaps *in* this very halt) creates a movement or 'ten[dency]' of its own. '[O]ne *tends to think* of explosions as the chief danger of mining' (passage 2, emphasis added).

Is it not significant that in the many Orwellian quotes dotted about the book there are hardly any brackets? Moreover, the text ends with 61 pages of Notes — another indication of the expansiveness of Woloch's style. Is it not significant that Orwell hardly ever used a note in his writings — perhaps the result of having never enjoyed nor endured a university education.

Yet buried in the book are some wonderfully original insights. To take a few examples: Woloch argues (p. 9) that Orwell's plain style is political not merely because of how he communicates ('familiarly and, thus, democratically') but also 'because *what* Orwell aspires to communicate is explicitly a politics' (italics in the original). He is particularly concerned to highlight the many extraordinary complexities of the plain style: for instance, Orwell's constant focus in *Wigan Pier*, *Down and Out*, 'A Hanging' and in the 'As I Please' columns on what we are 'liable to miss', 'reveals a strange blankness, or emptiness, at the deliberate heart of Orwell's work' (p. 23). Later, he describes this 'withholding at the center of his style' as the 'poetics of exclusion' (p. 67).

He goes on to argue that the opening of 'A Hanging' crystallises the sense of a basic emptiness that lurks within any representation. 'The stated bareness of the cells functions, on this register, as an ironic imagining of the hollowness of linguistic representation. It is a projection, within the story-world itself, of our nagging awareness that even the most topically grounded or referentially charged language is nothing but a tissue of words, if not lies.' For Woloch, the amorphous status of the work between 'documentary', 'essay', 'sketch' and 'story' highlights its *generic* uncertainty (p. 73) and 'ontological instability' (p. 74).

In his detailed examination of *The Road to Wigan Pier*, Woloch argues that 'the conceptual framework of Orwell's democratic socialism helps motivate a specific articulation of literary irony' (p. 118). He notes how the book opens with Orwell highlighting the gap between the experience of the working class and the observations of a middle class writer. 'If this tension between observer and experience informs the opening paragraph – like a kind of warning at the entryway of the essay – it is most notably reflected in the structure of the work as a whole, which gets divided into two parts when Orwell changes topics, swerving away from the workers in northern England to write about how the class divide poses problems for Socialist intellectuals' (p. 122). Thus, 'empirically grounded observation gives way to self-reflection' (ibid). On the five-page, eye-witness description of travelling through the tunnels to the coal face, Woloch argues that Orwell was making a 'theoretical' point: 'Attention to the difficult commute provides a brilliant image for a much more general process: the inevitable disjunction between a worker's experience of labor and the abstract definition of this labor under capitalism. The experience *of* work cannot be contained within the (wage) definition of this work by capital' (pp 130-131).

In his analysis of *Inside the Whale and Other Stories*, Woloch is fascinated by Orwell's use of the term 'semi-sociological' to describe it. The neologism 'hovers between technicality and familiarity, providing – if only by its alliterative, internally rhyming phonetic structure – a kind of bump in Orwell's famously plain style' (p. 145). Orwell concludes 'Inside the Whale' (the last essay in the collection) and his long evaluation of Henry Miller's *Tropic of Cancer* by stressing the 'impossibility' of writing in the contemporary world. Woloch continues:

> If *Inside the Whale* functions as such a pivot within Orwell's writing trajectory, it would suggest that a negativity inheres in the essay form itself, as Orwell conceives of it. The essay, as the most contingent form of writing, might always reflect its own transience – its own formal inadequacy – no matter how expressive, direct, or powerful its rhetorical and topical achievement (p. 147).

On the 'As I Please' weekly columns, Woloch suggests their enduring quality rests 'in the fragility of writing that these pieces – in their ephemeral topicality – both register and crystallize' (p. 187). And he argues that they are 'paradoxically, a telling exploration of both freedom (most essentially in their heterogeneity) and the nature of thinking (most essentially as they interweave immediacy and reflection)' (p. 203).

The focus clearly in *Or Orwell* is on the text. Yet it is difficult to consider Orwell's journalism without reference to his audience – and this is missing here. In his 'As I Please' columns, for instance, Orwell used two strategies to promote his notion of 'the community of the left': firstly, through columns focusing on literary, social, cultural or political issues; and secondly, and most imaginatively, through developing a close relationship to his audience. This relationship was crucial to the flowing of Orwell's journalistic imagination. While he realised that mainstream journalism was essentially propaganda for dominant financial, political and cultural interests, at *Tribune* he was engaging in the crucial debates with engaged, activist, politically-aware people who mattered to him.

It is also a little surprising that Woloch does not engage with the leading theorists in the growing academic field of literary journalism – such as Applegate (1996), Bak and Reynolds (2011), Butler (1981), Campbell (1998), Gross (1969), Hartsock (2000), Italia (2005), Schudson (1978), Sims (1984), Treglown and Bennett (1998) and Wolfe (1973).

In his discussion of Orwell's essay 'Charles Dickens', Woloch notes how he imagines Dickens' face: 'It is the face of a man of about forty, with a small beard and a high colour. He is laughing, with a touch of anger in his laughter, but no triumph, no malignity' (p. 180). Cleverly, Woloch also highlights the similar way in which Raymond Williams, in his short text on Orwell of 1971, also comments on his face: 'The thing to do with his work, his history, is to read it, not imitate it. He is still there, tangibly, with the wound in his throat, the sad strong face, the plain words written in hardship and exposure' (p. 178).

Continuing the 'face' theme, whenever I read Orwell's journalism my face, I guess, will be constantly creased in smiles. I love Orwell's droll wit, the flow and clarity of his prose, the range of subject matter, the extraordinary flights of his imagination. In contrast, as I read *Or Orwell* there will be a constant frown on my face as I struggle with the complex prose. But given the range of Woloch's insights – it's a struggle (just about) worth the effort.

- This review was first published in *George Orwell Studies*, Vol. 1, No. 1, 2016 pp 144-148.

Chapter 12

Far Beyond Mere Hackery: Orwell's Journalism

A review of *Seeing Things As They Are: Selected Journalism and Other Writings by George Orwell* (compiled by Peter Davison, published by Harvill Secker, £25)

Orwell, the journalist, has always been an inspiration to me – a model of a committed, radical, intelligent, witty, wonderfully imaginative writer who deploys the tools of journalism for their best purpose: as a crucial, morally urgent intervention in politics.

Paul Foot, the Socialist Worker/Trotskyite journalist, called him the greatest journalist of the 20th century. Timothy Garton Ash in his 'Introduction' to *Orwell and Politics* (of 2001) describes Orwell as the most influential political writer of the twentieth century.

Orwell's sunny, positive character shines, in particular, through many of the eighty 'As I Please' columns he wrote between 1943 and 1947 for the leftist journal, *Tribune*. The quality of the writing – the range of subject matter – the displays of intelligence, vast reading and wit are all simply dazzling. In these columns Orwell appears to be a man at the peak of his powers, playing with the genre, switching subject matter and tone effortlessly; one moment he is deconstructing the front page of a morning newspaper, the next he is constructing a mini-play about a family determined to drink their tea in the face of a V-bomb attack, recounting a racist conversation overheard in a Scottish hotel, campaigning for communal washing-up services or admitting a mistake over the authorship of a poem. Humour is always around the corner.

Orwell was, in effect, through his contributions to *Tribune* defining a new kind of radical politics. It involved reducing the power of the press barons, facing up to racial intolerance, defending civil liberties. Yet it also incorporated an awareness of the power of language and propaganda, a celebration of the joys of nature and an acknowledgement of the cultural power of both Christianity and Marxism. Above all, in the face of the vast political, cultural, economic factors driving history, it recognised the extraordinary richness of the individual experience – summed up in his idiosyncratic columns. Moreover, in his political and cultural essays Orwell is said to have done nothing less than invent the discipline of Cultural Studies as he examined such everyday artefacts as boys' weekly magazines and the seaside postcards of Donald McGill in their broader political, economic and cultural contexts.

Another impressive aspect of Orwell's journalism is the close relationship he developed quite instinctively with his readers. In his 'As I Please' columns Orwell can be seen, in many ways, as a proto-blogger, responding to letters sent to him directly or addressed to *Tribune*, inviting letters, asking readers to answer queries or point him towards a book, pamphlet or quotation he is looking for, running a competition for a short story or giving them a quirky brain teaser to answer.

Moreover, Orwell's commitment to the alternative media has always inspired me. Realising that the mainstream newspapers were basically propaganda for their wealthy proprietors, Orwell's main objective after his experiences in the Spanish civil war was to speak for and to socialists. It was thus his deliberate choice to concentrate his journalism on small-scale, left-wing publications in both Britain and the United States – *New English Weekly*, *Fortnightly Review*, *New Leader*, *Left Forum*, *Left News*, *Progressive*, *Politics and Letters* and *Gangrel*. Some of these survived for a couple of editions and then died.

The publication of a bulky, 485-page, new collection of Orwell's journalism, edited by Peter Davison, is clearly a cause for celebration. It includes more than 100 items: book, film and theatre reviews, BBC broadcasts, extracts from both his 'As I Please' columns and the 'London Letters' he contributed to the American leftist journal, *Partisan Review*; literary essays, letters – as well as poems. Stressing his journalistic achievement, Professor Davison comments astutely in his 'Introduction': 'Although Orwell continued to the end of his days to strive for success as a novelist, three of his nine "books" are the product of his journalism in a form in which he excelled: documentary reportage – *Down and Out in Paris and London*, *The Road to Wigan Pier* and *Homage to Catalonia*.'

So much of journalism is ephemeral and quickly forgotten. As Professor Davison points out, the mark of Orwell's genius is that so much of his journalism is still relevant – whether he is discussing 'Anti-Semitism' (p. 261), 'Skin Colour and Living Standards' (p. 250) and 'The Colour Bar' (p. 289) or 'Scottish Nationalism' (p. 411) and 'Polish Immigration' (p. 380). Professor Davison adds:

> And some of his journalism has a timeless quality. 'Woolworth's Roses' (p. 257) roused the ire of some readers of *Tribune* because it was deemed a piece of 'bourgeois nostalgia' ... but as Orwell correctly responded: 'One of the outstanding characteristics of the working class of this country is their love of flowers.'

The collection also serves to highlight Orwell's invention of a form of broadcast literary magazine which attracted leading poets, intellectuals and critics – such as T. S. Eliot, E. M. Forster and Ritchie Calder – and the 'spoken poetry magazine' complete with spoken editorial by Orwell (pp 172-173). Another of his inventions is shown in his hilarious 'Imaginary Interview with Jonathan Swift' (p. 192). In one section Orwell asks Swift: 'Tell me candidly, do we stink as we used to?' To which Swift comments: 'Certainly the smells are different. There was a new one I remarked as I came through the streets' – (sniffs) – Orwell responds: 'It's called petrol. But don't you feel that the mass of the people are more intelligent than they were, or at least better educated? How about the newspapers and the radio? Surely they have opened people's minds a little? There are very few people in England now who can't read, for instance.' 'That is why they are so easily deceived,' replies Swift.

As each year passes the Orwell industry expands a little and there are growing dangers of overlaps and repetitions. For instance, all of Orwell's journalism at *Tribune* (including all the 'As I Please' writings) has already been brought together in a volume (Politico's, 2006) edited by Paul Anderson who provides a wonderfully insightful 'Introduction'. Moreover, the greatness of the columns lies in the way they usually incorporate a range of topics, styles and tones. His column of 28 January 1944 is typical in that it binds together four very different topics drawn imaginatively from four contrasting sources: a news item, a letter from a reader, a barmaid's comment and a book he had just reviewed for the *Manchester Evening News*. By using just extracts from the columns (as in this collection) that richness, journalistic inventiveness and originality goes missing.

This selection also uses just two of the 19 despatches Orwell sent to the *Observer*, being edited by his friend David Astor, and the *Manchester Evening News*, while reporting from the Continent on the final days of the Second World War. Admittedly, all of Orwell's *Observer* writings between 1942 and 1948 have been brought together in a volume (London: Atlantic Books, 2003). Yet for any serious analysis of Orwell's journalism more examples were needed. After all, it is extremely interesting to compare the vitality, outspokenness, wit and narrative inventiveness of Orwell's reportage from the 1936-1937 Spanish civil war in *Homage to Catalonia* with his less assured (though equally fascinating) frontline reporting in 1945.

Orwell tended to look down on his journalism as 'mere pamphleteering' and a 'lesser' form of literature. He had a horror of hack reporting, despised the 'dreary sub-world of the freelance journalist' and maintained a constant attack on journalists as professionals. Typically, in *Homage to Catalonia*, he even joked on meeting a suspected, fat Russian agent in the Hotel Continental in Barcelona after the fighting ended there on 6 May 1937 that 'it was the first time that I had seen a person whose profession was telling lies – unless one counts journalists'.

Yet in his essay 'Why I write' (of 1946) Orwell said he wanted 'to make political writing into an art'. This volume proves conclusively that Orwell succeeded in achieving just that. As Prof. Davison comments (echoing the words of Rushbrook Williams, head of department at the BBC), Orwell's journalism far transcended hackery – being the work of 'a mind and a spirit of real and distinguished worth'.

- This review was first published at https://orwellsocietyblog.wordpress.com/2014/12/01/far-beyond-mere-hackery-orwells-journalism/, in December 2014.

Section 3

Orwell's Afterlife: Beyond 1950

Chapter 13

Appreciations: Just Months after He Died

One of the first appreciations of Orwell, published in June 1950 just months after his untimely death, came in a special edition of *World Review*. Interestingly, it mixes both celebration and critique. Orwell's personality as much as his writings clearly fascinated many – and this is reflected in the articles here.

Around selections from Orwell's Notebooks (from 18 May 1940 to 28 August 1941), which lie at the core of the journal, are contributions from a glittering array of (all male) journalists and intellectuals: Bertrand Russell, Tom Hopkinson, Aldous Huxley, John Beavan, Herbert Read, Malcolm Muggeridge and Stephen Spender.

World Review, published by Edward Hulton, described itself as 'a monthly devoted to literature and the arts and all other aspects of our cultural interests'. It had previously published Orwell's Appendix on Newspeak from his dystopian novel *Nineteen Eighty-Four* (then shortly to be published) though without any background explanation.

In a brief editorial, Stefan Schimanski says that Orwell felt, 'strangely enough', that his diary should not appear until ten years after the events described. 'Today, the records as he left them in his notebooks, have, indeed, the value of a document that brings to life a forgotten and short-lived period of high expectation.'

The first article (pp 5-7) – just a few hundred words – is by the philosopher Bertrand Russell. He highlights Orwell's 'admirable essay' on Dickens and compares *Animal Farm* with *Gulliver's Travels*. Swift's satire, he suggests 'expresses universal and indiscriminating hatred, Orwell's has always an undercurrent of kindliness'. But he concludes on a critical note (pp 6-7): 'The men of our day who resemble Goethe, Shelley or Wells in temperament and congenital capacity have mostly gone through, either personally or through imaginative sympathy, experiences more or less resembling imprisonment in Buchenwald. Orwell was one of these men. He preserved an impeccable love of truth, and allowed himself to learn even the most painful lessons. But he lost hope. This prevented him from being a prophet for our time.'

Next, Orwell's *Tribune* colleague T. R. Fyvel contributes a 13-page biography. It is split into seven sections: after a brief Introduction, the second section is a moving, personal memoir of his time visiting Orwell in hospital just before he died. He writes (p. 7): 'In this private ward, a square pane of glass is let into the door of each private sickroom, through which patient and caller can see each other. I visited him fairly often during these months, and my first glimpse of him was always through this glass, and always a slight shock, at the sight of his thin, drawn face, looking ominously waxen and still against the white pillow.' Orwell would then immediately start to chat. 'His need to plunge straight into conversation was more than ordinary shyness. It had something of the schoolboy about it. And to the last, even on his sick-bed, Orwell retained those boyish traits which were so marked in his character.'

But Orwell did not like talking about possible death. 'To the last he kept his form. He read newspapers carefully, watching out for journalist misuse of words – one of his pet worries – and noting down instances. The last piece of work he was contemplating was to be a study of Joseph Conrad. The interaction of the Continental and English mind held a special interest for him.' The last time he saw Orwell he seemed 'particularly cheerful' and they chatted about his plans to leave for Switzerland by 'special charter aircraft' and about their early schooldays.

In the third section, Fyvel examines Orwell's class background with special reference to his comments in *The Road to Wigan Pier*. He next moves on to Orwell's time at 'a preparatory school in the South of England' (St Cyprian's, in Eastbourne, though for libel reasons its name is never given) at Eton and then, at the end of section five, in the Indian Imperial Police in Burma. He comments (p. 13): 'In personal affairs, Orwell was always extraordinarily reticent, so shy as to be almost secretive. Though he seemed to like to deal in personal asides, e.g. "When I was fourteen or fifteen I was an odious little snob", this was always in terms of social classification: the self-revelation is only apparent. In his novels, on the other hand, he himself stands out; for, if he had sharp power of insight, he had much less of invention. From Flory, in his first novel, *Burmese Days*, to Winston Smith in *1984* [as the novel is consistently called throughout the journal, rather than *Nineteen Eighty-Four*], his last, all his heroes are Orwell himself, suitably transmuted.'

Section six (pp 14-18) moves rapidly through the biography taking in publication of *Down and Out in Paris and London*, *The Clergyman's Daughter* and *Burmese Days*, *Keep the Aspidistra Flying*, his essays on Dickens and Kipling, his fighting in the Spanish civil war, publication of *Homage to Catalonia* and finally of *Coming up for Air*. Orwell's success, he stresses 'remained confined to increasing prestige among a few discerning critics'. Fyvel adds in parenthesis: 'Once, in 1940, he told me that he reckoned – he loved making such calculations – that his literary earnings over the decade 1930-40 worked out at not quite three pounds per week.'

In the final section (pp 18-20), Fyvel returns to personal reminiscences. 'It was probably my second or third encounter with him which remained in my memory. It was at his small mews flat near Baker Street, in London, a rather poverty-stricken affair of one or two rather bare, austere rooms with second-hand furniture. I saw an extremely tall, thin man, looking more than his years, with gentle eyes and deep lines that hinted at suffering on his face.' Following publication of *Animal Farm* in 1945, to 'instantaneous success, especially in America', Orwell, for the first time in his life, became 'comparatively well off'. 'But I found him in character quite unchanged – and physically very tired. ... In spite of his many new friendships, he remained a solitary and a lonely man.'

In a section of the journal subtitled 'Revaluations', Malcolm Muggeridge, Orwell's friend, former intelligence agent and later editor of *Punch*, contributes a surprisingly highly critical assessment of *Burmese Days* (pp 45-48). He writes: 'Considered simply as a novel, *Burmese Days* is not particularly satisfactory. Most of the characters are stock figures, and most of the dialogue is intended rather to present them as such than to reproduce actual conversations.' He continues (p. 46): 'The description of the Europeans in their club, of their discussions about electing a "native" to membership, their quarrels and their drunkenness and their outbursts of hysteria, is somehow unreal.'

Perhaps in an attempt to offer some 'balance' he ends (somewhat unconvincingly) on a positive note: '*Burmese Days*, as I have said, is not on any showing a great novel. It is, however, extremely readable and, in some of its descriptive passages, brilliant.'

John Beavan, who next examines *The Road to Wigan Pier* (pp 48-51), was London editor at the time of the *Guardian*. Little did he know that he featured on Orwell's infamous 'little list' of crypto-communists handed over to the government's newly-formed secret propaganda outfit, the Research Information Department, in 1949. There is an attempt to understand Orwell's complex attitudes to class: 'As a child he was taught that the poor were dirty and immoral and he was denied their society, though they seemed to him to be the most interesting and friendly of people. He never quite got over this.' And Beavan ends: 'Orwell produced at least one book that touched men of his time deeply, and that even his slenderest writings helped many of us to examine our consciences with something of his fierce honesty.'

Poet Stephen Spender, in his short article on *Homage to Catalonia* (pp 51-54), also takes the opportunity to comment on his personality: 'He was perhaps the least Etonian character who has ever come from Eton. He was tall, lean, scraggy man, a Public House character, with a special gleam in his eye, and a home-made way of arguing from simple premises, which could sometimes lead him to radiant common sense, sometimes to crankiness.' On *Homage*, Spender (p. 53) says that it had encouraged him to reflect on the meaning of the phrase 'the living truth'. 'This has all too often in history been exploited in order to trample on human freedoms for the sake of some authoritarian teaching which is supposed to bring happiness in this world or the next. Orwell was extremely sceptical of the claim of any cause to represent "the living truth". But he himself in his own life was an example of "the lived truth", which is perhaps the most valuable truth anyone can offer to humanity.'

Tom Hopkinson, then editor of *Picture Post*, another Hulton publication, next looks at *Animal Farm* (pp 54-57). Actually, his stint at *Picture Post* was soon to be ended abruptly after Hulton objected to his publication in October 1950 of reports by James Cameron and photojournalist Bert Hardy of UN atrocities in the Korean War – and promptly sacked him. In his article, Hopkinson provides a précis of the novel, ending in glowing terms: 'Orwell's knowledge of farming helps to maintain the necessary faint illusion of reality. Nothing is shirked – even the relations of "Animal Farm" with its human neighbours. Everything is treated with combined lightness and assurance that suspend disbelief. ... *Animal Farm* is a work of genius in the lofty tradition of English humorous writing.'

The art historian, poet, literary critic, anarchist, pacifist and philosopher, Herbert Read, in considering *1984* over just two pages, provides a rather strange explanation for its success (pp 58-59). He writes: 'In his last years he saw only the menace of the totalitarian State, and he knew he had only the force left to warn us. It is the most terrifying warning that a man has ever uttered, and its fascination derives from its veracity. Millions of people have read this book. Why? It has no charm; it makes no concessions to sentiment. It is true that there are some traces of eroticism, but surely not enough to make the book, for those who seek that sort of thing, a worthwhile experience. An element of sado-masochism in the public may explain the strange success of this book.'

The novelist Aldous Huxley brings the collection of essays to a close with just half a page 'Footnote about *1984*' (p. 60) critiquing the novel and at the same time promoting his own ideas. In his celebrated *Brave New World* (1932), Huxley says he prophesied the production of 'Hypnopaedia'. It is now, he stresses 'an accomplished fact'. 'Pillow microphones attached to clock-controlled phonographs playing suitable recordings at regular intervals during the night are now being used quite extensively here by paediatricians who want to get rid of childish fears and bad habits, such as bed wetting, or to help backward children acquire larger vocabularies, and by students who want to learn foreign languages in a quarter of the time ordinarily required for the job.' And he ends with a jibe at Orwell: 'It looks very much as though the systematic brutality described in *1984* will seem to the really intelligent dictators of the future altogether too inefficient, messy and wasteful.'

Overall then, the various articles provide a fascinating if rather idiosyncratic insight into the early reception of Orwell.

- This essay was first published at https://orwellsocietyblog.wordpress.com/2017/01/18/orwell-appreciated-just-months-after-he-died/ in January 2017.

Chapter 14

Gordon Bowker: So Wonderfully Insightful into Orwell the Man and his Writings

Given that George Orwell specifically indicated in his will that no biography of him should be written, how does one justify just such an undertaking? One of Orwell's biographers, Gordon Bowker, who died aged 84 in January 2019, clearly thought a lot about this question. And in the end, his answer is tightly argued and persuasive.

He writes: 'He was certainly not antagonistic to the genre, as some have suggested. In fact, in his reviews and letters there is ample evidence that he valued literary biography as a means of illuminating an author's work.' And in a review of Lewis Mumford's biography of Melville, Orwell perhaps indicates the kind of work he may have liked: Mumford's 'analytical, interpretative method' exploring his ideas, his feelings, his urges, his vision of life was the one he favoured.[1]

Significantly, in the Preface of his biography of George Orwell (London: Little Brown, 2003), Gordon Bowker sets out his ambitions with these perceptive comments:

> Orwell himself was a man with deep feelings, which he attempted as far as possible to conceal. Yet, as he admitted, it was emotion that provided the driving force of his creativity. The main thrust of this book will be to reach down as far as possible to the roots of that emotional life, to get as close as possible to the dark sources mirrored in his work (p. xii).

And through the course of the 495-page text he succeeds in following Mumford's 'analytical, interpretative method', delving deep into Orwell the man – providing original and often profound insights into his writings and complex personality. Bowker's prose is always clear yet densely packed with meticulously researched information – and throughout he displays a deep knowledge of the politics and broader culture of Orwell's times.

Indeed, for an insightful, concise yet wide-ranging overview of Orwell, there is perhaps little to compare with Bowker's six-page Preface to the biography. He talks of how Orwell was 'fascinated by how things work, from pieces of machinery to human societies. ... This intuitive grasp of social patterns and processes, his sociological imagination, enabled him to develop into a writer of vision' (p. xii). Despite his reputation for honesty, 'he had a deceptive streak' (p. xiii):

> He deceived fellow tramps about his identify and true circumstances, he kept his family ignorant of what he was doing; he deliberately kept some of his friends apart in order to present them with different faces; he was deceptive in his sexual relationships; he concealed his true feelings behind a mask of reserve. The revelation that he co-operated with the IRD [the state's secret propaganda unit] left some of his old friends feeling badly deceived as to his true nature. He deliberately concealed himself behind a pseudonym.

He was also a man full of contradictions: 'So while he was against private schools, disliked Scots, and was a staunch atheist, he put his adopted son down for Westminster, chose to live among Scots on Jura and asked to be buried according to the rites of the Church of England' (p. xiv).

Bowker is particularly interesting throughout the biography when examining Orwell's sexuality. Here he writes: 'Like his fictional heroes, he had difficulty approaching women. In his teens, he was rebuffed by a childhood sweetheart; in Burma he indulged with prostitutes and is said to have had a child by a Burmese girl; in Paris in 1928 he lived for a while with a "trollop". ... Although part of him wished to emulate sexually unbridled writers like D. H. Lawrence, James Joyce and Henry Miller, the social and political climate of his age and the harsh obscenity laws propelled him towards literary puritanism' (ibid).

Bowker is at pains to acknowledge the unique insights thrown up by the previous biographies: Bernard Crick (1980) stressed the political context; Michael Shelden (1991) highlighted Orwell the literary man; Meyers (2000) 'acknowledged more the inner man' (p. xiii). And throughout, Bowker acknowledges as a crucial source, the recent publication of the 20-volume *Collected Works of George Orwell*, edited by Peter Davison (D. J. Taylor's award-winning biography was also to appear in 2003 so could not be acknowledged). But Bowker also turns up new and important information.

For instance, there is a lot new here on the family background of Orwell's mother. Her father, Frank Limouzin, was a timber merchant in Limoges, France, before emigrating to Burma in the late 1850s with his wife, Eliza. Ida, Orwell's mother, was their sixth (of eight) children who grew up in Moulmein, marrying Richard Walmsley Blair, a lowly sub-deputy opium agent, in June 1897. At the time Ida was 22, Richard 39. Eric Arthur Blair, their second child, was born on 25 June 1903. So much is already well known. Now Bowker goes on to reveal how the Limouzins of Moulmein sadly fell on hard times: Frank's

SECTION 3 - ORWELL'S AFTERLIFE: BEYOND 1950

boat-building company collapsed and so he moved into the rice business, 'losing much of his money in the process' (p. 10-11).

> His long-deceased brother William had co-habited with an Indian woman; now, in 1899, his second eldest son, Ida's brother Frank, fathered a child by a Burmese girl, Mah Hlim. There could well have been a scandal over this because Frank appears to have fled the country. ... In Burma in the early 1920s, Eric was to meet his grandmother Limouzin, and presumably his Eurasian relatives – Aunt Aimée, daughter of William and Sooma, and his cousin, Kathleen, daughter of Frank and Mah Hlin, just four years older than himself. On this feature of his mother's family, he remained silent, but in his first novel, *Burmese Days*, he gave the name Ma Hla May to the Burmese mistress of his tragic hero John Flory.

Previous biographers had suggested that Eric Blair, aged five, was sent as a day boy to an Anglican convent in Henley. But Bowker argues convincingly that it was, in fact, a Catholic convent run by French Ursulines exiled from France after religious education was banned there in 1903 (p. 21). He concludes that if Blair was, then, first taught by Catholic nuns, this would explain two enduring aspects of his complex personality: 'his unremitting hostility towards Roman Catholicism and an acute sense of guilt' (ibid: 22).

Drawing from new correspondence with Steven Runciman, one of Orwell's friends at Eton (which he attended from 1917-1921), Bowker reveals the (perhaps surprising) fascination of Blair with the occult. A senior boy, Phillip Yorke, had attracted the disfavour of both Blair and Runciman so they planned a revenge.

> As Runciman recalled, they fashioned an image of Yorke from candle wax and broke off a leg. To their horror, shortly afterwards, Yorke not only broke his leg but in July died of leukaemia. The story of what happened soon spread and, in somewhat garbled form, became legend. Blair and Runciman suddenly found themselves regarded as distinctly odd, and to be treated warily (p. 56).

Previously unpublished letters between Orwell and one of his early female friends in Southwold, in the early 1930s, schoolteacher Brenda Salkeld, reveal other aspects of Orwell. He opens up to her, saying how depressed he is at the slow progress of his career and how at times he was losing confidence in himself as a writer (p. 125). 'Brenda noticed how he enjoyed trying to shock her with tales of his exploits in Burma and to offend her sense of delicacy with risqué stories and his collection of rude seaside postcards' (p. 124).

Bowker also harvests a lot of material, extracted from newly available KGB archives, on how Orwell was hunted and spied on while in Spain in 1937, fighting for the republicans against Franco's fascists in the civil war. The man sent to Barcelona to spy for the KGB was David Crook whose reports on the Blairs (Orwell's newly-married wife, Eileen O'Shaughnessy, having joined him on the frontline) and his comrades Georges Kopp and John McNair were normally passed on to a Hugh O'Donnell, whose code name was O'Brien. As Bowker comments (p. 219):

> It seems unlikely that Orwell ever knew that Crook was spying on him, or that his contact worked under that name, but the fact that the character in *Nineteen Eighty-Four* who first wins the confidence of Winston Smith and then betrays him is given the name O'Brien must be one of the strangest coincidences in literature.

Towards the end of their time in Spain, in June 1937, the Blairs' flat in Hotel Continental, Barcelona, was raided by the Spanish secret police. All Orwell's diaries, press cuttings, letters to Eileen, fan letters about the recently published *The Road to Wigan Pier* and photographs were seized. Bowker adds (p. 222): 'Interestingly, one item taken, a French translation of Hitler's *Mein Kampf*, turned up in Crook's possession when he was arrested later on a trumped-up charge in connection with his spying activities.'

Following again Mumford's 'analytical, interpretative method', Bowker explores Orwell's personality in some depth. For instance, in discussing *The Road to Wigan Pier* (1937), his damning indictment of poverty, particularly among the miners, in northern England, Bowker highlights Orwell's obsession with dirt and foul smells: 'Stinks, stenches, reeks and odours of unimaginable repugnance swirl and permeate throughout his wretched worlds. ... Orwell was repelled by filth and evil odours, but sought them out as if to rub his own nose in them to exorcise his demons through self-inflicted suffering' (pp 197-198).

Nor did Bowker shirk criticising his subject. Here, for instance, he suggests that *Wigan Pier*'s main weakness lay in Orwell's 'inability to portray working class life from the inside'. 'He later admitted that only a proletarian writer could get beyond the surface of proletarian life, but in an age when the bourgeoisie was the dominant class, proletarian writers had yet to find their own voice' (p. 198).

Elsewhere, Bowker highlights Orwell's obsession with lists: 'He made lists of books, redundant metaphors, jargon words, Kiplingesque epithets, poets who characterised the century and "sentimental writers". ... He was still constructing lists (and collecting junk) at the end of his life, most controversially the list of those he thought were suspected subversives' (p. 19).

Particularly impressive are the short commentaries on Orwell's writings dotted about the biog. Take, for instance, the six pages devoted to *Nineteen Eighty-Four* (pp 385-390). He begins by identifying the literary influences: Zamyatin, Trotsky, Jack London, Belloc, Poe and M. R. James. Orwell's horror at the Inquisition, his experience of terror in Spain and of the propaganda operation at the BBC, of wretched wartime London and the mysteries of junk shops are all there.

> The conundrum 2 + 2 = 5 was taken from Eugene Lyons writing about the Soviet Five Year Plan (it also crops up in *Tristram Shandy*). His fascination with the Chestertonian paradox is there in the form of 'Doublethink'. ... as is his identification with Protestant martyrs, his penchant for nursery rhymes, his fascination with fiction factories (offering formulae for novel writing) and the paranoia that led him to arm himself against possible assassination (p. 385).

Bowker next moves on to explore the religious sub-text. Many of the names of the characters in the novel are those of persecuted religious and political dissidents: 'Rutherford, Scottish dissident condemned to be burned, saved himself by confessing under torture; Jones, Chartist leader, persecuted and imprisoned for sedition; Tillotson, seventeenth-century preacher against popery; Wither and Ogilvy, Civil War turncoats' (p. 386).

The strange relationship with his previous novel, *Keep the Aspidistra Flying*, is next explored. 'Gordon Comstock is in advertising, sickened by the fact that he is paid to mislead and swindle the public; Winston Smith is in the business of misleading and swindling through deliberate falsification. *Keep the Aspidistra Flying* attacks the money-god, *Nineteen Eighty-Four* attacks the power-god' (p. 388). Bowker's interpretation of Julia, Smith's promiscuous lover, is also pleasantly controversial, raising the possibility that she is actually luring Smith into a honeytrap:

> Julia seems to be a secret hater of the Party and Big Brother, seems to be a candidate for the dissident Brotherhood, seems to go off to be tortured after her arrest and finally seems to have been purged of her thought-crime. But in the world of the book she could, like O'Brien and Charrington [the owner of the junk shop where the lovers conduct their secret affair], also be a dissembler leading Winston straight into the arms of the Thought Police (ibid).

Bowker sums up astutely: 'On Airstrip One truth rests on ever-shifting sands, only pain and Room 101 are real. Such a reading gives the book a strangely modern character, making it a novel about the slippery, unstable nature of meaning' (p. 389).

Such a section is so typical of this wonderful biography: it's incisive, original, elegantly written conveying – concisely – a vast knowledge of Orwell and the many influences on his personality and writings. And every time I re-read the biography it never ceases to give me such enormous pleasure. Thank you, Gordon.

- Gordon Bowker, who was born on 19 March 1934, wrote a number of other literary biographies: *Pursued by Furies: A Life of Malcolm Lowry* (1994) (*New York Times* Bestseller and Notable Book of the Year) and *Through the Dark Labyrinth: A Biography of Lawrence Durrell* (1996). His biography of James Joyce, published in May 2011 in time for Bloomsday, was longlisted for the Carnegie Medal for Literary Excellence, was the runner-up in 2013 for the American PEN/Jacqueline Bograd Weld Award for Biography and was shortlisted for the PEN Center USA West Literary Award. After reading English, Sociology and Philosophy at Nottingham and London Universities, he worked as a lecturer and wrote dramas and documentaries for radio and television. He contributed pieces to a wide variety of magazines and newspapers including *London Magazine, Plays and Players*, the *Listener, Sunday Times, Times Literary Supplement* and *The New York Times*. He reported on the rise of the Polish trade union Solidarity for the *Illustrated London News*.

Note

[1] https://www.orwellfoundation.com/the-orwell-foundation/orwell/library/gordon-bowker-the-biography-orwell-never-wrote/

- This tribute was first published in *George Orwell Studies*, Vol. 3, No. 2, 2019 pp 71-76.

Chapter 15

Orwell and Leveson

How would Orwell have responded to the current controversy over press standards and the recent Leveson Report (of November 2012)? It's hard to know really – and there is a danger of projecting our own biases and obsessions on to Orwell.

That said, much of the Leveson debate seems to me to be missing the essential Orwellian point. Toby Young's recent blog in the *Daily Telegraph* was typical. He accused the Media Standards Trust, which administers the annual Orwell Prize, of supporting attacks on press freedom simply because they backed (along with the Hacked Off campaign) some kind of legal underpinning for the new regulatory system. And he claimed both organisations were 'anti-tabloid'. He ended with this flourish:

> Orwell's dislike of high-mindedness, piety, sanctimony, snobbery – all the vices of the Left-wing intelligentsia – is a constant theme running through his work. Anyone familiar with his essays – in particular, his views on press freedom, the 'boiled rabbits of the left' and the common people of England – can be in no doubt that he would have summoned all his powers as a journalist to pour vitriol on the panjandrums behind the Hacked Off campaign. For the Media Standards Trust to give out a journalism prize in his name, given its close association with this lobby group, is a disgrace to his memory. They should rename it the Beatrice Webb Prize or the H. G. Wells Prize and stop traducing the name of the finest journalist this country has ever produced.

Orwell, he claimed, was a maverick challenging the orthodoxies of the left. Yet, hasn't Young misunderstood Orwell's dissident spirit. Orwell was, indeed, unorthodox in that he had little time at all for the mainstream, corporate press (his work for David Astor's *Observer* was an exception). He devoted most of his time to left-wing journals such as *Tribune, New English Weekly, Fortnightly Review, The Highway, Left News, Left Forum, Gangrel*. Some of these lasted only a few issues and then died. He didn't mind: he was deliberately engaging in crucial political debate with people who mattered to him.

Orwell never failed to criticise the left press (particularly over its reporting of the Spanish civil war and Soviet communism) and leftist intellectuals although he sympathised with them. But they were an authentic audience compared with what Stuart Allan has called 'the implied readers or imagined community of readers' of the mainstream press. And the left press is predictably completely ignored in the whole Leveson circus.

Most seriously the Leveson process has marginalised the importance of the economic structure of the press and its impact on standards. As Orwell wrote in his banned preface to *Animal Farm*:

> Unpopular ideas can be silenced, and inconvenient facts kept dark, without the need for any official ban. Anyone who has lived long in a foreign country will know of instances of sensational items of news – things which on their own merits would get the big headlines – being kept right out of the British press, not because the Government intervened but because of a general tacit agreement that 'it wouldn't do' to mention that particular fact. So far as the daily newspapers go, this is easy to understand. The British press is extremely centralised, and most of it is owned by wealthy men who have every motive to be dishonest on certain important topics.

The Leveson process is, then, best understood as largely spectacular theatre – too trapped within the system it is attempting to reform to have any lasting effect. It has provided the illusion of moral intent by the state and its propaganda institutions – the leading media corporations – when, in reality, the system is run on ruthless profit-oriented principles.

Thus, Leveson's priorities and those of the mainstream media covering it have reflected dominant values and sourcing routines: celebrities, leading journalists, proprietors and politicians dominated proceedings while 'ordinary' people (such as the parents of murdered schoolgirl Milly Dowler) were allowed to play their harrowing bit-parts in the Great Leveson Theatre Show before being condemned to obscurity in the wings.

Revelations about the intimate, collusive links between politicians and Fleet Street were also all too predictable. Such ties have long been analysed and documented by countless academics. And while politicians may wring their hands in guilt over being too intimate with the press in the past, Leveson is hardly likely to change this since newspapers remain far too closely integrated into the dominant structures of political, economic, cultural and ideological power.

Moreover, newspapers' ties to the intelligence services are as important as those to politicians – yet Leveson had little interest in investigating these. The Hutton Inquiry into the strange death of weapons inspector Dr David Kelly had the opportunity to examine in some detail the links between hacks and spooks – but missed it.

Indeed, how Orwell may well have enjoyed mocking Toby Young, Hacked Off and the whole Leveson circus.

- This essay was first published at http://www.orwellsociety.com/2013/01/14/orwell-and-leveson/ in 2013.

Chapter 16

A Deliberately Provocative, Fascinating Feast of Racy Writing and Orwellian Musings

A review of *Orwell's Nose*, by John Sutherland, Reaktion Books, London pp 256

So now we have it. Following John Ross's *Orwell's Cough* (2012), John Sutherland, Emeritus Lord Northcliffe Professor of English at University College London, has come up with *Orwell's Nose* (subtitled, intriguingly, *A Pathological Biography*). Who knows: next there'll be *Orwell's Ear* followed by *Orwell's Throat* (Sutherland concedes that *Orwell's Bum* 'may be an obliquity too far').

The *Nose* certainly arrives lauded with praise from diverse Fleet Street reviewers: on the cover Jay Parini celebrates it as a 'shrewd and riveting book'. But it is a distinctly odd affair.

Take, for instance, its chaotic structure. Sutherland begins by telling us that his interest in Orwell's 'smell narratives' (as he calls them) began a few years ago when he lost his sense of smell. So in a 39-page Preface, Sutherland proceeds to write what could be considered a highly original and witty academic paper exploring the role of smell in Orwell's *oeuvre*. But there is no stopping him. Next (from pages 51 to 250) comes Sutherland's stab at a brief biog of the celebrated writer of *Nineteen Eighty-Four*. Tagged on to the end comes an appendix presenting an imaginary Orwellian 'smoking diary' (which ideally could have been integrated into the Preface) and a close analysis of the 'smell narrative' of the 1935 novel *A Clergyman's Daughter*.

There is still a lot to welcome. Sutherland has clearly had a great deal of fun in composing his little, idiosyncratic contribution to the ever-expanding Orwell canon. It's bursting with jokes and word play. Hardly a page passes without a juicy quip appearing. For instance, according to Sutherland (p. 29), Orwell diagnosed the malaise of socialism in 1936 'nose first': 'Socialism, at least in this island, does not smell any longer of revolution and the overthrow of tyrants, it smells of crankishness, machine-worship, and the stupid cult of Russia. Unless you can remove that smell, and very rapidly, Fascism may win.' Sutherland adds: 'It is hard to think of it inspiring a rousing call ("We Must Reform our Smell, Comrades") at the annual Labour Party Conference. But it is echt Orwellism.'

Moreover, according to Sutherland, Orwell's attitude to class was 'above all else, a matter of smell': 'English society was arranged, hierarchically, from the toffee-nosed to the Great Unwashed, with the Lifebuoy-carbolic-washed middle classes squashed, uneasily, between the underclass stink and aristocratic, Bond Street perfumer (or, for the male, Imperial Leather) fragrance' (p. 154).

Sutherland's 'smell narratives' are undoubtedly fascinating. For instance, he notes that in John Flory's lovemaking in *Burmese Days* 'erotic, nasal stimulus was a major part of the oriental package' (p. 15). When George Bowling, in *Coming Up for Air*, rhapsodises on the smells of the churches of his childhood in Lower Binfield, 'Orwell's discrimination of the sniff reaches a pitch of sheer nasal virtuosity'. And in Henry Miller, who in *The Tropic of Capricorn*, raved about the 'peculiar sweetish smell of the Metro stations' Orwell found 'the most congenial nasal Francophile. A brother of the nose'. And so on. Sutherland has also done his counting: there are, apparently, fifty occurrences of the word 'smell' In *The Road to Wigan Pier*.

Approaching Orwell in this way from quirky, 'oblique, self-indulgent angles' (in Sutherland's own words) can also lead to some intriguing new perspectives. On his time serving in Burma with the Imperial Police Service between 1922 and 1927, Sutherland suggests Orwell was essentially an intelligence officer: 'The Burmese police force, like its parent Indian forces, was not primarily an instrument for maintaining law and order but one for gathering intelligence and nipping any possible uprising in the bud. Internal espionage ("IPS is Watching You") was its reason for being' (pp 104-105). He continues: 'He was not moved around because he gave dissatisfaction but because he was good at his job: a competent spy in policeman's uniform. He was shrewd, fluent in native languages and observant, and could write the kind of clear English that made for a good analytic report' (p. 105).

Andrew Gow, Orwell's Classics tutor at Eton, also plays an intriguing role in this biog. It was he who stressed to Orwell's father, Richard Blair, that having finished a lowly 137th out of 168 in the final school examinations, it would be a disgrace to the college even to allow him to apply to Oxford or Cambridge (p. 73). Eric had written a 'scurrilously homophobic limerick' for one of the school's papers with clear allusions to Gow. Was this his way of wreaking revenge on his tormentor? But then, strangely, when Orwell returned from Burma in 1927 Gow invited him to stay briefly with him at Trinity College, Cambridge, where he had gained a fellowship. At High Table, Blair sat next to the poet A. E. Housman. What was going on? Was Gow, friend to the master spies Anthony Blunt and Guy Burgess, working in intelligence? '...it is relevant that before the Second World War MI5 employed mostly former Indian policemen. Orwell, to indulge the most far-fetched of speculations, may have been viewed as a possible recruit' (p. 111).

The references at the end of the *Nose* indicate only a limited look at the vast literature on Orwell (for instance, Beci Dobbin's essay 'Orwell's squeamishness' in *Orwell Today*, 2012 pp 62-78 would have been a useful resource). Thus, in the absence of deeply-delving research, Sutherland is left following hunches, raising (often meaningless) questions – and, at worst, spreading scurrilous gossip.

For instance, on page 43 he describes Orwell's second wife, Sonia Brownell, as a 'gratifyingly easy lay (allegedly Connolly [editor of *Horizon*] would pimp her out to potential backers. of his magazine)'. On page 53, he wonders: 'Did Richard Blair console himself with native women in the long years of absence from his family?' He even suggests (p. 55) that Orwell may have witnessed or heard behind closed bedroom doors his father's 'attempts to reclaim "conjugal right", that male right to legally rape an uncooperative spouse'. Of Orwell's friend Brenda Salkend, he writes (p. 59): '... the surmise is that she never slept with him, despite his urgent requests.' Of Mrs Wilkes, his teacher and tormentor at St Cyprian's prep school, he wonders whether 'she may have been menopausal in Blair's last years at the school' (p. 67). These strange sexual preoccupations and speculations continue throughout the text: on page 77, he writes: 'Orwell surely masturbated. Boys' schools, then and now, floated on a sea of frustrated juvenile sperm.' And so on.

On top of all this, there are a number of errors: for instance, Fredric Warburg is spelled incorrectly (p. 33); biographer Bernard Crick is said (p. 47) to have founded the Orwell Society (he didn't).

The *Nose*, then, is a deliberately provocative, fascinating feast of racy writing and Orwellian musings: a spiffing wheeze celebrating Orwell as the 'virtuoso of the nostrils'. But it ends up an ideas hotchpotch in need of a ruthless editor.

- This review was first published in the Orwell Society's *Journal*, No. 10, 2017 pp 23-25.

Chapter 17

Mrs Orwell – A Review and a View

A review of *Mrs Orwell*, by Tony Cox: Old Red Lion, London, directed by Jimmy Walters

The reviews (*Guardian, The Stage* etc) of *Mrs Orwell* have generally been very kind. Certainly the actors are all excellent and it makes for a very entertaining theatrical experience. Peter Hamilton Dyer, who plays Orwell, has a sort of Orwellian profile and Cressida Bonas, as Sonia, looks appropriately glamorous and debonnaire.

But there are many problematic elements in the play and production. Orwell begins coughing a lot and he does sound very ill (though the make-up department has made no effort to make him look pale and haggard). But after a while he stops coughing, starts shouting, cracks jokes and even gets up and walks about. Though Orwell stoops a bit he generally seems perfectly OK. And that feels all wrong. Then suddenly towards the end he begins coughing again; the room and bed is empty and he's gone and died. Strange. (The actual script interestingly includes an Anglican wedding service conducted by the hospital chaplain and with Orwell dressed in a red velvet smoking jacket looking 'unexpectedly grand and military' but this wasn't included in the production we saw).

The playwright clearly had a problem: depicting a man close to death, very ill, coughing a lot and lying in a hospital bed does not offer a great many theatrical opportunities. So he uses the dialogue to provide a sort of worthy, educational, Eamonn Andrews *This is Your Life*-ish overview of Orwell's life (his time in Burma with the prostitutes, his guilt over his empire service leading to his need for atonement with the down-and-outs, fighting in Spain, getting shot, his daily routines with his son Richard on Jura etc) rather than portraying him 'realistically' as a dying man.

The play is called *Mrs Orwell* yet, in fact, the playwright misses the opportunity to focus more on her – for instance, her relationship with Cyril Connolly, her feelings about her former lover Maurice Merleau-Ponty, her views on Orwell's work and contemporary writings in general. Too often in the histories the women in the lives of 'Great Men' (Mrs Bach, Mrs Dickens, Mrs Joyce, Mrs Mahler etc) are marginalised – here was a chance to put the spotlight on Sonia. But still the real emphasis of the play is on Orwell, the man. What a shame.

For a man so political as Orwell there is very little politics in the play. When 'politics' is discussed it often feels 'wrong'. For instance, Orwell's attack on 'feminists and pacifists' seems to hark back to the second section of *The Road to Wigan Pier* – views he'd surely outgrown by 1949. And while Orwell was very ill he kept on reading. The play shows him dipping into just Somerset Maugham's *The Razor's Edge*. In fact, he had read that earlier at Cranham sanatorium in the Cotswolds. And by the time he arrived at University College Hospital, in London, he needed spectacles to read. Moreover, at UCH he read a vast amount: Dante's *Divine Comedy*, trying to teach himself Italian by reading it in the original, all of Poe's stories, a humorous novel by Cyril Alington, his old-Etonian headmaster, Connolly's *Enemies of Promise*, Compton Mackenzie's *Sinister Street*, two novels by Henry Green, Malcolm Muggeridge's new novel *Affairs of the Heart*, E. H. Carr's *The Romantic Exiles* – and so on. In total, he devoured 144 books during his final year – 27 of them for the second time. The play in no way captures Orwell's hunger for reading that lasted right up to his dying days.

The set seems odd too: more like an ordinary bedsit in Pimlico than an expensive private ward in a hospital (no medical equipment close at hand). And I did not get a real sense of the late 1940s in the production. The script indicates various production elements (such as sound mix of BBC's *Third Programme*, milk bottles on doorstep/MPs on hustings/*Workers' Playtime* on the radio) which would have helped convey this – but for some reason they were not incorporated into the production. Orwell actually wrote a detailed description of the contents of his room No. 65 at the hospital (including a wireless) – and the set designer could have exploited it perhaps more effectively.

Edmund Digby Jones conveys painter Lucian Freud's sinister creepiness well. But his comments on Simone de Beauvoir (suggesting that he had slept with her, that she was boring in bed simply competing with her partner, Jean-Paul Sartre, over the number of lovers they could have) were silly. Orwell's stressing the importance of 'learning how to make dumplings' when proposing to Sonia is recorded in Hilary Spurling's biography of her. But Sonia's comment that she was about to meet de Beauvoir and Sartre at the Ritz would appear to have little basis in reality. Sonia was clearly an excellent editor at *Horizon* who could thrive quite happily amongst the leading writers and intellectuals of her day – Koestler, Auden, J. R. Ackerley, Marguerite Duras, Mary McCarthy, Edna O'Brien, Ian Fleming. The play stresses her animal sexuality – her striking intelligence (which also clearly appealed to Orwell) was not conveyed.

There are a number of other factual errors: for instance, the American publishers are called Harcourt Price (p. 12 in the script published by Oberon Books and available at the theatre) when it should have been Harcourt Brace.

All that said, the play made for a totally unforgettable experience. Indeed, it's not very often that I travel to London on a Sunday to watch a play with fellow Orwell Society members in a tiny theatre at the back of a pub where the locals are noisily watching the Spurs/Chelsea derby on the box.

- This review as first published at https://orwellsocietyblog.wordpress.com/2017/08/30/mrs-orwell-a-review-and-a-view/, in August 2017.

Chapter 18

The BBC – And The Political Economy of Broadcasting

Room 101 is well-known as the place where Winston Smith, the anti-hero of George Orwell's dystopian masterpiece *Nineteen Eighty-Four*, is tortured. Named after the number of a meeting room at the BBC, it is often thought to sum up his loathing of the corporation, its programmes and his time spent there – as a talks producer for the Eastern Service from 1941 to 1943.

But, in fact, Orwell's attitudes to the BBC were complex, ambivalent (mixing considered praise with blunt criticism from a radical, socialist perspective) and often highly original. After resigning from the corporation, he became literary editor of *Tribune*, and his writings for this leftist journal (from 1943 to 1947) reveal some of his most fascinating ideas about the BBC – and journalism and broadcasting in general.

In particular, Orwell used his regular 'As I Please' column in *Tribune* to discuss a vast range of issues – such as racism, the power of language, post-war reconstruction, nationalism, the cost of books, the poor, superstitions, his love of nature and so on – and amongst them was the BBC.

BBC Talks Programmes 'Are Mostly Ballyhoo'

His first foray came in 21 January 1944 when discussing rumours of the introduction of large-scale commercial broadcasting and the dropping of the Forces programme after the war. He writes:

> People are vaguely aware that they don't like the BBC programmes, that along with some good stuff a lot of muck is broadcast, that the talks are mostly ballyhoo and that no subject of importance ever gets the honesty of discussion that it would get even in the most reactionary newspaper. But they make no effort to find out, either in general or particular terms, why the programmes are bad or whether foreign programmes are any better or what is or is not technically possible on the air (Anderson 2006: 86).

While working for the BBC he was concerned solely with broadcasting English programmes to India. 'This did not save me from being constantly buttonholed by angry people who asked me whether I could not "do something about" some item on the Home Programme which is like blaming a North Sea coastguard for something that happens in central Africa.'

His column on 17 March 1944 is given over entirely to a discussion of the many expressions in political literature: the dead metaphors, 'pamphletese', euphemisms, rhetorical tricks and so on. Intriguingly, BBC news bulletins are included in a list of 'the perversions of the English language' (ibid: 111).

Next, in a column on 7 April 1944 in which he engages in an extraordinarily original content analysis of the 21 January 1936 edition of the *Daily Mirror*, Orwell highlights the way in which most newspapers 'remain completely reckless about details of fact'. 'Many people frankly say that they take in such and such a paper because it is lively but that they don't believe a word of what it says.' In contrast, the BBC had gained prestige since 1940. 'I heard it on the wireless' was now almost equivalent to 'I know it must be true.' He continues:

> So far as my experience goes the BBC is much more truthful in a negative way than the majority of newspapers and has a much more responsible and dignified attitude to news. It tells less direct lies, makes more effort to avoid mistakes and – the thing the public probably values – keeps the news in better proportion (ibid: 124).

BBC 'Better than the Dailies'

In many respects, as a *Tribune* columnist, Orwell proved himself to be a proto-blogger. One time he is responding to comments and criticisms from readers, inviting letters, running a short story competition or giving his readers a quirky brain teaser to answer. At other times he is asking them to answer queries or point him towards a book, pamphlet or quotation he is looking for. So typically, in his column of 21 April 1944, he follows up a letter published in *Tribune* criticising his view that the BBC offers a better source of news than the daily papers. He says:

> It was not my claim that anyone likes the BBC or thinks it is interesting or grown up or democratic or progressive. I said only that people regard it as a relatively sound source of news. ... untrue statements are constantly being broadcast and anyone can tell you of instances. But in most cases this is due to genuine error and the BBC sins much more by simply avoiding anything controversial than by direct propaganda. And after all – a point not met by our correspondent – its reputation abroad is comparatively high (ibid: 128).

Most of the newspapers, he says, continued to publish without any query as to their truthfulness American claims to have sunk the entire Japanese fleet several times over. 'The BBC to my knowledge, developed quite early on an attitude of suspicion towards this and certain other unreliable sources.'

In his column of 2 June 1944, Orwell returns to his fascination with language, in particular the 'magical properties of names'. He writes: 'Nearly all human beings feel that a thing becomes different if you call it by a different name. Thus when the Spanish civil war broke out the BBC produced the name "insurgents" for Franco's followers. This covered the fact that they were rebels while making rebellion sound respectable' (ibid: 144).

The position of the artist in modern centralised, capitalist society is the subject of his 8 September 1944 column in which he reviews Sir Osbert Sitwell's *A Letter to My Son* – and the role of the BBC comes in for severe criticism. He writes:

> When you see what has happened to the arts in the totalitarian countries and when you see the same thing happening here in a more veiled way through the MOI and the BBC and the film companies – organisations which not only buy up promising young writers and geld them and set them to work like cab-horses but manage to rob literary creation of its individual character and turn it into a sort of conveyor belt process – the prospects are not encouraging (ibid: 186).

Another Damning Critique of the BBC

Orwell offers another damning critique of the BBC in his 27 October 1944 column where he discusses C. S. Lewis's *Beyond Personality* (a series of reprinted broadcasts on theology). He writes: '...the cotton wool with which the BBC stuffs its speakers' mouths makes any real discussion of theological problems impossible, even from an orthodox angle' (ibid: 199).

Finally, on 14 February 1947, in one of his last 'As I Please' columns, Orwell tackles the subject of Scottish nationalism and the associated language issues. He writes that, in Gaelic-speaking areas, Gaelic is not taught in schools and this is beginning to cause resentment. 'Also, the BBC only broadcasts two or three half-hour Gaelic programmes a week and they give the impression of being rather amateurish programmes' (ibid: 364). Orwell ends by suggesting it would be easy to buy a little goodwill by putting on a Gaelic programme at least once daily.

Conclusion

In conclusion, it can be seen that Orwell places his critique of the BBC in his 'As I Please' columns in the context of a broader discussion about journalism and broadcasting in general, language, propaganda and censorship. He shows himself particularly aware of the political economy of broadcasting, and while he draws on his own experience of working for the BBC in the early 1940s, many of his insights, critiques and preoccupations remain acutely relevant to any discussion of broadcasting today.

Reference
Anderson, Paul (ed.) (2006) *Orwell in* Tribune: *'As I Please' and Other Writings 1943-7*, London: Politico's

- This essay was first published as 'Beyond Room 101' in the Orwell Society *Journal*, Vol. 11 Autumn 2017 pp 8-10.

Chapter 19

Orwell – the Proto-blogger

The current celebration of Orwell Week has certainly got Fleet Street's pundits pondering how he may have responded to today's social, cultural and political controversies. While there may be a danger of merely projecting our own obsessions and biases on to the Great Man, I'm going to enter into the spirit and stick my neck out on a few, perhaps surprising, points.

First it's clear to me Orwell would have been at home in the blogosphere. Indeed, he might even be considered a proto-blogger. Take a look at those 80 wonderful 'As I Please' columns he contributed to *Tribune* between 1943 and 1947 and see the amazingly close relationship he instinctively established with his readers. So often he responds to letters sent to him directly or addressed to *Tribune*. At other times he is running a short story competition or giving his readers a quirky brain teaser to answer. Elsewhere he invites letters, asks readers to answer queries or even point him towards a book, pamphlet or quotation he is looking for.

Not only did Orwell respond to letters but, as Peter Davison's *Collected Works* show, his columns often provoked correspondence, both critical and supportive, from readers. For instance, following his criticisms of newspapers carrying pictures of French Nazi collaborators on 8 September 1944, a reader wrote: 'How much longer must your readers be affronted by the quite patently pro-Fascist, neo-Jesuit posturing of George Orwell. He writes in the wrong periodical.'

Orwell's close relationship to his readers was crucial to the flowering of what many consider the greatest journalism of the last century. While he realised mainstream journalism was basically propaganda for wealthy newspaper proprietors, at *Tribune* he was engaging in the vital political debate with people he often criticised – but who mattered to him.

Secondly, Orwell, who was always keen to stress journalists' responsibility to preserve high standards of English, would have found much to criticise in Fleet Street's churnalism of today. In 'Politics and the English language' (April 1946), he called for an end to 'dying metaphors', 'pretentious diction', 'meaningless words' and the jargon of political writing. He wrote: 'In our time, political speech and writing are largely the defence of the indefensible. ... Thus political language has to consist largely of euphemism, question-begging and sheer cloudy vagueness.' He urged us all to 'jeer loudly' whenever we heard or read some 'worn-out and useless phrase'.

Today, along with the militarisation of our politics and culture goes the militarisation of our language. How Orwell would have mocked Fleet Street for trotting out so often the dull, all too predictable, unimaginative, worn-out metaphors of warfare, fighting and battle. Looking at just a small crop of mainstream newspapers there are countless examples – across all the sectors, tabloid, mid-market and 'up-market' and in all areas: sport, politics, business, arts reviewing, travel writing.

As I write today (25 January 2013), *The Times* has a headline 'General Paterson wants YOU to fight the Great Ash War' over a parliamentary sketch by Ann Treneman about the ash dieback disease. A feature by Ian Sample in the *Guardian* is headlined: 'On the frontline against antibiotic resistance'. On 18 January, the *Guardian* carried the heading: 'Store wars: Winners and losers in battle for festive sales.'

On 19 August last year, the *Observer* carried a story: 'New generation of eco-activists takes war to Europe's seas.' A report in the next day's *Guardian* Media section, a story headlined 'A decisive blow in copyright wars' reported: 'In the ongoing "content wars" between those who run sites that offer links to all sorts of content, and the people who don't always want those links to exist, Vickerman's conviction marks the conclusion of a remarkable battle.' Vickerman is later described as 'the latest victim in the content wars'.

Virtually any noun can be accompanied by the 'battle', 'war', 'attack' or 'fighting' metaphor in the journalistic lexicon. For instance, to take a few examples: in the *Daily Mail* there was the headline: 'Family at war over Subo's millions.' The *Observer* colour supplement the following day had a main headline 'Mummy wars' while inside the copy ran: 'The war at home. Motherhood is the new battleground. ... A self-confessed "slack mother" reports from the frontline.' The *Sunday Express* headlined: 'Carpet wars as MPs camp out' over a story about MPs changing offices in parliament. And so on and so on… This is not clever punning; it's just lazy journalism.

Orwell was always optimistic in his language campaigning. In 'Politics and the English language', he argued that 'the decadence of our language is probably curable' and he highlighted the way in which a few 'silly words and expressions' had been discarded from the language through 'the conscious action of a minority'. So is it not important now to follow Orwell's example and jeer every time we see a crass, militaristic metaphor – and work as journalists and consumers of the media in every possible way to eliminate them from our language?

Finally, I wonder if Orwell would continue to hold his damning views about journalism education today. In two 'As I Please' columns (on 6 October 1944 and 17 November 1944), he actually follows up a letter from a reader and exposes what he sees as the shortcomings of 'schools of journalism and the whole business of extracting fees from struggling freelance journalists'. He comments: 'If these people really know how to make money out of writing why aren't they just doing instead of peddling their secret at 5s a time?'

And he concludes: 'Isn't it rather curious that the "Fleet Street journalist", "established authors" and "well-known novelists" who either run these courses or write the testimonials for them are not named – or, when named, are seldom or never people whose published work you have seen anywhere. If Bernard Shaw or J. B. Priestley offered to teach you how to make money out of writing, you might feel there was something in it. But who would buy a bottle of hair-restorer from a bald man?'

Perhaps we can end, then, with one certainty: Orwell would have had little time for me as a journalist academic.

- This essay was first published in 2013 at https://orwellsocietyblog.wordpress.com/2013/01/26/orwell-the-protoblogger/.

Chapter 20

The Orwell/Self Spat: What it Reveals about Contemporary Culture

The recent spat between the novelist Will Self and George Orwell is interesting, in particular, for what it reveals about contemporary culture. Firstly it demonstrates the central place of celebrities (in this case, literary celebrities) in determining the dominant agenda in the media landscape.

The coming together of Will Self – the author of ten novels, a number of collections of non-fiction, his work translated into more than 20 languages – and George Orwell – one of the most celebrated writers of the last century, author of *Animal Farm* and *Nineteen Eighty-Four* – is, in terms of conventional news values, nothing short of gold dust. And then for Self to dare to accuse Orwell of being a 'talented mediocrity' backed by a present-day 'language police' who seek to impose 'good old-fashioned prejudices' on a 'living, changing' tongue adds just that necessary bit of controversy to thrust the whole kerfuffle high into the headlines.

Another crucial element of the controversy is the speed with which it exploded in the media. Self made his comments in a 'Points of View' in the BBC's *News Magazine* (see http://www.bbc.co.uk/news/magazine-28971276) on 31 August 2014. In no time, the media was on to the story – reporting the comment directly, seeking reactions from various academics and Orwellians, or carrying responses from opinionated journalists on the spat. And these media reports were quickly commented on by members of the public. For instance, amongst a selection of comments carried on the BBC website was this Orwellian, witty one from Nathaniel Price, of London: 'All writers are mediocre, but some are more mediocre than others.'

Thus, the controversy confirms the trend towards an ever-narrowing consensus in news values. The BBC reports and immediately the rest of the media (and not just Fleet Street) sheepishly follow suit. Type 'Will Self Orwell mediocrity' into the Google search engine and 1,180,000 results are shown. There's the *Independent*, the *Daily Telegraph*, *MSN UK News*, the *Guardian* (with 726 follow-up comments), *contactmusic.com*, http://www.booktrade. info, *theweek.co.uk*, *artsjournal.com*, *moviecitynews.com* and so on. And various blog sites such as *beattiesbookblog.blogspot.com*, *gnayabchohan. wordpress.com* join in the fun. Most of these sites carry long, follow-up discussions. For instance, on *http://www.metafilter.com* (which describes itself as a 'community weblog'), the comments run amazingly to more than 10,700 words.

Moreover, the internet means that this consensus is not just confined to the UK. The controversy quickly spread across the globe. For instance, in the US, *Salon.com* carries an excellent answer to Self from Laura Miller (http://www.salon.com/2014/09/03/george_orwell_was_not_a_language_fascist_why_we_keep_misinterpreting_his_words/). In Australia, the *Conversation* website (committed to 'academic rigour and journalistic flair') has Howard Mann, a lecturer at Monash University, Melbourne, commenting: 'We live in an age when permatanned, rich white males shout over one another on television and this counts as public debate' (see http://theconversation.com/will-self-george-orwell-and-whats-he-newspeaking-about-31239).

Orwell had a great sense of humour, was a maverick constantly challenging groupthink and a master of self-effacement and droll self-criticism. Indeed, he may well have agreed with the late Christopher Hitchens when he wrote: 'George Orwell requires extricating from a pile of saccharine tablets and moist hankies; since he's become an object of sickly veneration and sentimental over-praise, employed to stultify schoolchildren with his insufferable rightness and purity.' A large part of Orwell may well have secretly admired Self's debunking...

- This essay was first published at https://orwellsocietyblog.wordpress.com/2014/09/07/the-orwellself-spat-what-it-reveals-about-contemporary-culture/, in September 2014.

Chapter 21

'Two Titans of the Fight for Individual Freedom'

A review of *Churchill and Orwell: The Fight for Freedom* (London, Duckworth Overlook) by Thomas E. Ricks

Thomas E. Ricks is a distinguished American journalist and his linking Churchill and Orwell ('two titans of the fight for individual freedom', according to the publicity blurb) might appear to the publishers a perfect, popular mix.

Thus he writes (p. 3): 'Despite all their differences, their dominant priority, a commitment to human freedom, gave them common cause. ... Together in the mid-twentieth century these two men led the way, politically and intellectually, in responding to the twin totalitarian threats of fascism and communism.'

During his brief journey through the biographies of his two heroes, Ricks fixes on some fascinating linkages. For instance, he writes (p. 2): 'Their paths never crossed, but they admired each other from a distance and when it came time for George Orwell to write *1984*, he named his hero "Winston". Churchill is on record as having enjoyed the novel so much he read it twice.'

But more often the links appear too contrived. 'The events of the Battle of Britain,' he writes (p. 130) 'and then the Blitz carried class implications to which both Orwell and Churchill were sensitive.' Or, again, on p. 154, he comments awkwardly: 'Orwell was occasionally better attuned to British politics than Churchill was, and that seems to have been the case early in 1942.'

The book could be seen to provide an original, polemical overview of Orwell to readers who may otherwise have missed his writings. But don't expect any original insights: on *Down and Out in Paris and London*, he comments (p. 34): 'In several places in the book, Orwell limns the status structure within a segment of proletarian society – a concern that seems quite British in an unconscious way on his part'; the novels of the mid-1930s are dismissed as 'close to unreadable' (p. 37) while *Homage to Catalonia* is hailed as 'wonderful' on more than one occasion. According to Ricks, it's 'his first great book' which ends 'beautifully' (pp 75-80).

Inevitably, errors crop up. Richard, Orwell's adopted son, is said to have been born in Newcastle (p. 181); later, Orwell is said to have purchased a pistol from a friend telling him that he feared a communist attempt to kill him (p. 183): Orwell may well have asked to borrow the gun from the novelist Ernest Hemingway in Paris while covering the final days of the Second World War for the *Observer* and *Manchester Evening News* (though some question whether this meeting ever actually happened). And so on.

Ricks offers a very US-centric view of the twentieth century and reproduces, uncritically, Christopher Hitchens's observations (p. 153) that Orwell exhibited a 'curious blind spot' and that he 'never visited the United States and showed little curiosity about it. ... America, in other words, is the grand exception to Orwell's prescience about the century in which he lived'. In fact, as John Newsinger stresses in a paper in the launch issue of *George Orwell Studies* in 2016, the US was, in many ways, an important influence on him. There were the cultural and literary influences (Henry Miller, Jack London etc); the impact of US servicemen in Britain during the war; his relationship with New York intellectuals and the journal *Partisan Review*, and, finally, his post-war thinking regarding the ideas of James Burnham, conflict with the Soviet Union and the British Labour government's alliance with the US.

Aspects of the biographies which do not fit into the overall theme are quietly ignored. Thus, for instance, Churchill, supposedly the great defender of freedom, was quite happy to promote the secret coup against the democratically elected Prime Minister of Iran, Mohammad Mossadegh, in 1953. It gets no mention here.

Yet, in the absence of any original research, this book could set a new trend for publishers keen to cash-in on Orwell's amazing Amazonian sellability: soon there could be *Gandhi and Orwell* and *Marx and Orwell* and so on. You have been warned.

- This review of *Churchill and Orwell* by Thomas E. Ricks, appeared in the Orwell Society *Journal*, Vol. 11, autumn 2017 pp 22-23.

SECTION 3 - ORWELL'S AFTERLIFE: BEYOND 1950

Chapter 22

Jura Days

Some thoughts on The Orwell Society visit to Jura, 8-11 June 2018

The Road to Crinan Pier
Maryline, my partner, and I drove up on Thursday night from Lincoln up to Penrith: the massive sky above the Cumbrian Pennines dazzlingly golden red in the setting sun. In the morning we head north, the drive around Glasgow somewhat hairy as cars around us weaved swiftly in and out of the lanes, past the beautiful Inveraray (with its kitsch castle), its buildings standing sturdy, white and impressive on the shores of Loch Fyne; and finally right on to the B841, over beautiful landscape and alongside the canal to Crinan Harbour and pier. After the warm welcomes with the fellow Orwellians we set off in the ferryboats (Venture West and Shannick) to Craighouse, 21 nautical miles away on Jura: 17 men and six women from all parts of the globe (reflecting the enormous reach of Orwell's reputation): Australia, Spain, Germany, California, New Mexico – and, of course, England, Scotland and Wales.

A Fisherman's Daughter?
There are 6,000 red deer on Jura (named after the Norse for 'deer island') and Orwell once described it as 'ungettable to'. But now we have finally got to it. And so my main aim (as a proper journo) is to secure a scoop. First, I need to speak to the oldest of the 200 inhabitants of the island. Perhaps they have memories of the Great Man never yet recorded? Maryline and I spend the first morning walking down the (surprisingly busy) beautifully scenic coastal road under the hot sun to Jura Forest where I speak to a chap (wearing just shorts and big boots: he was just back from his honeymoon) who says the oldest person on the island is a Drew Fairman. But on seeing shortly afterwards the island's postman getting out of his van, I run up to him, wondering if he will corroborate that name. 'Oh no,' he says. 'Drew's not your man. Try Nancy Maclean. She lives at Glenasdale on the seafront – just as the road turns off to the cemetery at Keils.'

So I bang on her door. A white-haired, old lady in slippers shuffles to the door. 'Do you remember seeing George Orwell?' I ask bluntly. 'Oh yes,' she replies. Wow! Could it be true? Have I the Great Scoop on my hands that has eluded Davison, Taylor, Meyers, Shelden, Bowker, Crick and Co? We want to get back to the village hall for the showing of two films (*Wildflower*, very moving, about Orwell's first wife, Eileen O'Shaughnessy, and *The Crystal Spirit*, excellent, with Ronald Pickup as GO and script by Alan Plater) so I arrange with Nancy to come back at 5 pm.

In the meantime, my imagination goes into overdrive. Could the many Orwellian mysteries still remaining be about to be resolved? For instance, why had Winston Smith's anti-Party co-conspirator and lover been called Julia? Could it have been the name of a glamorous fisherman's daughter Orwell had secretly dated on the island? And why was Winston's friend-turned-torturer called O'Brien? Could he have been a car mechanic on the island who had helped him so many times after the truck given by Georges Kopp broke down? My exclusive source, Nancy, I am confident, will help solve all the riddles. Moreover, it was exciting to imagine where she had met him – perhaps at a dance in the village hall where he may have appeared a little gauche and over-pensive – constantly puffing on a cigarette as he peered at the gathered, jovial islanders.

I want to inspire Nancy's memory with a few gifts so we ask at the village shop what goodies she likes. 'Oh yes,' they say, 'she likes chocolates. And, by the way, would you mind delivering her paper to her?' So with a box of chocolates and some biscuits (plus newspaper) I, nervously expectant, and Maryline (both of us having conspicuously shuffled out of the film showing a little early) are ushered into her living room overlooking the sea. Nancy, looking quite elegant, says she is 89. She had married and lived on the island most of her life. She giggles a lot. How many times had she seen Orwell? 'Several,' she says. And that was about all she could say. How did Orwell look: was he tall, brooding, clutching a book? 'Ordinary.' Oh well: at least I'd spoken to someone on the island who had seen Orwell. But then, on reflection, I'm left wondering: had she really?

Such, Such Was the Joy!
Our visit on the Sunday morning to the remote house where Orwell had written *Nineteen Eighty-Four* in the years before his untimely death at just 46 in 1950 proved to be the high point of the trip.

We are warmly welcomed by the owners, the Fletchers, and served fruit cake, tea, coffee and cordial. And what a pleasure it is to hear Richard Blair recounting (with deep affection and often wry humour) his memories of being with his father, other relatives, friends (such as Richard Rees) various hangers-on (such as Paul Potts) and neighbours (such as Bill Dunn who went on to wed Orwell's sister Avril) at the house. Here was the place where he had fallen and cut his head, here he had fallen sick after smoking surreptitiously a pipe; here was the little bedroom where Rick had shed 'buckets of tears' when his nanny, Susan Watson, had left (after falling out with Avril); here the kitchen where breakfast was taken and (quite numerous) visitors entertained; here the dining room where they had dinner and high tea; Orwell always punctilious in his daily routine wanting long stretches alone in his room upstairs to write. In the surrounding fields he had grown vegetables, oats, made hay, planted fruit trees and reared chickens. The azaleas which Orwell had planted in front of the house are thriving – thanks to the Fletchers driving away the wild goats. Indeed, Orwell the gardener is a subject well worth exploring, says Richard. In a letter from Barnhill to George Woodcock, on 9 August 1947, Orwell writes that 'Richard likes to roll about in the hay stark naked'. Quips Richard: 'Ah, but he didn't say with whom!' Richard also remembers being taken away when the chickens were killed – just hearing their desperate, dying squeals in the background.

And here finally is the upstairs room looking out across the fields to the sea beyond where Orwell had composed the great novel either at the table or in the bed – forever smoking and kept warm by the paraffin heater (its fumes adding to the 'disgusting' smells). Today there is a generator for electric lighting and charging phones: in Orwell's day there were candles, open fires, Tilley paraffin lamps – but the water ran hot and cold.

All houses reflect aspects of their owner's personality. And how Barnhill does just that. For instance, it reflects Orwell's love of the outdoors and nature; his sturdy, practical side that saw him mixing with the down-and-outs in Paris and London and mucking in with the militiamen in the trenches during the Spanish civil war. It reflects his extreme and profoundly unconventional character.

But above all, it strikes me as I walk about the house, that the splendid isolation of Barnhill (23 miles north of Craighouse up a road that deteriorates to a track for the last five miles) captures Orwell, the ultimate outsider. Yet throughout his life Orwell used the distance he cultivated to look deeply and critically into things: poverty, the courage of his Spanish comrades, the growth of totalitarianism, the corruption of language and so on. His friendship with fellow old-Etonian David Astor, the journalist and future editor of the *Observer*, had not only led to his renting Barnhill in the first instance (Astor owned a lot of land on the island and had recommended the house as a one-off place to holiday in) but had introduced him to the world of intelligence. Yet while Orwell became involved with the secret state he was clearly alarmed at seeing the extent of intelligence's collusion with elites in both the East and West, its social, political and economic powers and its penetration into the daily lives of ordinary citizens. And isolated on Jura, he used his amazing imaginative powers to compose the novel, *Nineteen Eighty-Four*. Had he written a polemic against the secret state we would not have been visiting Jura: Orwell knew that he could most effectively confront so many crucial issues only through a novel, with its extraordinary cultural resonance.

Coming up for Blair
And so, after Barnhill, we take the ferryboats up to Corryvreckan, the world's third largest whirlpool, named after Breckan, the Viking captain who fell in love with a Scarba chieftain's daughter. It was here where Orwell, Richard and his young cousins, Henry and Lucy Dakin, had almost drowned in the summer of 1947 during an ill-fated dinghy ride. As Orwell wrote in a letter to Celia Kirwan on 20 January 1948 (from Hairmyres Hospital, East Kilbride): 'We did have a very nasty accident in the famous whirlpool of Corrievreckan (which comes into a film called *I know where I'm Going*) & were lucky not to be drowned. The awful thing was having Richard with us, however he loved every minute of it except when we were in the water.' Publicity on the island is profoundly reassuring about the safety of our trip: waves can reach up to 30 ft, they warn, and the resulting turbulence can be heard 10 miles away. But in the end, the sea for our visit is placid and calm. And Richard is able to point at the very rock where he, his father and young relatives scrambled on to – only to be rescued luckily a few hours later by a passing lobster fisherman who had spotted the fires they had lit. As Richard points out, if, in some terrible accident, Orwell had struck his head on the rock and drowned there would have been no *Nineteen Eighty-Four* – and we would not be on Jura that day...

While, the stormy seas were missing on our trip (luckily) so were other things:

- Midges: Quentin Kopp, the amazingly efficient organiser of the trip, extremely well supported by wife Liz, had warned us about the threat of midges on the island and the newspapers were reporting on the dangers of unprecedented plagues of insects (wasps, ants, daddy-long-legs as well as midges) across the whole of Scotland. In the end: mercifully nothing.

- Rain: which normally people expect in Scotland. But not a drop fell during our stay. All the locals were amazed as they had already experienced two weeks of sunshine. As the *Scottish Sun* reported (with perhaps an excess of alliteration) on 2 June: 'Scotland is set to bask in a searing heatwave as rocketing temperatures start a sizzling summer this month.'

- Crowds: the front page of the current edition of the lively, news-packed local, independent, fortnightly journal for Islay and Jura, *Ileach* (on sale at the village hall for £1.40) reported on the large crowds attracted recently to the Fèis Ile festival with 'seemingly endless queues' outside the famous whisky distilleries on the island. By the time we arrived, the crowds had dispersed.

But we did see seals swimming in the sea, sea eagles flying high above the trees and rhododendrons flowering on the hills in the distance.

Appendix: Richard Reading

While at Barnhill, Richard Blair reads to us part of the handwritten letter Orwell had sent to Sonia Brownell (later to be his second wife), on 12 April 1947 trying to entice her up to the island. In typical, Orwell style, he lists meticulously the details of the trip: from 8 am boat train leaving Glasgow Central for Gourock; then joining boat for Tarbet arriving about 12 noon; bus to West Tarbet to join boat for Craighouse, arrived 3.30 pm. If she wants to go by plane he lists those details. He suggests she brings a raincoat and if possible stout boots or shoes. He adds: 'I am afraid I am making this all sound very intimidating.' Indeed, Sonia was duly intimidated and never visited Barnhill during Orwell's lifetime. As Mrs Nelson, of Ardlussa, who came to know Orwell reasonably well, writes in a pamphlet on sale at the Jura Hotel (which served us excellent meals throughout our stay): 'In January 1950, she came to stay with us at Ardlussa. Robin [her husband] took her to Barnhill which she saw for the first time and where she went through Eric's papers. She was clearly upset by its lack of comfort and amenities and felt that she could not have lived there without drastic modernisation.'

Towards the end of the letter to Sonia, Orwell writes: 'Meanwhile take care and be happy.' While Orwell is so often associated with the gloom of the dystopian vision of *Nineteen Eighty-Four*, what strikes me throughout his writing is also his constant humour: his wish to make his readers happy and the *joie de vivre* he conveys through his play with language and ideas – and the flowering of his creative imagination and intelligence. Indeed, it was an unforgettable privilege to hear Richard Blair (always accompanied by his wife Eleanor) share with us his happy memories of his very special times with his father on Jura.

- This essay was first published at https://orwellsocietyblog.wordpress.com/2018/06/18/jura-days-2018/, in June 2018.

Chapter 23

Retracing the Steps of George Orwell

A review of *Sur Les Traces de George Orwell*, by Adrien Jaulmes, Paris, Équateurs, 2019

Adrien Jaulmes, chief reporter at *Le Figaro* and award-winning war correspondent, bases his new book on a great journalistic idea: retrace the steps of Orwell across the globe (at Eton, in Burma, in Paris, amongst the poor in the north of England, in Spain – and finally on the remote Scottish island of Jura) and see what remains in each of these places of his legacy.

The text is clearly aimed at a general newspaper readership who are expected to have little knowledge of Orwell – the man and writings. Thus, a considerable amount of time in this slender, fascinating text is given over in each chapter to reproducing sections from the celebrated works – 'Such, Such Were the Joys', *Burmese Days*, *Down and Out in Paris and London*, *The Road to Wigan Pier*, *Homage to Catalonia* and *Nineteen Eighty-Four* – and to spelling out the basic details of the biography.

In one of the best chapters, Jaulmes visits the sites where, in 1937, Orwell fought alongside the POUM militiamen against Franco's fascist forces in Aragon, northern Spain. On the road from Saragossa, around 250 kilometres west of Barcelona, he spots a sign indicating '*Ruta Orwell*' which leads to some reconstructed civil war trenches. Jaulmes speaks to Victor Pardo, journalist, historian and author of *Orwell, Toma Café en Huesca* (*Orwell, a Coffee at Huesca*). Pardo comments: 'The Aragon front was important because it protected Barcelona even if it was not the most active region in the war. The Republicans wanted to take over the city of Huesca – but they never succeeded' (pp 106-107).

Many of Jaulmes' comments on Orwell the man are perceptive. For instance, he writes: 'Orwell was never as happy as when he was on the frontline. In England or in France, his attempts to make contact with people had most often been failures. Here, for the first time, he found himself totally accepted by his comrades. Among the volunteers, Spanish and foreign, no one cared about their social background. No one commented on his old-Etonian accent. England and its rigid class system seemed far away' (pp 109-110).

Jaulmes next meets Miquel Berga, Professor of English Literature at the Pompeu Fabra University, Barcelona, who tells him: 'More than the war,

SECTION 3 - ORWELL'S AFTERLIFE: BEYOND 1950

the days of May [when he witnessed communist attempts to destroy the anarchists and Trotskyists in Barcelona] particularly marked Orwell. Both his politics and writings were transformed by this experience which influenced the rest of his work' (p. 117).

Jaulmes even suggests (a little controversially) that O'Brien, who first befriends Winston Smith and then tortures him at the end of *Nineteen Eighty-Four*, is based in part on Georges Kopp, Orwell's comrade and commander on the frontline.

In Barcelona, with the historian Nick Lloyd (spelled incorrectly with just one L), he sees that most of the décor of Orwell's period remains intact: for instance, in a corner of Catalonia Square, the central telephone building (the focus of much of the fighting during the 1937 May days) is now occupied by the mobile telephone company, Movistar. The Hotel Colon of Orwell's day is now a shop selling telephones and computers. Jaulmes comments: 'The portraits of Lenin and Stalin and the revolutionary slogans which decorated the building during Orwell's time have been replaced by an internationally recognised logo: in place of the red flags there is now the white apple of the famous American company' (p. 121).

Walking down the Ramblas, he sees a plaque indicating the place where Andreas Nin, leader of the POUM, stood just before his arrest in June 1937. At No. 122, the Hotel Falcon no longer stands – replaced by a shop selling jeans. The Poliorama, where Orwell took up a roof-top position to observe the May days fighting, is now a venue for flamenco shows – and special authorisation is needed to climb to the roof. Next, at the Café Moka, often frequented by Orwell, a waiter says, a little embarrassed: 'We are going to install a special "Orwell Room" in the basement, complete with books and portraits' (p. 122).

Jaulmes reports: 'In 1987, the town council decided to create an Orwell Square in the Gothic Quarter. Ironically, it was there where a few weeks later the city's first surveillance camera was installed in anticipation of the Olympic Games' (p. 123).

Earlier, following Orwell to the town of Katha in Burma (renamed Kyauktada in *Burmese Days*) where he was stationed in 1926 during his five years as an imperial policemen, Jaulmes meets Nyo Ko Naing in the Zone Cafe. A portrait of Orwell hangs on a wall close to television sets broadcasting a football match and a small altar dedicated to Buddha. Nyo Ko Naing has discovered a map of the town dating back to 1911 and a dozen of the buildings from that period remain standing. A large red-brick building is advertised as 'Orwell's building', even though it was actually then occupied by the district commissioner, and Nyo Ko Naing has helped found the Katha Heritage Trust with the aim of transforming the building into a museum dedicated to Orwell. The wooden house occupied by the doctor and Indian friend of John Flory, Veraswami, still stands as does the Church of St Paul where, in the novel, Flory is publicly humiliated – but the Lackersteen's home was destroyed in an earthquake in 1986 (p. 56).

Jaulmes goes on to meet Thurein Win, the Burmese translator of Orwell's works, who argues that those five years as an imperial policeman (1922-1927) actually inspired a linked trilogy about oppression: *Burmese Days*, *Animal Farm* and *Nineteen Eighty-Four* (p. 61).

In a chapter titled 'Le Robinson de Jura', Jaulmes narrates his journey, along with members of the Orwell Society, to the remote farmhouse, Barnhill, on the Scottish island where Orwell bashed out *Nineteen Eighty-Four* in his dying days (I was actually on that very same trip). He writes: 'The house has hardly changed since Orwell's days. The rooms are small and rural. The narrow windows look out on to the surrounding fields or the sea. ... the chipped earthenware bathtub is the same one as used by Orwell. ... The only heat is provided by pipes from the coal stove' (pp 130-131). Jamie Fletcher, a descendant of the family which let the house to Orwell, and his wife, Damaris (known as Mimsie), continue to rent it out to holiday-makers from time to time. Mimsie says she tries to dissuade folk from coming: 'I like to warn visitors: some of them after all can be a little put off by the conditions of life here' (p. 131).

Jamie, who grew up on Jura, was too young to retain any memory of Orwell but he remembers well his sister Avril, who came to the island to help look after his young son, Richard. 'I was a little afraid of her; she even resembled him physically: moustache included...' (p. 132). The Orwell Society members, led by Richard – now retired – and Quentin Kopp, son of Orwell's commander in the Spanish civil war, are described as being 'completely transported on visiting the rooms once inhabited by their Great Hero'. And Jaulmes watches as they explore every nook and touch the very table where Orwell wrote his masterpiece 'as if these places had conserved something of the spirit of the master' (p. 134). But Jaulmes does reproduce uncritically the myth that Orwell chose the title *Nineteen Eighty-Four* simply by reversing the order of the last two numbers in 1948 (p. 139). It is more likely that Orwell used the title of a poem written by his first wife, Eileen O'Shaughnessy, celebrating the 50th anniversary of her school in Sunderland in 1934 – and looking ahead another 50 years.

For his early chapter on Eton, Jaulmes speaks to Alex Renton, author of *Stiff Upper Lip*, a book highly critical of public schools. But Renton moderates his criticisms for Eton: 'If the school trains its pupils for the establishment, it also produces a certain number of independent spirits. An Etonian will tend to say that if the majority think one way, he will think differently. In this sense, Orwell was a perfect product of the school' (p. 22). Renton has done much to expose bravely the high levels of sexual abuse at private schools. In 2014, for instance, he wrote a personal memoir in the *Guardian* of his time at Ashdown House in the early 1970s where he suffered appalling sexual abuse from a staff member – and reported the findings by a *Times* investigation of a 'surge in criminal prosecutions' at 130 private schools, 20 of them feeders to Eton. Would it not have been interesting to discuss that with Renton?

Jaulmes rightly says that Orwell remained an old-Etonian to the very end (p. 32). And leaves it at that. Would it not have been good to mention, briefly, all the old-Etonians who played such crucial roles throughout Orwell's life: such as Andrew Gow, Richard Rees, L. H. Myers, Cyril Connolly and David Astor?

The final chapter considers Orwell's legacy today – in particular his recent appropriation by intellectuals of the political right in France (of particular interest to readers of *Le Figaro*). The journalist Ben Judah takes the opportunity to take a swipe (somewhat gratuitously) at Orwell and the left in general for their allegedly anti-Jewish prejudices (p. 152). But Jaulmes ends with a quote from Quentin Kopp which stresses Orwell's 'clear language and his great honesty': 'He was open to the facts and never hesitated to change his opinion, a quality which is too little evident today' (p. 153).

- All the translations from the original French are by the author.
- This review first appeared at https://orwellsocietyblog.wordpress.com/2019/12/07/retracing-the-steps-of-george-orwell/, in December 2019

Chapter 24

Orwell, the University and the University of Life

Orwell the Cultural Icon

Let's first consider Orwell's place in society as nothing less than a cultural icon. Is it not extraordinary that hardly a day goes by without the global media referring to Orwell – while the word Orwellian is equally prominent. It is used as a pejorative adjective to evoke totalitarian terror, the falsification of history by state organised lying; the use of euphemistic language to camouflage morally outrageous ideas and actions. Or it is used as a complimentary adjective to mean 'displaying outspoken intellectual honesty, like Orwell'. Does any other writer occupy such a place? I doubt it. In the debate over Edward Snowden's revelations in 2013 about NSA global surveillance, Orwell's Big Brother society of *Nineteen Eighty-Four* was a constant reference point.

His contribution to the broader culture is vast. Orwell himself gave to the English language a whole host of new words, phrases and striking aphorisms. He was the first person to use the phrase 'Cold War'. Other phrases and words he invented which have slipped effortlessly into everyday English include 'Big Brother', 'newspeak' (and variants such as 'nukespeak' and 'massacrespeak'); 'doublethink' (and variants such as 'groupthink'); even 'Room 101' (the name of a television series of dubious quality) – all from *Nineteen Eighty-Four*.

Moreover, many of his aphorisms are regularly referred to in the media. For instance, there's 'During times of universal deceit, telling the truth becomes a revolutionary act' and 'Early in life I had noticed that no event is ever correctly reported in a newspaper.' Others include: 'Every war when it comes, or before it comes, is represented not as a war but as an act of self-defence against a homicidal maniac.' 'Freedom is the right to tell people what they do not want to hear,' and 'In our age there is no such thing as "keeping out of politics". All issues are political issues, and politics itself is a mass of lies, evasions, folly and hatred.' And there's 'The great enemy of clear language is insincerity.'

SECTION 3 - ORWELL'S AFTERLIFE: BEYOND 1950

Orwell and Higher Education

English Studies

Orwell acquired international fame for his great novels *Animal Farm* (1945) and *Nineteen Eighty-Four* (1949) and not surprisingly the study of these and his other novels and essays is embedded in English programmes in schools, colleges and universities across the globe. The recent publication of a volume containing all of Orwell's poetry by Orwell Society founder member Dione Venables should also help focus academic attention on that previously ignored aspect of his overall vast output.

Cultural Studies

Moreover, Orwell virtually invented the discipline of Cultural Studies with his commentaries on so many of the manifestations of popular culture which fascinated him – crime novels, boys' weeklies, women's magazines, cups of tea, Woolworth's roses, common lodging houses, the common toad and handwriting. Such subjects have tended to be considered too trivial and unworthy of attention by the intellectual and cultural elite.

In one of his most celebrated essays – published in Cyril Connolly's *Horizon* in September 1941 – he examined the seaside postcards of Donald McGill and, as he wrote, 'their endless succession of fat women in tight bathing-dresses and their crude drawings and unbearable colours'.

Intelligence Studies

Orwell also occupies a place in intelligence studies, highlighted in James Smith's recently published *British Writers and MI5 Surveillance 1930-1960*. Files of Special Branch and MI5 released a few years ago reveal that Orwell was followed closely by British intelligence throughout his career – from the time he began writing for radical journals in Paris at the end of the 1920s. But Orwell's links with the secret state in the end became somewhat ambivalent (as I have examined in a number of essays) – particularly after he befriended David Astor who was very involved in SOE, the military arm of intelligence during the Second World War. It is likely that Orwell travelled to the Continent in 1945 on some kind of intelligence mission for Astor under the cover of writing for the *Observer* – and his decision on his deathbed to hand over a list of crypto-communists to the Information Research Department (a newly set up propaganda operation of the secret state) has been the subject of a heated controversy ever since.

Journalism

Orwell may be best known as a novelist. But for me, ever since I first joined a newspaper in my home city Nottingham in 1970, Orwell the committed, progressive journalist has been an inspiration.

Moreover, as an academic since 1984 I have used Orwell's writings in a wide range of programmes. At the University of Lincoln I set up (with the backing of John Pilger) the only undergraduate BA in investigative journalism – and not surprisingly Orwell's investigations into poverty in *Down and Out in Paris and London* and *The Road to Wigan Pier* are seminal texts which all students without any exception love to devour.

In my teaching of media ethics too, Orwell's decisions to live amongst the beggars, prostitutes, and hop-pickers, to actually go down a mine to experience first-hand the miner's experience have usefully raised all kinds of issues for students – about authenticity, commitment and the supposed 'truthfulness' of eye-witness reporting. His essential commitment to alternative non-corporate newspapers and journals also highlights important ethical and political issues for students (swamped as they are by the corporate media) to consider.

At Lincoln I also set up the MA programme in War, Journalism and Human Rights and here again Orwell's writing on his experiences fighting on the Republican side in the Spanish civil war and his frontline despatches for the *Observer* and *Manchester Evening News* at the end of the Second World War are crucial texts.

Literary Journalism

Also at Lincoln my teaching of literary journalism (exploring the political economy of the text and the ways in which journalism exploits the techniques mostly associated with high literature) has very often used Orwell's writings as models. The genres covered by Orwell are so fascinating: film and book reviews, political polemic, columns, essays, war reporting, letters, diaries, memoir. His aim, he says, is 'to make political writing into an art'. And in that he succeeds.

Media/Journalism Studies

While Orwell is often celebrated for virtually inventing the discipline of Cultural Studies, he is less well known for anticipating the emergence of Media/Journalism Studies and Media Sociology with his innovative, detailed deconstructions of the press. He constantly questioned the notion of press freedom, stressing the impact of advertisers and proprietorial control on content – and highlighting the close integration of mainstream newspapers with dominant financial, political and military interests and their essential propaganda role for the wealthy. Orwell also adopted many other original ways of examining the press: for instance, deconstructing an issue of the *Daily Mirror* and cheap women's newspapers – to highlight the manufacture of the 'sunshine mentality' – and even damning journalism training at the time.

Significantly, his reflections on the press culminate in the creation of Winston Smith, the anti-hero of his dystopian masterpiece *Nineteen Eighty-Four*. For Winston is a media worker at the satirically named Ministry of Truth altering the records of *The Times* to conform to the current dogma.

Conclusion

In conclusion, it's intriguing to consider that Orwell never went to a university. Yet, in effect, his whole life can be considered an educational project. He had an enormous appetite and curiosity about life – a deep desire to understand himself and the times he was living in. And through his wonderfully original and often witty writings he was seeking to encourage us all to join him on his journey.

- This essay is based on the keynote speech at a conference jointly organised by the Orwell Society and Goldsmiths College, University of London, on 7 January 2016.

INDEX

A Clergyman's Daughter 49, 59, 72, 127, 140
Acton, Harold 13, 32, 55
Adam, Eugéne 61
Ami du Peuple 7
Anarchist 35, 61, 76, 129, 163
Animal Farm 1, 6, 8, 49, 53, 54, 116, 126, 128, 129, 138, 153, 164, 167
'As I Please' 1, 4, 5, 8, 22, 35, 54, 65, 66, 77-78, 83, 117, 119, 120-121, 122, 146, 148, 149, 150, 152
Astor, David 3, 12, 13, 14, 24n1, 26, 30, 31, 36, 39-43, 50, 51, 52, 55, 73, 79, 83, 122, 137, 159, 165, 167
Ayer, A. J. 'Freddie' 13, 31, 36n7, 41, 55

Barbusse, Henri 24n6, 26
BBC 3, 8, 13, 15, 21, 26, 29, 30, 34, 39, 46, 47, 49, 52, 60, 74, 79, 83, 113, 121, 123, 135, 144, 146-149, 153
Beavan, John 6, 126, 128
Beddoe, Deirdre 16, 58
Bellamy, Edward 47-48
Bevan, Aneurin 14, 42
Bissell, Norman 52-55
Blair, Richard Horatio 15, 41, 49, 53, 54, 61, 104, 143, 156, 158, 159, 160, 161, 164
Blair, Richard Walmsley 110, 132, 141, 142
Bluemel, Kristin 58, 60, 61
Bowker, Gordon 6, 15, 23, 24, 26, 29, 30, 32, 52, 64, 70n5, 73, 79, 83, 89, 90, 91, 95, 103, 104, 108n6, 111, 131-136, 157
'Boys' Weeklies' 117

Buddicom, Jacintha 59, 60, 61, 67
Burmese Days 27, 49, 58, 72, 73, 127, 128, 133, 141, 162, 163, 164
Butler, Samuel 91, 100, 101, 108n3

Camus, Albert 14, 31, 55
Campbell, Beatrix 16, 58, 59, 119
Catholic 35, 59, 83, 84, 133
Chaplin, Charlie 24n5, 33, 111, 112
Chesterton, G. K. 7, 61, 135
CIA (Central Intelligence Agency) 6, 31, 32, 35, 41
Colls, Robert 6, 17, 52, 60, 67, 69, 111
Combat 14, 31
Coming Up for Air 49, 72, 127, 141
Committee for European Federation 3, 13, 31, 55, 117, 119, 120, 121, 122, 146, 148, 149, 150, 152
Communists 26, 27, 28, 29, 30, 31, 32, 33, 34, 35, 36, 46, 53, 61, 156, 163
'Confessions of a Book Reviewer' 114
Congress for Cultural Freedom 31
Connolly, Cyril 12, 30, 39, 67, 79, 90, 91, 98, 103, 142, 143, 144, 165, 167
Conrad, Joseph 54, 59, 127
Cox, Tony 7, 143-145
Crick, Bernard 6, 24n8, 30, 52, 60, 61, 67, 69, 70n5, 74, 78, 79, 89, 108n1, 111, 132, 142, 157
Crook, David 29, 79, 134
Crook, Tim 10, 20
Crossman, Richard 24n5, 33
'Crypto-communists' 3, 6, 14, 33, 36, 42, 128, 167
Cultural Studies 9, 66, 79, 110, 120, 167, 168

Daily Express 26, 77
Daily Mail 151
Daily Telegraph 31, 70n1, 137, 153
Daily Worker 27, 28
Davison, Peter 14, 31, 37n12, 60, 72, 73, 75, 85n4, 116, 120-123, 132, 150, 157
Dickens, Charles 2, 39, 79, 81, 82, 92, 100, 101, 117, 119, 126, 127
Down and Out in Paris and London 1, 4, 58, 59, 62, 69, 72, 75, 80, 98, 103, 121, 127, 155, 162, 168
Dwan, David 21, 23, 52

Encounter 31
Ethical Space: The International Journal of Communication Ethics iii, 10, 112
Eton 3, 12, 13, 24n6, 26, 30, 31, 32, 40, 54, 73, 96, 107, 127, 129, 133, 141, 144, 159, 162, 164-165

Fascist 26, 28, 35, 52, 74, 77, 134, 150, 162
FBI 32, 37n11, 45
Fierz, Mabel 60, 61
Figaro 7, 162, 165
Fleming, Ian 13, 30, 36n3, 50, 144
Fortnightly Review 121, 137
Franklin, Bob 1
'Funny not vulgar' 81
Fyvel, T. R. 52, 127-128

Gangrel 121, 137
George Orwell Studies iii, 10, 25, 46, 55, 71, 109, 119, 136, 156
G. K's Weekly 7, 26
Gollancz, Victor 27, 28, 48
Gow, Andrew 54, 141, 165
Graves, Ruth 60
Greenwood, James 62
Guardian 85n1, 128, 143, 151, 153, 165

Hemingway, Ernest 13, 31, 32, 41, 45, 53, 55, 156
Hitchens, Christopher 16, 59, 73, 154, 156
Holden, Inez 15, 60, 61
Homage to Catalonia 1, 4, 5, 22, 28, 58, 59, 63, 75, 121, 122, 127, 128, 155, 162
Homosexuality 4, 56, 63, 64, 69, 103-104
Hopkinson, Tom 6, 126, 129
Horizon 30, 39, 42, 58, 67, 69, 79, 80, 90, 142, 144, 167
Hulton, Edward 13, 50, 126, 129
Hunter, Lynette 23, 75, 90, 94
Huxley, Aldous 6, 47, 48, 49, 126, 129

Information Research Department (IRD) 3, 14, 24n2, 33, 34, 36n7, 37n15, 42, 128, 167
'Inside the Whale' 91, 117, 118
Inside the Whale and Other Stories 117, 118
Intelligence Studies 167

Jackson, Lydia 60
Jaques, Eleanor 15, 60
Jaulmes, Adrien 162-165
Jeffreys-Jones, Rhodri 44-46
Jones, Audrey 60
Journalism Studies 9, 168-169
Joyce, James 2
Jura 14, 15, 41, 49, 51, 53, 132, 143, 157-161, 162, 164

Keep the Aspidistra Flying 49, 98, 111, 127, 135
Kipling, Rudyard 81, 91, 100, 127, 134
Kirwan, Celia (née Paget) 3, 14, 15, 33, 42, 60, 61, 74, 160
Knight, Maxwell 32
Koestler, Arthur 14, 33, 42, 61, 144
Kopp, Georges 29, 74, 134, 158, 163

Kopp, Quentin 160, 164, 165
Koven, Seth 62

Lashmar, Paul 33, 34
Lawrence, D. H. 2, 54
'Lear, Tolstoy and the Fool' 81
Left Forum 121, 137
Leveson Inquiry 137-139
London, Jack 47, 49, 62, 135, 156
Lucas, Scott 33, 73
Lucky Star 65, 66
Lynskey, Dorian 5, 15, 17, 47-48, 52

Manchester Evening News 1, 2, 3, 13, 40, 41, 122, 126, 168
Manchester Guardian 31
Mannin, Ethel 28, 36n2
Margaret, Lady Rhondda 5, 111
Marks, Peter 44, 46, 68, 80, 81, 83, 88, 94, 116
Martin, Kingsley 48
Marxist 28, 39, 120, 156
McEwan, Sally 53, 60
McGill, Donald 1, 58-71, -81, 82, 85n1, 121, 167
Media Standards Trust 137
Metropolitan Police 27, 28
Meyers, Jeffrey 6, 17, 58, 70n5, 73, 79, 84, 89, 112, 113, 132, 157
MI5 3, 26, 29, 30, 32, 34, 36n6, 37n12, 141, 167
MI6 13, 28, 31, 34
Miller, Henry 118, 132, 141, 156
Miller, Max 68, 80, 112
Monde 24n6, 26
Muggeridge, Malcolm 6, 13, 31, 41, 55, 74, 83, 85n3, 126, 128, 144

New English Weekly 121, 137
New Leader 28, 121
Newsinger, John 10, 33, 36n2, 60, 65, 156

Nin, Andreas 163
Nineteen Eighty-Four 1, 4, 5, 6, 9, 12, 14, 15, 16, 18, 20, 22, 23, 26, 29, 32, 33, 36, 42, 44, 47, 49, 50, 51, 52, 53, 59.69, 72, 78, 79, 95, 99, 101, 114, 116, 126, 127, 134, 135, 140, 146, 153, 158, 160, 161, 162, 163, 164, 166, 167, 169; newspeak 6, 18, 50, 78, 79, 126, 166

Observer 1, 2, 3, 13, 26, 30, 39, 40, 41, 53, 55, 73, 83, 122, 137, 151, 156, 159, 167, 168
Orwell, George *film reviewing* 110-115; homoeroticism 4, 58, 63-64, 69; humour 72-87, 120; misogyny 58, 59, 73; *New Man* 4, 58, 61, 64, 104, 105; *proto-blogger* 8, 121, 147, 150-152
Orwell Society 2, 5, 10, 43, 51, 142, 145, 149, 156, 157, 164, 167, 169
Orwell, Sonia (née Brownell) 6, 7, 14, 15-16, 42, 50, 52, 53, 54, 60, 61, 108n1, 142, 143-145, 161
O'Shaughnessy, Eileen 12, 15, 24, 29, 41, 52, 53, 60, 61, 110, 134, 158, 164
OSS (Office of Strategic Services) 32, 33

Pacifism 8, 36
Partisan Review 5, 40, 48, 121, 156
Patai, Daphne 16, 18, 20, 58, 59, 91, 108n6
Picture Post 129
Pilger, John 34, 168
Politics and Letters 121
'Politics and the English language' 1, 41, 150, 151
Popham, Anne 60
Potts, Paul 53, 158
POUM (Partido Obero de Unifacación Marxista or United Marxist Workers' Party) 28, 74, 76, 162, 163
Priestley, J. B. 24n5, 33, 152
Progressive 121
Punch 31, 85n3, 128

Read, Herbert 6, 126, 129
Rees, Richard 72, 158, 165
Reuters 34
Ricks, Thomas, E. 155-156
Runciman, Steven 133
Russell, Bertrand 6, 126

Salkend, Brenda 15, 110, 133, 142
Schimanski, Stefan 126
Scotland Yard 3, 26, 45
Secret state 3, 12-14, 22-24, 26-38, 44-46, 51, 132, 159, 160, 167
Self, Will 153-154
Sexuality 2, 4, 5, 6, 12, 15, 16, 17, 18-19, 20, 33, 42, 44, 47, 50, 58-71, 79-81, 88, 89, 92-93, 103-105, 110, 132, 142, 144, 165
Shakespeare, William 67, 69, 81
Shaw, Bernard 91, 152
Shelden, Michael 6, 17, 33, 112, 132, 157
Sinclair, Upton 45, 47
Smith, James 34, 167
Smith, Stevie 60, 61
Socialist Workers Party 46
'Some thoughts on the common toad' 83-84
Special Operations Executive (SOE) 13, 26, 30, 31, 36n7, 50, 55, 167
Spender, Stephen 6, 108n6, 126, 128-129
Spurling, Hilary 6, 15, 52, 144
Stansky, Peter 6
St Cyprian's prep school 5, 32, 49, 64, 72, 88-109, 127, 142
'Such, Such Were the Joys' 4, 5, 49, 58, 64-65, 67, 69, 72, 88-109, 162
Sunday Express 151
Surveillance 3, 4, 12, 14, 22, 27, 29, 34, 36, 44-46, 49, 51, 98, 99, 114, 163, 166, 167

Sutherland, John 63, 67, 93, 95, 98, 111, 140-142
Swift, Jonathan 79, 81, 122, 126

Taylor, D. J. 6, 14, 15, 24n7, 26, 33, 37n13, 47, 49-51, 52, 70n5, 73, 82, 96, 102n8, 110, 111-112, 132, 157
Thackeray, William Makepeace 81, 82, 100, 102
'The Art of Donald McGill' 1, 4, 58-71
The Highway 137
'The Lion and the Unicorn' 1, 7, 30, 39
The Road to Wigan Pier 1, 27, 28, 40, 59, 61, 75, 98, 117, 118, 121, 127, 128, 134, 141, 144, 162, 168
Time and Tide 5, 111
Times 9, 151, 169
Tolstoy, Leo 47, 81
Tribune 1, 4, 5, 8, 9, 13, 14, 22, 24n2, 31, 35, 40, 52, 53, 54, 65, 74, 77, 83, 110, 114, 117, 119, 120, 121, 122, 127, 137, 146, 147, 150
Trotsky/Trotskyist 8, 26, 28, 29, 35, 74, 76, 120, 135, 163
Tulloch, John 5, 75, 112-114
Twain, Mark 47, 81

University College Hospital, London 14, 52, 54, 144

Venables, Dione 60, 108n7, 167

Wadhams, Stephen 52
Walton, Kay 60
Waugh, Evelyn 54
Wells, H. G. 47, 48, 49, 61, 100, 126, 137
Wheatley, Dennis 13
'Why I write' 75, 89, 96, 97, 98, 107, 123
Wilde, Oscar 2, 64
Williams, Kristian 64
Williams, Raymond 119

Williams, Rushbrook 123
Wilson, Harold 35
Windmill 31, 83
Wodehouse, P. G. 31, 36*n*4, 81, 82, 83, 85*n*3
Woloch, Alex 89, 90, 116-119
Woodcock, George 52, 159
Woolf, Virginia 2, 65
World Review 6, 126-130

Zamyatin, Yevgeny 47, 135

www.ingramcontent.com/pod-product-compliance
Lightning Source LLC
Chambersburg PA
CBHW051100160426
43193CB00010B/1257